writings on
RECONCILIATION
and RESISTANCE

writings on

RECONCILIATION
and RESISTANCE

by WILL D. CAMPBELL
edited by RICHARD C. GOODE

CASCADE Books · Eugene, Oregon

WRITINGS ON RECONCILIATION AND RESISTANCE

Cascade Books
A Division of Wipf and Stock Publishers
199 W. 8th Ave., Suite 3
Eugene, OR 97401

www.wipfandstock.com

ISBN 13: 978-1-60608-128-0

Cataloguing-in-Publication data:

Campbell, Will D.

    Writings on reconciliation a d resistance / Will D. Campbell; edited by Richard C.
Goode

    xiv + 238 p. ; 23 cm. Includes bibliographical references and index.

    ISBN 13: 978-1-60608-128-0

    1. Reconciliation—Religious aspects. 2. Christianity—20th century. 3. Social action.
I. Goode, Richard C. II. Title.

BT734.2 C25 2010

Manufactured in the U.S.A.

Contents

RESISTANCE

Introduction

Watching friends and students discover Will D. Campbell has been a great joy. A few have even become self-professing "Campbellites." Some had previous knowledge of Will, but, for whatever reason, had never given him due consideration. Others have been completely unaware of his life and work. Whatever their respective backgrounds, when they "get" Will, the proverbial light goes on, because Will has helped them see Christianity in a new way. More than some new persuasive argument, Will provides a witness. As my friend, David Dark, might describe, Will's example and encouragement "rearranges our mental furniture," and provides an alternative "script for what is realistic and right." When Will talks "gospel," it's not "just another peaceful, easy feeling." When Will talks of reconciliation, he presents a "blazing, bloodred question mark against whatever we consider common sense . . . breaking the pavement of countless cultural status quos."[1] Given a hearing, Will can describe a Christianity that is scandalous and objectionable, shockingly exhilarating and frighteningly attractive. He often jokes how he is an author of rare books. In fact, Will is a rare human being, with an exceptional voice and vocation. The title of this volume also reflects that character. Rather than terms in tension, for Will resistance grows out of reconciliation. Precisely because we are reconciled, professing disciples must live an irrepressible conflict against the principalities and powers—the idols—that divide and dehumanize. If this volume helps additional individuals simply hear and consider what Will has to say, my hopes will be fulfilled.

For those who have not read much (or any) of Will, perhaps this collection will encourage further investigation into his writing. Ideally, after surveying this volume's offerings, readers would rush out, or quickly log on, and find Will's longer works. Will maintains that he has neither sought nor desired disciples, but he has seldom passed up an opportunity to have a good conversation—and his writing often serves as his invitation to such rich conversations.

---

1. David Dark, *The Sacredness of Questioning Everything.* (Zondervan, 2009).

Introduction

This collection is designed as a continuation of *Crashing the Idols: The Vocation of Will D. Campbell.*[2] That volume introduces Will's life and thought, reprints his first book, *Race and the Renewal of the Church*, and then offers an essay arguing for the ongoing relevance of Will's life and work. Campbell, in other words, is more than an interesting southern preacher, civil rights activist, or cultural gadfly. Will represents a Radical tradition in Christian history that is far from the escapist, withdrawal-minded, or passive strategies that some historians, ethicists, and theologians associate with the Radical (Anabaptist) tradition. The Radical tradition of Campbell and others seeks not so much to *do* something amazing. Because the truly amazing thing has already been achieved, Radicals strive to *be* an incarnation of the scandalous *kerygma* in the midst of, and very much for, the world. Instead of shock-jock activists, Radicals are simply salt. Instead of awesome powerbrokers they are leavening agents. To be sure, this incarnation is not the typical script for making a difference in the world. Although Radicals seek neither coercive control, nor traditional forms of political power, their incarnation is, nonetheless, an intentional engagement in-and-for the world. Getting to know Will, therefore, should shatter the stereotype that the Radicals (i.e., the Anabaptist tradition) are so narrowly fixated with either their own purity or the afterlife that they refuse to get "dirty" in the affairs of this world.

Those who read the chapter in *Crashing the Idols* entitled "Incarnating Radical Christianity in the American South: The Importance of Will Campbell," will see how that essay spends significant time describing Will's theological neighborhood (i.e., his friends, colleagues, and fellow travelers). Some readers of that essay may no doubt want more of Will's writing. To make a plausible case for the importance of Will, they might say, requires more of Will's own words. This volume is a conscious effort to meet that request. Smashing the idols requires incarnating reconciliation while resisting the principalities and powers.

For those who have not yet read the "Incarnating Radical Christianity in the American South," no need to worry. All are invited to jump into this volume and enjoy Will for Will's sake. This collection can stand on its own, if need be. *Crashing the Idols* will provide considerably more context behind the selected pieces offered here, but one can benefit from Campbell's writings here without having read that volume.

2. Eugene, OR: Cascade, 2009.

The architecture of this collection is thematic rather than chronological. Although such a structure may obscure the evolution of Campbell's thought over time, it does allow the reader to chart one's own path of discovery, and to see the depths of Campbell's thinking on particular issues. In other words, the reader can enjoy selected sections at one's own discretion and interest, rather than feeling the need to read in linear fashion from beginning to end. Given Will's often unstructured and uncontrollable tendencies, it seems only fair to invite the reader to follow suit.

If Will were writing many of these pieces today, I am confident he would use more gender-inclusive language. Such vocabulary would only fit his commitment to reconciliation. He composed many of these essays and sermons, however, in an era before the push for inclusive language was widespread. In the writings presented here, the language is as originally published or delivered.

An editorial introduction is provided for most readings, to set some context for the piece. Far from comprehensive, these introductions are offered as an aid to synthesize the readings, and to highlight the theme of the section (e.g., Will's views on "reconciliation" and "resistance"). These introductions may also help explain some of the internal references within the selection that may not be self-explanatory.

Special gratitude and thanks are due to the staff at the University of Southern Mississippi's McCain Library and those at the University of Mississippi's Special Collections. Both were helpful and patient with my own "research conversation" with Will as I explored their archival holdings. The staff of the Southern Baptist Historical Library and Archive also helped locate a few scattered items in their holdings. Likewise, the staff of the Beaman Library at Lipscomb University—successfully led by Will Campbell's good friend Carolyn Wilson—was helpful in filling numerous interlibrary loan requests. Ms. Andrea Blackman of the Civil Rights Collection at the Nashville Public Library also deserves thanks. The consummate professional, she is a good friend and valued colleague. Hopefully it will not sound patronizing for me to say that librarians are some of my favorite people. They seem incessantly interested in learning and knowing—my kind of folk. Mr. Jonathan Melton and Mr. Benjamin Oliver, Lipscomb students and "Campbellite" converts, also provided assistance and conversation along the way. Mr. Craig Katzenmiller has likewise provided valuable support and assistance to the project.

Introduction

I would also like to thank my family. Candyee has always been an understanding partner, patiently listening as I think out loud. Most of the time, she even manages to look interested, no matter how preliminary my ideas may be at a given time. Our daughters, Anastasia ("Ana") and Mary Elisabeth, have never quite understood Dad's obsession with books, but they are always good sports about it. (Mary once told her kindergarten teacher that her Daddy didn't really have a job. "He just sits in his office all day.") As Ana and Mary continue to grow and chart the course of their lives, I pray that in their respective ways they will incarnate, in-and-for the world, the reconciliation achieved in Christ and that they will resist the idolatrous principalities and powers that tempt, distract, and divide us all.

Finally, a word of thanks to Will. Time often separates historians from their subjects. What a thrill to talk with Will, to sit in his cabin and explore the nuances and implications of his work and writing. I will forever count him as one of my mentors.

Let us bless the Lord.
Thanks be to God.

Richard C. Goode
Lipscomb University
Nashville

Introit *

CONTEXT: *Given Will Campbell's vigorous iconoclasm toward the institu-tionalized church, one could develop the misperception that he lacks any se-rious faith commitment. Campbell's resistance to the political principalities and the denominational powers should not, however, inspire doubts about his commitment to the Christian kerygma. Campbell's criticism is always inspired by an unflagging allegiance to God's Kingdom. These excerpts from his reflections on the Lord's Prayer provide a hope-filled "opening prayer" to the body of Will's writing.*

Sometimes we confuse the things we wish *for* with the things we hope *in*. We *wish* for a world in which there would be no crime, no war, no disease, no wanton destruction of the forests nor poisoning of the streams, no discrimination on the basis of race, gender, or religion. To say that this has not come true is a gross understatement. Our *hope* is in the Lord. And then in a kingdom. His kingdom. Our frail assumption is that it is a king-dom in which the things wished for would be taken for granted. We are bold to ask the Father to bring His reign to earth. Thy kingdom come.

Are we serious? Or do we pray the prayer assuming that the kingdom of God would be pretty much like the kingdom of Caesar? Maybe a few more sacred art pieces to adorn the walls and cute little cherubs picking flowers all day while some empyrean Muzak beams Handel's oratorios from above. But otherwise not much change.

Not so. The prayer has become tough now. Earlier it has been gentle and comforting. Baby talk to a caring sire, followed by a sort of cheering section: May your name be holy! Yea, Abba! Abruptly Jesus begins to tell them what it is appropriate for them to ask for. And the very first peti-tion is so outrageous. So far beyond the limits of what we honestly want because it would totally change the world we live in.

* Excerpt from Will D. Campbell, *God on Earth: The Lord's Prayer for Our Time* (New York: Crossroad, 1983), 22–ff., and 64. Reprinted with permission.

Since we are not the Father, we can but speculate as to what His kingdom would be. But from what we learned of Him from the person of Jesus we can make certain assumptions.

Because the morality of God is perfection we would assume that His kingdom would be one without crime. But if crime were removed from the present era the economy would collapse. Our brother/son, Webb Campbell, is a student of law. In a reign without crime he would have to change his professional direction. No crime, no lawyers. Licenses for marrying, driving, hunting, and the regulation of commerce would not be necessary, so courthouses would be useless except for keeping the census. And what would be the point of that? Sell the courthouses and give the money to the poor. If none breaks the law there is no need for legislatures to pass and repeal laws. And no judges, sheriffs, JPs [Justices of the Peace], bail-bond companies, prison guards, wardens, warrant servers, court clerks, or bailiffs. No contractors to build jails and no staff to run them. Police departments, highway patrolmen, the FBI and private investigators would be unemployed. And what need for a president, vice president, 100 senators, 435 congressmen and their staffs? Let them go to work in something useful. (Wonder how often the Senate chaplain says the Lord's Prayer on the Senate floor.) Guess all of us had better be careful how we pray for a kingdom without crime.

Pray: Thy kingdom come.

A kingdom without war? Do we want it? More than half the economy is somehow related to it. No Pentagon? Army, navy, marine corps, and their academies? No fifty billion dollars for weapons this year? No munitions manufacturers, barracks builders, vending machines for the troops? Not even bus drivers to take anti-nuclear demonstrators to New York or hotels to house them and restaurants to feed them. No United Nations on Manhattan Island. How many millions of people are making their living in war-related industries? What would we do with them?

Better be careful how we pray for a reign without war. Yet Jesus said, "Pray, Thy kingdom come."

A kingdom without disease? No doctors, nurses, medical schools, hospital administrators and orderlies. No health insurance policies, drug manufacturers, pharmacists, paramedics, or Hospital Corporation of America.

When you pray, say: Thy kingdom come.

A kingdom with air birds could fly in, and streams fish could swim in and Boy Scouts could stoop and drink from on their hikes. But where would we pour the acrid smoke and foul leavings, the residue of our indulgences? Perchance no clamoring for the indulgences?

Thy kingdom come?

St. Paul talked about the kingdom. Neither male nor female. Black nor white. Educated nor ignorant. No discrimination. And what would that cost?

What if we pray the prayer just one time too many and it is answered?

It is already answered. The advent of a utopian society is not the only way to view these words of Jesus. Another approach is that the kingdom is already here, has been ushered in by the Son of the Father, Jesus himself. And the call to the kinfolks of God is for our participation in it. Just live what already is. That which *is* has been revealed by this Son of the Father. Our joint heir. The kingdom of which he spoke is locked in relentless combat with the kingdom of this world, the kingdom of evil. We are praying that the kingdom of the Father will win. Which it already has. We are choosing between the two, offering our services in this ministry of reconciliation.

We wish. We also hope. Our wish is for the things we desire. Our hope is in the Lord. Who made heaven. And also earth. The prayer Jesus taught us is that the kingdom is for us.

"Thy kingdom come."

More than once, the prayer of Jesus is an offer to abdicate, to yield the will, the freedom with which we are endowed back to the will and freedom of the endower. Yes, Thou hast given us a kingdom, but we want *Thy* Kingdom to come. *Thy* will to be done over the free will Thou has given to us. Thou has given us the earth and told us to have dominion over it, to subdue it, and run it. Now we are asking that things be on earth the way they are in heaven. And yes, the humanistic unbeliever is right: it's a cop-out. We are asking for help, for rescue, redemption. We are asking for Grace, that something be done for us which we cannot do for ourselves. It is the total dependency of the child again. We are God's little cop-outs. And why not? God is God is God is God is God.

RECONCILIATION

A. With the Thomas Colemans

CONTEXT: *Preaching on 2 Corinthians 5 and the Christian's "ministry of reconciliation" is one thing. By 1965, Campbell had a well-established, and well-earned, reputation for supporting the civil rights movement. His book* Race and Renewal of the Church *articulated his commitment to reconciliation with the African-American community. It is quite another, and altogether scandalous, thing to explain in no uncertain terms that incarnating reconciliation is radically comprehensive—embracing victims and offenders, heroes, and "villains."*

In the following two pieces, Campbell explains his understanding of the unique imperative to "be reconciled" (in the Greek, katallagete*). The first source is perhaps the best known of all Will Campbell's writing. From his autobiography,* Brother to a Dragonfly, *Campbell explains the moment in 1965 when P. D. East helped him comprehend what it means to be reconciled—especially when it comes to the most egregious and reprehensible among us (i.e., the Thomas Colemans of the world).*

"Law and Love in Lowndes County" captures Campbell's attempt in 1965 to convey to the readers of Katallagete *the breadth and depth of reconciliation. By the time of the essay's publication, the wheels of injustice had already moved swiftly in Selma, Alabama. Less than two weeks after Officer Coleman had shot Jonathan Daniels and Richard Morrisroe on August 20, 1965, an all-white jury acquitted the deputy. Here, in just the second issue of* Katallagete, *while the death of Jon Daniels was still sharply felt, Campbell published a shocking, even outrageous, essay where he counsels forgiveness and reconciliation with all the Colemans of the world. Reaction to Campbell's essay was swift and strong. Some reacted to the essay positively, while others were infuriated. Either way, the essay illustrated the extent to which 2 Corinthians 5 informed Campbell's worldview.*

1

Excerpt from *Brother to a Dragonfly**

Joe [Campbell] came to the door and called us in. "Brother, you know a Jonathan Daniels?" "Yea. Sure. I know Jon Daniels. Why?" "Well, he's dead." Joe had heard a news bulletin but had no details. It was not hard to believe for I had been with Jonathan at a conference a few weeks earlier and knew what he was about.

He was a student from the Episcopal Theological Seminary in Cambridge, Massachusetts who was involved in registering black citizens to vote in Lowndes County, Alabama. A few days earlier I had learned that Jon was in jail in that county along with a number of others. We waited to hear the national news which carried a detailed account.

Jonathan and Richard Morrisroe, a Roman Catholic priest from Chicago, had just been released from the Lowndes County jail in Hayneville. Because of some confusion in a telephone conversation there was no one there to meet them when they, and twenty-five others, had been released. Jonathan, Richard, and two black students [Ruby Sales and Joyce Bailey] stopped at a small grocery store on the edge of the little town. Despite the fact that the majority of the woman's trade was black people, she became alarmed at their presence and called a special deputy named Thomas Coleman who arrived on the scene before the four could finish their cold drinks and leave. Armed with his own shotgun he fired as the four were leaving the premises, killing Jonathan instantly with the first shot, turning immediately upon Father Morrisroe, the pellets from the second shot leaving him mortally wounded on the gravel outside the little one-room, unpainted shack which was the store. The two young

* From Will G. Campbell, *Brother to a Dragonfly* (New York: Continuum, 2000), 217–22. Reprinted with permission from The Continuum International Publishing Group.

black women fled in terror and were unharmed. Coleman went to the telephone and called Colonel Al Lingo, Commissioner of Public Safety in Alabama, and told him, "I've just shot two preachers. You better get on down here."

That was the news. That was all we knew. My young friend Jonathan Daniels was dead and his friend lay mortally wounded, listed in critical condition. I sat in stunned silence. Joe snapped the television off and came over and kissed me on the head. "I'm sorry, Brother." P. D. [East] said nothing.

I made some phone calls to get more details and to see if there was something we should be doing. Joe and P. D. sat in a silent room, mourning with me over the death of a friend, saying little, forgetting to turn the lights on when darkness came. When I re-entered the room they were speaking in whispers, like people do in a funeral parlor when there is a casket in the room. I could see them outlined against the street light which cast a beam through a crack in the venetian blind, reflecting itself in a huge mirror and returning across the room to bring form to these two big men sitting facing each other as if playing chess. P. D. spoke first. "Well, Brother, what you reckon your friend Mr. Jesus thinks of all this?" I allowed that I guessed he was pretty sad about it. He stood up and turned an overhead light on, went to the kitchen and came back with some beer and cheese. He spoke again as his hulking frame sank into a bigger chair. "Brother, what about that definition of Christianity you gave me that time? Let's see if it can pass the test."

Years before, when P. D. had his paper going, he liked to argue about religion. Most of it was satire, but I would often take it upon myself to set him straight on one theological point or another. He had long since deserted and disavowed the Methodist church of his foster parents, had tried being a Unitarian, and had taken instruction from the local rabbi and was considering declaring himself a Jew. He referred to the church as "the Easter chicken." Each time I saw him he would ask, "And what's the state of the Easter chicken, Preacher Will?" I knew he was trying to goad me into some kind of an argument and decided to wait him out. One day he explained.

"You know, Preacher Will, that church of yours and Mr. Jesus is like an Easter chicken my little Karen got one time. Man, it was a pretty thing. Dyed a deep purple. Bought it at the grocery store."

I interrupted that *white* was a liturgical color for Easter but he ignored me. "And it served a real useful purpose. Karen loved it. It made her happy. And that made me and her Mamma happy. Okay?"

I said, "Okay."

"But pretty soon that baby chicken started feathering out. You know, sprouting little pin feathers. Wings and tail and all that. And you know what? Them new feathers weren't purple. No siree Bob, that damn chicken wasn't really purple at all. That damn chicken was a Rhode Island Red. And when all them little red feathers started growing out from under that purple it was one hell of a sight. All of a sudden Karen couldn't stand that chicken any more."

"I think I see what you're driving at, P. D."

"No, hell no, Preacher Will. You don't understand any such thing for I haven't got to my point yet."

"Okay. I'm sorry. Rave on."

"Well, we took that half-purple and half-red thing out to her Grandma's house and threw it in the chicken yard with all the other chickens. It was still different, you understand. That little chicken. And the other chickens knew it was different. And they resisted it like hell. Pecked it, chased it all over the yard. Wouldn't have anything to do with it. Wouldn't even let it get on the roost with them. And that little chicken knew it was different too. It didn't bother any of the others. Wouldn't fight back or anything. Just stayed by itself. Really suffered too. But little by little, day by day, that chicken came around. Pretty soon, even before all the purple grew off it, while it was still just a little bit different, that damn thing was behaving just about like the rest of them chickens. Man, it would fight back, peck the hell out of the ones littler than it was, knock them down to catch a bug if it got to it in time. Yes siree Bob, the chicken world turned that Easter chicken around. And now you can't tell one chicken from another. They're all just alike. The Easter chicken is just one more chicken. There ain't a damn thing different about it."

I knew he wanted to argue and I didn't want to disappoint him.

"Well, P. D., the Easter chicken is still useful. It lays eggs, doesn't it?"

It was what he wanted me to say. "Yea, Preacher Will. It lays eggs. But they all lay eggs. Who needs an Easter chicken for that? And the Rotary Club serves coffee. And the 4-H Club says prayers. The Red Cross takes up offerings for hurricane victims. Mental Health does counseling, and the Boy Scouts have youth programs."

I told him I agreed and that it had been a long time since I would not have agreed but that that didn't have anything to do with the Christian faith. He looked a little hurt and that was when he asked me to define the Christian faith. But he had a way of pushing one for simple answers. "Just tell me what this Jesus cat is all about. I'm not too bright but maybe I can get the hang of it." The nearest I ever came to giving him a satisfactory answer was once when I blasted him for some childish "can God make a rock so big He couldn't pick it up" criticism of the faith. He blasted right back. "Okay. If you would tell me what the hell the Christian faith is all about maybe I wouldn't make an ass of myself with I'm talking about it. Keep it simple. In ten words or less, what's the Christian message?" We were going someplace, or coming back from someplace when he said, "Let me have it. Ten words." I said, "We're all bastards but God loves us anyway." He swung his car off on the shoulder and stopped, asking me to say it again. I repeated: "We're all bastards but God loves us anyway." He didn't comment on what he thought about the summary except to say, after he had counted the number of words on his fingers, "I gave you a ten word limit. If you want to try again you have two words left." I didn't try again but he often reminded me of what I had said that day.

Now, sitting in the presence of two of the most troubled men I have ever known, I was about to receive the most enlightening theological lesson I had ever had in my life. Not at Louisiana College, Tulane, Wake Forest, or Yale Divinity School. But sitting here in a heavily mortgaged house in Fairhope, Alabama. P. D. East and Joseph Campbell, as teachers. And I as pupil.

"Yea, Brother. Let's see if your definition of the faith can stand the test." My calls had been to the Department of Justice, to the American Civil Liberties Union, and to a lawyer friend in Nashville. I had talked of the death of my friend as being a travesty of justice, as a complete breakdown of law and order, as a violation of federal and state law. I had used words like redneck, backwoods, woolhat, cracker, Kluxer, ignoramus, and many others. I had studied sociology, psychology, and social ethics and was speaking and thinking in those concepts. I had also studied New Testament theology.

P. D. stalked me like a tiger. "Come on, Brother. Let's talk about your definition." At one point Joe turned on him, "Lay off, P. D. Can't you see when somebody is upset?" But P. D. waved him off, loving me too much to leave me alone.

"Was Jonathan a bastard?"

I said I was sure that everyone is a sinner in one way or another but that he was one of the sweetest and most gentle guys I had ever known.

"But was he a bastard?" His tone was almost a scream. "Now that's your word. Not mine. You told me one time that everybody is a bastard. That's a pretty tough word. I know. Cause I *am* a bastard. A born bastard. A real bastard. My Mamma wasn't married to my Daddy. Now, by god, you tell me, right now, yes or no and not maybe, was Jonathan Daniels a bastard?"

I knew that if I said no he would leave me alone and if I said yes he wouldn't. And I knew my definition would be blown if I said no.

So I said, "Yes."

"All right. Is Thomas Coleman a bastard?"

That one was a lot easier. "Yes. Thomas Coleman is a bastard."

"Okay. Let me get this straight now. I don't want to misquote you. Jonathan Daniels *was* a bastard. Thomas Coleman *is* a bastard. Right?" Joe the Protector was on his feet.

"Goddammit, P. D. that's a sacrilege. Knock it off! Get off the kid's back."

P. D. ignored him, pulling his chair closer to mine, placing his huge, bony hand on my knee. "Which one of these two bastards do you think God loves the most?" His voice now was almost a whisper as he leaned forward, staring me directly in the eyes.

I made some feeble attempt to talk about God loving the sinner and not the sin, about judgment, justice, and brotherhood of all humanity. But P. D. shook his hands in a manner of cancellation. He didn't want to hear about that.

"You're trying to complicate it. Now you're the one who always told me about how simple it was. Just answer the question." His direct examination would have done credit to Clarence Darrow.

He leaned his face closer to mine, patting first his own knee and then mine, holding the other hand aloft in oath-taking fashion.

"Which one of these two bastards does God love the most? Does he love that little dead bastard Jonathan the most? Or does He love that living bastard Thomas the most?"

Suddenly everything became clear. Everything. It was a revelation. The glow of the malt which we were well into by then seemed to illuminate and intensify it. I walked across the room and opened the blind, staring directly into the glare of the street light. And I began to whimper. But the crying was interspersed with laughter. It was a strange experience. I remember trying to sort out the sadness and the joy. Just what was I crying for and what was I laughing for. Then this too became clear.

I was laughing at myself, at twenty years of a ministry which had become, without my realizing it, a ministry of liberal sophistication. An attempted negation of Jesus, of human engineering, of riding the coattails of Caesar, of playing on his ballpark, by his rules and with his ball, of looking to government to make and verify and authenticate our morality, of worshipping at the shrine of enlightenment and academia, of making an idol of the Supreme Court, a theology of law and order and of denying not only the faith I professed to hold but my history and my people— the Thomas Colemans. Loved. And if loved, forgiven. And if forgiven, reconciled. Yet sitting then in his own jail cell, the blood of two of his and my brothers on his hands. The thought gave me a shaking chill in a non-air-conditioned room in August. I had never considered myself a liberal. I didn't think in those terms. But that was the camp in which I had pitched my tent. Now I was not so sure.

2

"Law and Love in Lowndes"*

If one thing is clear in the New Testament it is the central theme of the triumph of grace over law. While St. Paul stopped short of a rigid antinomian position, a complete disregard for law, he did make it clear that to abide *in* grace is more radical than to abide *by* law. And such law as he did emphasize was not law in the sense of entreaties of the state to make us behave, but an ethic, the fruit of the spirit, resulting from being "in Christ." Far more radical than law was the acceptance of this freedom.

Unless and until the Christian civil rights movement goes to the white segregationist—or the Negro segregationist—with that radical word we will continue to be little more than a pitiful addendum to the humanistically oriented organizations which got along quite well without us during our long period of silence and inactivity.

The real issue now is the *failure of law* in the racial crisis. (If anyone sees a few recent "convictions" as a denial of this let him understand that "failure of law" does not have to do with conviction or acquittal but with the fact that the acts were committed.) So to go on crying, "More law!" or "Better law!" or even "Federal law!" is to beg the question. It is akin to using aspirin for a headache long after it is discovered that the headache is caused by a brain tumor. There is no question that aspirin is a remarkable drug and continues to have its place even in the presence of a brain tumor. But to rush around to find better aspirin—aspirin with buffering, aspirin that will dissolve minutes faster, aspirin with a combination of ingredients—simply because that is all the pharmacist could provide, is to place too much confidence in the pharmacist and too little in his allies of medical science. The patient is dying. We are suspicious of surgery for brain tumors because Dr. John R. Brinkley and other quacks used it to

* From *Katallagete*, December 1965, 11–14. Reprinted with permission.

graft goat reproductive organs onto human beings with the claim that it would restore one to youthful vitality.

The Christian doctrine of grace is suspect in the area of civil rights because "the South has had that preached to it for two hundred years and it hasn't done any good." The only trouble with that claim is that it simply is not true. The folk religion of the South has been a religion of law, not of grace, and it continues to be such. As Harry Caudill observed in his recent book, *Night Comes to the Cumberland*, concerning the Appalachian South, we also have never been the Bible Belt in the sense of a depth of understanding of the Bible. He points out that many rural folk of that area—and the same is true of the lower South—did not even have Bibles, and if they had them seldom could read them.

The religion that developed in the South was a strange combination of Indian lore, old wives tales, bits of stoic doctrine passed on by the educated aristocracy, and superstitions based on biblical quotations remembered from the time the Methodist or Baptist itinerant preacher spent the night on his way to Natchez.

The religious problem of the South is not biblical literalism but biblical illiteracy.

When religion in the formal sense did move South, it was generally in the form of a rigid legalism, and for much the same reason that legalism is what we are promoting today in civil rights. That reason is to solve a problem, to get people to behave in a certain way. It was assumed that it would *work*. The drunkenness, knife fighting, and general unruliness of the frontier South was not conducive to the success of mine, mill, and field. What better way to control that than to proclaim that the Devil will get you if you don't watch out. . . .

And it failed. The South has the finest laws but without a corresponding relationship to its crime rate. . . .

Legalism is failing again. Whether we can see it or not, it is failing. It fails because the first lesson man learned was how to deal with the requirements of the law. From Eve to Thomas Coleman it has been the same. The way to handle law is to interpret it. Thus, "Thou shalt not steal," means children should not take apples from other children's lunch baskets, but it does not have anything to do with price fixing, or cheap labor, or the stock market. "Thou shalt not commit adultery," means unless your wife doesn't understand you. "Thou shalt not kill," means one man does not take a gun and shoot a fellow he admits he hates, but it does not apply to a nation killing thousands of men, women, and children whom it claims to love.

Yet, if we seem now to advocate the repeal of recently enacted civil rights laws or oppose the passage of others we are being less than clear. And certainly we are not suggesting that love and law are contrary to each other. The point is that those of us who should be interested in relating the two seem not to be relating them at all but to be promoting the one and ignoring the other. The further point is that the one we insist on promoting continues to let us down.

If law is for the purpose of preventing crime every wail of a siren calls out its failure. Every civil rights demonstration attests to the courts' inability to provide racial justice. Every police chief who asks for a larger appropriation because of the rising crime rate is admitting his own failure. Every time a law has to be *enforced* it is a failure.

The simple fact is that for the Christian, law is an inadequate minimal. Do not even the publicans [say] the same? If this is all we have to offer the world then, Jesus Christ was of all men most mad.

Still we hear, "But the Thomas Colemans must be restrained." Exactly! Then where is the fruit? When will he be restrained? The truth is that he now sees a truce being signed between his two traditional enemies, Negro leaders and the federal government. No doubt, this has been necessary in moving in the direction of simple justice, especially when he has declined offers to be a party to the truce. Be that as it may, the rejections continue, the killings go on, the hostilities mount and intensify, perhaps to be set loose wholesale again on another day when the Feds and marchers have all gone home, or turned to stopping the war with Venus, and what we see as the gains of this day turn out to be the rack rent of that day.

If the argument now is on the basis of what will work, then let us put it there.

Few criminologists today see punishment, and especially capital punishment, as an effective deterrent to crime. I have had the frustrating experience during the past six months of working with a group on a frantic, around-the-clock basis in an effort to abolish capital punishment. The argument that got the most votes in the legislature was the above finding of leading criminologists. Since that time some of those same individuals have marched in the streets over the acquittal of Thomas Coleman. When they hear, "You are after revenge," they reply, "No, not revenge. Preventative." Now this is sheer madness.

What then do with say? Certainly we cannot say we are not interested in stopping the killings all around us. Any Christian who is not involved to his maximum in correcting the injustices of the Southern region had best examine his commitment to Christ. Certainly we cannot say we are not interested in the success of the civil rights movement. Too long we debated the number of angels on a needle point while our brothers were in chains. Certainly we cannot advocate retreating from the world into the security of established religion. God knows that didn't work! But the question is, what is one's maximum involvement? Is it law or is there a still deeper issue and involvement?

What distinctive word, what message of hope does the Christian have for the racial crisis? It may be that he has no word of hope in the sense that hope is understood generally. But he certainly has a distinctive word. That word is *The Word. The Word* become flesh.

And that *Word* leads us to the death of Jonathan Daniels and our response to it. What can one say when a brother whom we have set apart and sent forth is dead? We can say, "Our brother is dead. Let's go bury him." Then we can say a benediction. And perhaps nothing more is appropriate.

But we who set Jon Daniels apart and sent him forth have said far more than that. We got immediate appointments with the highest official of the Department of Justice. We pressured through releases and statements and marches and court stays for federal intervention. We have said such things as: "We must have federal initiative and involvement in the investigation and prosecution of murders . . ." And now we are considering civil proceedings of our own against the murderer of our brother. We have indicated that the President is a scoundrel for not "doing something." And worst of all we have said that unless the conditions which we have set forth are met, Jonathan will have died in vain.

Yes, that is the worst of all because nothing, absolutely nothing, any of us do or do not do now will cause his death to have been in vain. That is out of our hands. He can never have died in vain because he loved his killer. By his own last written words he loved his killer. (If one is looking for a martyr in it all, to die at the hands of one you love for a cause in which you believe strongly enough to let the beloved kill you is coming mighty close.) If he had loved only the Negroes with whom he lived and ate and worshipped it might have been different. Then one might set up conditions and issue ultimatums in order to get mileage out of his death, in order to have his death "mean something." But since he loved his murderer his death is its own meaning. And what that means is that Thomas Coleman is forgiven. If Jonathan forgives him, as he did when he came to love him, then it is not for me to cry for his blood. Any act on my part which is even akin to "avenging" his death is sacrilege. Vengeance negates martyrdom. It never confirms it. The sacramental act was Jonathan's, not mine.

When he loved his killer he set him free, for that is what love is. We might at least have learned that much from two thousand years of punishing Jews for killing Christ.

But apart from that, for the Christian to invoke the law of the state in this case is as absurd as it would have been for the early Christians to have gone to court following the death of Polycarp in 155, or for the Gospel Missionary Union to have lobbied for a war with Ecuador when Nathaniel Saint was killed at the hands of a savage Jinaro Indian mob in 1958. Jonathan was as certainly an evangelist as Polycarp. He was as certainly a missionary as Nathaniel. And any time a Christian is set apart and sent forth to proclaim the bold and offensive *Word*, death is apt to be the outcome. While I cannot find it within me to rejoice in this death, we at least must know that what happened was the worst that they could do, that all Satan can produce is death and that that enemy has been conquered by *The Word*. . . .

And might the truth of the matter be that we don't quite . . . trust the central theme of the gospel, the triumph of grace over law.

The notion that a man can go to a store where a group of unarmed human beings are assembled, fire a shotgun blast at one of them, tearing his lungs and heart and bowels from his body, turn on another and send lead pellets ripping through his flesh and bones, and that God will set him free is almost more than we can stand. But unless that is precisely the case then there is no gospel, there is no good news. Unless that is the truth we are back under law, and Christ's death and resurrection are of no account.

When Thomas killed Jonathan he committed a crime against the state of Alabama. Alabama, for reasons of its own, chose not to punish him for that crime against itself. And do we not all know what those reasons were?

When Thomas killed Jonathan he committed a crime against God. The strange, the near maddening thing about this case is that both these offended parties have rendered the same verdict—not for the same reasons, not in the same way, but the verdict is the same—acquittal.

The Christian response here is not to damn the "acquittal *by law*," but to proclaim the "acquittal by *resurrection*." One frees him to go and kill again. The other liberates him to obedience in Christ. Acquittal by law was the act of Caesar. Render unto him what is his. The state, by its very nature and definition, can do anything it wills to do—Hitler proved that much. Acquittal by resurrection was the act of God. And he has entrusted us with that message.

Thomas also committed a crime against Jonathan. And Jonathan rendered a similar verdict when he loved him.

But he also committed an offense against us, against those of us who set Jonathan apart and sent him forth. Thus far we have come out worst of all.

Perhaps it is because we are afraid of the Colemans of this world. Perhaps it is because he rebuffed us in the Delta and elsewhere. But worse than either of these it may be that we just plain do not love him.

The blood that is on our hands is more than that of Daniels and [James] Reeb, [Michael] Schwerner and [Herbert] Lee, [James] Chaney and [Andrew] Goodman, [Medgar] Evers and [Jimmy Lee] Jackson. The blood that is on our hands is the immortal souls of the Coleman and the [Lawrence] Raineys. They did it in the name of Jesus Christ.

That makes them blasphemers. If we, the righteous ones, the children of light, can offer them only law for their deliverance we are approaching the point of joining them in that offense.

If he persists in his blasphemy, and we in ours, we may yet be integrated with him—but in Hell. What then have *we* overcome?

B. With All the Imprisoned

3

Good News to Prisoners*

CONTEXT: *For Campbell, the theological mandate of 2 Corinthians 5 for criminal justice continued well beyond Thomas Coleman and 1965. Seven years after his P. D. East-prompted epiphany, Katallagete dedicated a double issue to the theology and politics of crime and justice in America. Contributors to the issue all had first-hand encounters with the criminal justice system in one capacity or another.*

Campbell and Holloway introduced the issue with yet another classically objectionable Katallagete essay. This time they advocated not just forgiveness of one notorious offender, but the abolition of all prisons and the release of all prisoners, period. Everyone from James Earl Ray (the convicted assassin of Martin Luther King Jr.) and Lt. William Calley (convicted for the murder of twenty-two My Lai civilians in Vietnam), to more "popular" prisoners such as Angela Davis and the Berrigan brothers. Because of the reconciliation achieved by Jesus Christ, the principality known as "the penal system" had to go.

Committed to the application of that plea, Campbell and the Committee of Southern Churchmen launched Southern Prison Ministries to rethink and rework Christian relations with the incarcerated.

Why [in Luke 4:16–30] did Jesus use that Isaiah passage [Isaiah 61] to announce that the news from God was *good*?

Talk to prisoners. Be a prisoner. Here is the clear account of what Jesus says about prisoners and prisons. It is not we Christians on the outside—safe with our money, respectability, and connections—who tell

---

* From Will D. Campbell and James Y. Holloway, "The Good News from God in Jesus Is Freedom to the Prisoners," *Katallagete*, Winter–Spring 1972, 2–5. Reprinted with permission.

the prisoners the Scriptures. It is the prisoners who tell us. This is what *Katallagete* is all about.

Jesus read a passage of gospel from Isaiah, and announced that God was coming through on his promises, reconciling all men to each other, and to Himself. The hatred, warfare, and death between and among us is over: God is with us the way He is with us in Jesus. The promises, "fulfilled in your hearing" in Jesus, come not in law, but in life. The promises are not about moral principles, but people; not generalizations, but specifics; not pieties about God, and man, but deeds between them. *Immanuel!* God is with us! God with us, not "for-example-prisoners," but with prisoners, specifically, literally. A concrete deed as a first notice about the meaning of reconciliation. Freedom to prisoners!

The announcement then, and now, throws us into fear, trembling and terror because it shatters our worship of self; that is, our money, career, social security, law-abidingness, morality, education, politics, and culture. It is the announcement from God which frightens us to install new locks on our doors, burglar bars on our windows, sign up in the neighborhood security system, submit to more taxes for more police protection, abrogate lofty, school-book political principles about individual rights and due process, and believe that everything that is against our middle-income morality is political conspiracy or organized crime. In Jesus God proclaims freedom for those in prison. The prisoners are to be turned loose. Literally. This is the good news *from God*. In Jesus God is not reform. Not rehabilitation. Nor parole. In Jesus God is freedom. Liberation. Freedom to the criminals inside the walls of stone and so to criminals on the outside who use prison as a shield against what is done against one another, against God, and against the criminals that are hidden from sight inside the walls of stone.

Jesus' news is specific, immediate, indifferent to moral codes. It is an event as close to us as brothers, children, neighbors, bedrooms and bars, and the poor and black who stand as judgment on our citizenship and our confessions about Jesus as Lord. *Criminals* are proclaimed free by God's deed in Jesus, and that, literally: "*Today* in your very hearing this text has come true." It is difficult to be more specific than that. We do not believe that Jesus was speaking of enlightened chaplains who, using the latest techniques of pastoral counseling, lead the prisoners into an adjustment—into a life of great books, celibacy, good behavior points. Nor was He talking of the chaplains who through the art of preaching win a soul here and there to a decision which says, "I am free wherever I am, for 'if God be for us who can be against us?'" What Jesus is talking about is unlocking the doors, dismissing the warden and his staff, recycling the steel bars into plowshares, and turning the prisoners loose. But let us be clear at all points. This means James Earl Ray as well as Angela Davis; William Calley as well as Phil and Dan Berrigan.

Well. Of course Jesus' neighbors in the congregation at Nazareth were dismayed and angry: "*Today* in your very hearing this text has come true." The *one* thing society cannot do is free the prisoners. Society can only *make* prisoners, and rehabilitate, adjust and then parole them . . . *to itself.* Society cannot free the prisoners. Thus does Jesus' word from God undermine the claims of absolutism lurking in all political orders— whether religious (Israel) or secular (Rome). All any political order can do is to rest its legitimacy and make its distinctions between criminals and free men on the basis of power deals and arrangements. It is never good news to say to those who stake their lives on the political order and its distinctions that God frees the prisoners. Now, and here, not there and later, God announces freedom to prisoners. Literally, not symbolically. That is how God in Jesus overcomes society. No guns. No plastic bombs or napalm or anti-personnel missiles. No conspiracy that will have to be tried in a court of law. In Jesus God is freedom to the prisoners. Society is overcome. Not destroyed. Overcome.

In his time Jesus had to go. God was made a prisoner and executed. To good religious people, as a religious fanatic; to good citizens, and a political "king." But in any case, he had to go. Society's law in both religious and political dimensions makes Jesus a prisoner and executes him in the company of other criminals. And as a wise man reminds us, there, at Jesus' crucifixion at the place called The Skull, there "was the first Christian fellowship, the first certain, indissoluble and indestructible Christian community . . . directly and unambiguously affected by Jesus' promise and his assurance . . . to live by this promise is to be a Christian community." Thus, in their time John the Baptist was a criminal, a prisoner, and executed so; thus, Paul, Peter, and others in the earliest communities who confessed Jesus as Lord; thus the prophets through whom God had spoken his words of reconciliation "to our fathers of old." Prison and the threat of prison were the necessary part of the life of Jeremiah, Amos, Isaiah, Micaiah, Joseph, Samson. . . . The news that God proclaims freedom to the prisoners is the word that overcomes society and politics.

It is the word and deed of freedom which overcomes the words and deeds of inhumanity. Society and politics can *only* answer by crucifixion, as God answers crucifixion by freedom, liberation, resurrection.

Prison is all that society and law know to do when there are violations of its codes, values, moralities, prejudices. Society and society's law cannot acquit, liberate, reconcile, free, resurrect. Rehabilitation? What would the prisoners be "rehabilitated" *from*? And *to*? *From* the very codes, values, arrangements, moralities, and prejudices which put them in prison? *To* a society that sees men—all men or any man—as sovereign over these codes, values, arrangements, moralities and prejudices? Never. Society can *only* "rehabilitate" the man from himself and his violations of the codes which placed him in prison, and *to* the society which lives by these codes. That is all society can ever know to do to those it judges "criminals." Jesus' word about this arrangement is not that it is "bad" and must therefore be destroyed, but that it is inhuman, unfree, of the order of necessity, death . . . but, that God overcomes it.

So the proclamation about freedom to the prisoners: the news from God in Jesus is *an other* word, a Word about, and to, men. Prisoners are proclaimed free, delivered from the walls of stone: a paradigm, a first-sign, but a literal one, to all men, inside and out of prison, a notification about the specifics of the gospel—specifics, according to Paul, that occur "while still in life . . . a new order has already begun." It is the good news from God that is an outrage: a concrete action. A deed. Freedom. Resurrection.

So the Bible looks at prisons without illusion. Their accounts of men in prison, and why they are in prison, are straightforward without rhetoric, whether men are imprisoned by Philistines or Israelites, Babylonians, Judeans or Romans. No explanation is to be found, nor is one needed, about violations of due process or about a system of justice gone mad under the pressure of external enemies or internal tyrannies. Both Testaments understand *all* prisoners to be *political* prisoners. Murderers, rapists, sodomists, insurrectionists, assassins, thieves of millions in a stock fraud or a loaf of bread to keep the family alive—the only thing society can do with those it judges criminals is to make prisoners. Therefore, to the Scriptures, it is always, in Dr. Menninger's phrase, "the crime of punishment,"—a situation more characterized by inhumanity's necessity than by a delicate and evil conspiracy. . . .

All this takes us back to Jesus, and to Calvary. . . . We hear no call for prison reform. We do not find instructions to the disciples to become involved in prison reform. Visit the prisoners, yes. But visit them as the prisoners Jesus talked about: no questions asked about their "crimes," about their "motives," else we tell a lie about the quality of the good news from God. Here is *another* basis for "visit the prisoners," inasmuch as those separated from the Lord at the final judgment would have visited the prisoners had they known that *Jesus the Lord* was in jail. Yet, they didn't, and we don't because we deny the Lord is a criminal. "Visit the prisoners" has never been taken seriously by the churches. Yet, we constantly discover men and women who have been in various types of prisons for decades without *one single visitor* having signed their record card. We have suggested on other occasions that each institutional church adopt three prisoners purely and simply for purposes of visitation—so that at least once each week every man and woman and child behind bars could have one human being with whom he could have community, to whom the prisoner could tell his story. And the visitor his. We have advocated that because we are convinced that this elementary act of charity alone would provide all the prison reform that society could tolerate. And we're not talking about visiting Phil and Dan [Berrigan]—in truth, they "visit" us when we talk to them in prison, not we, them—but about visiting the poor and the unknown and forgotten. For brutality and injustice is meted out far less often to those the world is watching than to those who are ignored by the world.

But it is not of reform that our Scriptures speak. Rather, it is that prisoners remind us again that Jesus is not a social reformer. So neither were (and are) those who call him *Lord! Lord!* God's good news in Jesus to the prisoners calls us to the reality that Jesus means *freedom*, not *reform*. That is what Jesus' life *is*, and does. Those who call him *Lord! Lord!* are ambassadors of, witnesses to, freedom to the prisoners, not messengers of reform of prisons. (The fate of Quaker "reforms" in an earlier century might serve as a plumb-line for the realism of the gospel at this point.)

Perhaps it is not good news to Jewish or Roman or to any society to proclaim freedom to those whom society has made prisoners. Perhaps it is to blur if not reject the distinctions between innocent and guilty on which societies necessarily exist. Those who call him *Lord! Lord!* should never forget what happened when Jesus first spoke about freedom to the prisoners. He was speaking to his own people, his friends and neighbors and relatives: ". . . they were infuriated. They leapt up, threw him out of the town, and took him to the brow of the hill on which it was built, meaning to hurl him over the edge"—the town, *his* town, Nazareth, like all towns built on moralities, prejudices, codes, fears, power arrangements, prestige, and a worship of security. And finally Jesus' people, religion and secular people, did the only thing they knew to do with him: make him a criminal, imprison him, and execute him along with others they had judged criminals and prisoners.

And that is why the news from God in Jesus is good. All society knows to do about criminals and prisoners is to do what they did to Jesus and to those executed with him. But God in Jesus did and does free the prisoners. Resurrection. Jesus is prisoner in *our* place. He is executed in *our* place. So that we might be free. So that we might be resurrected. "Free?" Yes, free to be with God and with neighbors and enemies the way Jesus was with God and with neighbors and enemies. But free also in and from prisons of stone and concrete.

The texts, but more critically the lives of Jesus and the prisoners admit of no demythologizing, no re-mythologizing, no hermeneutic contortions, no theologizing about symbolic or other hidden meanings. Jesus proclaims freedom to the prisoner. That is the good news in its first-fruits. Men's crimes against God and therefore against society are taken up, they are assumed by the imprisoned and executed Jesus. Jesus in *our* place. But we in *His*. Free. Resurrected. So why not "free the prisoners?" God has. All of us, inside and outside prison. "Worldly standards have ceased to count in our estimate of any man" (2 Corinthians 5:16). So what could the "prisoners" freed do to us that we are not already doing to ourselves? Murder us? Pervert us? Steal from us? Use us? Lie to us? Is not the freedom that Jesus means the very option to humanity that the murderer, conspirator, dope-pusher and user, sodomist and thief cannot find in the prisons and the paroles of society?

. . . It is not to oppose "reform" of prison life, but to overcome prison, to preach and live the good news of freedom to the prisoners as a first-fruit of freedom to us all.

We cannot blot out Christmas and Easter. Jesus became a criminal and prisoner of society and was executed for *us*. *All! Everyone!* When we call him *Lord! Lord!* we are therefore calling upon a Lord who was and is a prisoner. . . . We cannot take refuge in our law-abidingness, our good citizenship and economics, for our Lord was himself executed as a criminal and thus brings freedom, resurrection, to them.

If, as we believe, the first certain Christian community was those three criminals and prisoners at their execution on Calvary, then we who call him *Lord! Lord!* must bear witness to His promise to the criminals and prisoners: "I tell you this: today you shall be with me in Paradise."

The good news from God in Jesus is freedom to the prisoners.

4

Exchange of Letters with Chaplain Amos L. Wilson, Tennessee State Prison

CONTEXT: *A Boston Globe reporter once asked Will why he reached out in compassion to a man recently convicted of an especially heinous crime. "Because I feel deep compassion for that man," Campbell explained. "But why?" the reporter continued. "Why would you feel compassion for any man that brutal?" "Because he's a prisoner of the state," Campbell responded. "Jesus admonished us to visit with prisoners—no questions asked." "I'm afraid I don't understand," the confused reporter fired back. "Why extend this man the courtesy—unless you're some kind of a goddamn Christian?" "Well," Will confessed, "I guess I am some sort of a goddamn Christian."*

Chaplain Amos Wilson, of the Tennessee State Prison, may have never read Campbell's Katallagete *editorials, but in early 1973 he encountered Campbell's brand of theological iconoclasm. The brief exchange below not only highlights Campbell's view of prisons, but also his low esteem of institutions and civil governments. Tony Dunbar, mentioned in the exchange, was one of the first to work for the Committee of Southern Churchmen's Southern Prison Ministries.*

Letter from Chaplain Amos Wilson to Will Campbell*

Dear Dr. Campbell:

During the last three months or so two men have presented themselves to us as, in part, related to the Committee of Southern Churchmen, and interested in assisting at the Tennessee State Prison. They have approached

---

* Dated January 30, 1973. Printed on Tennessee State Prison letterhead.

us in markedly different manners, and I would like to briefly summarize our perception of and response to them.

The first to call on us was Anthony Dunbar. He came in a demanding way. He talked about establishing a volunteer visiting program, an activity with which I have been working. However, he exhibited no interest to cooperate with my program, he was vague as to how he would establish his, he was elusive about the goals of his program, and the men he seemed most interested in visiting were, in my opinion, among the most sociopathically oriented men in the institution. More recently he attempted to have his name added to the mailing and visitation list of a resident, and his technique appeared less than honest. Because of his shortage of candor, we are not interested in working with Tony.

The second man to call on us was Ernie Collins. He approached us with an attitude of cooperation. He inquired about the programs functioning and those in planning stages. He projected a curiosity to learn the range of our programs for the purpose of selecting the program or programs he could support. Ernie seems to be active, trying to recruit some volunteers to assist with tutoring in the school program.

I am writing this description of how we perceived Tony and Ernie as an explanation of why we resisted one man and attempted to cooperate with the other.

Sincerely,
(signed)
Amos L. Wilson,
Chaplain

Letter from Will Campbell to Chaplain Amos Wilson*

Dear Mr. Wilson:

This is in response to your recent letter. I cannot respond in an official manner. By that I mean that I gathered that your letter was written as an officer of the State, an employee of the prison which the State maintains for those who have offended it. I cannot address you, nor any other man, as an officer of the State. I have absolutely nothing to say to an agent of the

---

* Dated February 2, 1973. Printed on Committee of Southern Churchmen letterhead.

State. I do have something to say to a brother Christian and minister. Our baptism is the highest thing we have in common. Or we have nothing in common. So I address you as brother. I am not known for great displays of piety so I trust that that does not come through as such. It is just something that I believe so firmly as to try to make it paramount in dealing with any fellow human being. It is based on my own Anabaptist tradition and on a passage from 2 Corinthians which our little group uses so often that we are inclined sometimes to think we wrote it first: "With us, therefore, worldly standards have ceased to count in our estimate of any man. Even though once they counted in our understanding of Christ, they do so now no longer." Since "prison official" or "employee of the State" are worldly standards, or human categories, as one translation has it, I will try to stay away from even thinking them.

So, Brother, let's talk about the Faith for a moment. Letters are not a good way to do that for each one gives the writer license to be in complete charge for the duration of his time while the reader cannot respond in appropriate places. I wanted to "bust out" at several points as I read your letter. I'll bet you will have the same experience while reading mine. Letters also carry the hazard of sucking the writer into the vortex of self-righteousness and pride. But for the moment it's the only medium we have.

I cannot comment on the comparative personalities or approaches of the two men you mentioned. Both of them are, in my judgment, outstanding men and worthy of being received as Christian brothers. I commend them both to you as such. At the same time, each of them, in my judgment, is capable of being misunderstood on any given day. As are we all. I have certainly never thought of Mr. Dunbar as being "demanding" and I must say that it would take far more evidence than you cited to convince me that any technique he used was "less than honest." My suggestion at this point is that the three of us get together at a convenient time and discuss these specifics and go from there.

But back to the Faith. That paragraph, obviously, was my own lashing out. When you say that you are not interested in working with Mr. Dunbar I am not in the least offended. It is quite possible that you shouldn't work with him and it may well be in the interest of the faith that neither of you work with the other. But that is not to say that there is not a place for each of you. Not all are endowed with the same gift. I have been visiting prisons for many years now and have never met but one chaplain. Not because I did not wish to be of service to them if I could, but because I did not feel that they needed me. And, to be candid, I did not feel that I needed them in the ministry I was there to perform. Though I do not know the details of your program, nor even Mr. Dunbar's, it is quite possible, in my own understanding of the gospel, that you are not even trying to do the same thing. It is instead my feeling that if each prisoner had his own chaplain and his own daily visitor from the outside there would still be no overlapping of ministry. I can only speak from my own understanding of the Faith. And in that understanding, as cited above, there is no such thing as "prisoner" where the gospel is concerned. That too is a human category, a worldly standard. God has not made us prisoners. Man does that. Christ came proclaiming their release, from the time of his inaugural until the moment of his own death as a prisoner of the state. When I visit the prison I am not there to assist the prison. That is the job of the state. The state created it and I do not question its authority to do so. By definition, the state can do anything it wants to do. That is what the state is. When I come it is because a brother human being is there and needs me. If he does not need me he has only to make that known and I will not return. But if he does need me, and indicates that he does, then I will make every possible effort to continue to see him. I do not expect the state to assist me in that venture. And I am well aware that it can prohibit it if it so desires. If, in the name of the state, it feels that I am a threat [then] that is its right and perhaps even its obligation. But, in the name of the Faith, I will fight it, knowing before the fight begins that I will lose.

I feel that I must also comment on your statement that Mr. Dunbar "... seemed most interested in visiting ... among the most sociopathically oriented men in the institution." As a Christian I do not know what the word means. I know that it is a euphemism for what in the culture used to call "psychopath," and later "character disorder," but in the Christian understanding I did not know what those words meant either. Worldly standards, human categories again. And I am not suggesting that they do not have to be dealt with. All I am saying is that those categories no longer count in my estimate of a suffering human being.

Again, Brother, let's get together and witness to one another. If we can I will enter the conversation fully aware that the label "agent of the Lord" can be just as much a human category or worldly standard as "agent of the state." For it is not those who say, "Lord, Lord . . ." So. Let's get together and have a beer and try to learn to love one another as The Man has loved us. Right now I doubt if either of us does.

AD MAJOREM DEI GLORIAM (I hope)
(signed)
Will D. Campbell

POSTSCRIPT: *Sometime after this exchange, Chaplain Wilson's denomination discussed revoking his orders. One of the first individuals to come to his defense was Will Campbell. Thus, even in subtle and seemingly simple ways in his life, Campbell has illustrated his commitment to reconcile and restore good relationships with—rather than demonize and defeat—his neighbor.*

C. With the "Rednecks"

CONTEXT: *In the 1950s and early '60s, Campbell understood that African Americans were often American society's "least of these." Thus, he cast his lot with them. As the decade of the '60s unfolded and African Americans attained civil rights, however, Campbell came to believe that American society was substituting "Rednecks" as the new, preferred "least of these" group. True to form, Campbell humbly cast his lot with them—seeking to illustrate reconciliation with these ostracized sisters and brothers.*

In the five pieces that follow, Campbell resists the honor-shame paradigm of justice. Christianity rejects such zero-sum equations, in which one group gains their rights by defeating and suppressing those who had oppressed them. Incarnated reconciliation celebrates a beloved community in which all are included and valued—in this case even the scorned and undesirable Klansman.

5

Homily to a Liturgical Conference*

Hello, I'm your happy homilist for the evening. Welcome to the country version of the liturgical conference. Jim Collonini ("Collonini," now that's a name for a vice president if I ever heard one) called and said: "We are inviting you to attend the liturgical conference this year." Being a low-church Baptist that was not exactly the most unequivocal proposition I had ever had made to me. But I played it vague—just in case he got around to mentioning some handsome honoraria figure. When he didn't, I said: "Look Jim, I think you have the wrong man. I'm a Baptist preacher, I come from Mississippi, I really don't know anything about liturgics." I protested that I really didn't know anything about liturgics but that I had once met a priest in Arkansas who just might be interested in attending. He said, "Well we don't care anything about your knowledge of liturgics, we are inviting you to give the homily." Now what would you expect a redneck fundamentalist preacher to say to a statement like that? Hominy I know about, but I said, "What in the hell is a homily?" just like that, right there on the electronic horn. "What in the hell is a homily?" And he said, "You know, a sermon." And I said, "Oh." Then he said, "Well, whatever you do, we're going to call it a homily."

So let this be the homily. Let the homily be a lamentation for us, the sick and dying. Let it be the shedding of a silent tear for our condition. Let it be repentance. Let it be the casting out of demons. Let it be a song of reconciliation. Let it be a consideration of the ole time religion.

Let this homily be those haunting world of the Jewish Cantor, the funeral dirge, "O what is man that thou takest knowledge of him"—plaintive yet filled with hope, reminding us that first and last with all men is the

---

* Undated manuscript, Will Campbell Papers, University of Southern Mississippi.

affair with the almighty and reminding us of the words of Pius XI that we are all spiritual Semites.

And let the homily be the ole time religion of Pentecost. Let the homily be these familiar sounds. Sounds which many in this room have sought to alter.

Let the homily be the from the Albany civil rights movement in Georgia. Hear the ole time religion of a mass meeting in a black church house, since burned to the ground.

Or let the homily be the words of Josh White, the prophet. His words of forty years ago when he tried to tell us and we would not hear:

> Southern trees bear a strange fruit
> Blood on the leaves and blood at the root
> Black body swinging in the Southern breeze
> Strange fruit hanging from the poplar trees.

We would not, could not hear it. Already our sins were too grievous, already our hearts were so hard that we could not even repent, even if we had wanted to. We thought the strange fruit hanging on the poplar trees was talking about a lynch mob in Georgia or Mississippi. Lord have I ever been in a lynch mob? I have kept the commandments. I have eaten the flesh and drunk the blood. When was it I saw you naked, or in prison, or hungry? We thought Josh White the prophet was talking about a gang of redneck Southerners, hanging a black accused rapist from a tree. We could not look then at Rochester, and Watts, and Harlem, and Chicago, and Cleveland, and Detroit, and Baltimore, and Boston, and Washington. We, the Yankee liberals, could see the mote, but none could behold the beam. We could not, would not, hear the Lord saying to us:

> I hate, I abhor your new moons and Sabbaths. Your appointed feast, my soul hateth. Even when you spread forth your hands, and make many prayers, I will not hear, sayeth the Lord for your hands are full of blood.
>
> I hate, I abhor your stained glass windows, your cathedrals, your mahogany altars, your pretty catechism cards, your beautiful chimes and organs, your ancient vestments, your chaste nuns, your celibate monks. Even when you celebrate the Mass, I will not hear, for your hands are full of blood.

We could read the words, but the blood was invisible. We had not killed. We had not lynched. We HAD NOT EVEN *HATED*! The blood of Emmitt Till and Medgar Evers and Samuel Hammond and Delano Middleton and Henry Smith and Mickey Schwerner and Andy Goodman and James Chaney and Martin Luther King, their blood was not on our hands. And it is true. I have no guilt over that. They are alive, delivered by resurrection. The blood that is on our hands is the immortal souls of those who pulled the triggers. For they did it for us. They did it for patriotic reasons. They did it for America. Believe me now when I say they did it in the name of Jesus Christ, so protect the faith. Our hands are full of blood. Strange fruit hanging.

But let the homily not be a eulogy for the dead. Of eulogies we have had enough. Let the homily be a lamentation for the dying, for the sick and dying. From our dead black brothers let us hear if we will listen tonight:

> Weep not for us o ye sons and daughters of Jerusalem, but weep for yourselves and your children. For the time is nigh when you will cry out to the mountains "Cover us" and to the rocks, "Fall on us."

Yes, let the homily be a lamentation for the dying, for us the sick and dying. And let it begin right here with these gathered, these of the Holy Mother Church of us all. For it was religion, Christian religion, more than Caesar, that has killed our black brother. Let the homily be the casting out of demons. The power of exorcism is not mine. The casting out of demons requires orders never bestowed upon me. It requires fasting which I have not done. But there are demons in this place, in the church houses. If you want some concrete, direct action project when you return home, if you were ordained, exorcise the demons in your congregation, a power bestowed upon you in one of the earliest orders. But instead of casting them out, we have given them the seats of honor. We have nursed them at our bosom. Yes, let the homily be a lamentation for us the sick and dying.

Let the homily be a song of reconciliation with our brothers in the Ku Klux Klan. Let us repent for what we have done to them. Several months ago the Columbia Broadcasting System did a documentary film which was called "Ku Klux Klan: The Invisible Empire." It showed the horror of such things as lynching and floggings, night riding and bombings, the castration of Judge Aaron in Alabama, the murder of four Sunday school children at prayer in Birmingham. All dreadful crimes. But there were many important things they did not tell us. They did not tell us that the same thing produced them as produces the violence born of frustration and deprivation in the black ghetto. The film did not tell us that the white redneck ghetto is produced by the same social forces as produces the black ghetto.

It did not tell us about a man, who is a friend of mine who is a leader in the Ku Klux Klan. I have no parish. I have no pulpit, and he has no church that wants him. So, you might say, I am his priest and pastor. Mr. CBS did not tell us about how his father left him when he was six years old. How his mother went to work in a textile sweat shop where for 37 years, she sewed the seam down the right leg of overalls. They did not tell us about how this boy was sent to reform school; how he ran away because he was a big boy and joined the army at 14, was jumping out of airplanes when he was 16, leading a platoon when he was 18. How for 17 years he learned *from us* the fine art of torture, interrogation, and guerilla warfare.

The film did not tell us that the same social forces produced the Klan's violence that produced the violence of Watts, Rochester, Cleveland, Washington, and Nashville, and will produce much more. They did not tell us that the Klansmen are victims of the same social isolation, depriva-tion, economic conditions, rejections, under and unemployment, broken homes, ignorance, poor schools, no hospitals, bad diets, all the rest.

They only told us that only the Ku Klux Klan has a record of vio-lence as an organization in America. What of Ford? What of the textile industry sweat shops? What of the American Legion? What of the State Department?

And we revolutionists, do we think we will win? No, we will not win. But that is our sad vocation. That is our holy call. Not to stage a revolu-tion, but to be a revolution already staged. We follow the fads. We make the fads so sacred that our children's children puke and create new ones. O, how we look for a sign, but there is no sign except the sign of Jonah, three days and three nights in the belly of a whale. A kooky Jew boy three days and three nights in the belly of the early [missing in text]. Lord have mercy upon us. Christ have mercy upon us. Acquittal by resurrection. There is no other hope. The revolution is accomplished. It is over. It is fin-ished. The truce was signed on a jagged tree. O when will we ever learn?

6

Excerpt from "Our Grade Is 'F'"*

We wish to talk about another failure. It concerns a subject that has been implicit in our efforts since this journal began four years ago. This is the failure of the church and society to distinguish between the so-called black problem and the problem of the poor whites. Our nation has refused to see this distinction, we suspect, partly because of our accumulated guilt and partly because we assume that the problem of race offered more promise of solution. We white liberals romanticized the racial problem and sought to identify with the civil rights movement either by ignoring the poor whites or by seeing movements which manifest themselves most often in such groups as the Ku Klux Klan as a police problem, pure and simple.

A few years ago the Columbia Broadcasting System did a documentary film called "The Ku Klux Klan, An Invisible Empire." It showed the horror of such things as the murder of Messrs. Goodman, Chaney, and Schwerner in Mississippi; the castration of Judge Aaron in Alabama; the murder of four Sunday School children in Birmingham—who would deny that they were dreadful crimes? But as always, there were many important things which were not put before the audience, most important being the conditions which produced these people. The same thing produced them that produces, and is producing, and will produce more violence in the black ghetto. These same things are producing the white ghettos and will produce the violence, the rioting and all the rest.

The film did not tell us about a man, who is a friend of ours, and a leader in the Ku Klux Klan. It did not tell about how his father left him when he was six years old, how his mother went to work in a textile sweat

* From Will D. Campbell and James Y. Holloway, "Our Grade Is 'F,'" *Katallagete*, Fall 1969, 8–9. Reprinted with permission.

ship where for 37 years her job was to sew the seam down the right leg of those overalls. The outside right leg, for 37 years: Never the inside of the right leg, never the left leg, but her job for 37 years was to make the seam down the right side of the overalls and that was for 40 cents an hour and generally for not more than two days a week. They did not tell us about how this boy ran away because he was a big boy, joined the Army at 14, was jumping out of airplanes as a paratrooper when he was 16, was leading a platoon when he was 18. The film didn't tell how for 17 years he learned the fine arts of torture, interrogation, and guerilla warfare.

The film said only that the Ku Klux Klan has a record of violence as an organization. What of the textile industry sweat shops? What of the American Legion? (What of us—and how much do you pay your maid or your maintenance personnel? How many hungry children are there in your town tonight?)

The film did not tell us that the same social forces produced the Klan's violence that produced the violence of Watts, Rochester, and Harlem, Cleveland, Chicago and Dayton, Tampa, Houston, Atlanta, Baton Rouge and Nashville. Because the Klansmen are of the same stuff, victims of the same social isolation, deprivation, economic conditions, rejections, under-and-un-employment, broken homes, working mothers, ignorance, poor schools, no hospitals, bad diets, all the rest. Does one have to wonder why the film did not tell us?

The invisible empire? Yes, there is an invisible empire in America, but it is not the Ku Klux Klan.

There is a film of an invisible empire which needs to be made. It should be of the evil and cynical white aristocracy, the few not in the South, but in America, who profited from the sale of human flesh. It should include those who tried to do something about their plight in the Populist movement and Farmers' Alliance in the 1890s. It should report how the poor, ignorant rednecks were told that if they persisted in their egalitarian activities, their daughters would be ravished *en masse* by blacks. Then the camera should be turned slightly to the northeast, to the little city of Springfield, Massachusetts, where can be found what is said to be the richest street in the world, built not with Yankee ingenuity, but with the sale of rum and slaves. Let there be a few frames for a beautiful upper-class church edifice there and for its pastor who several years ago said at a very fashionable luncheon that his most annoying problem was that he had one usher who insisted on walking down the aisle in the offering procession in a gray flannel suit instead of the traditional morning cutaway which the other five ushers wore. Let that portion of the film conclude with this same pastor asking of a fellow clergyman from the South in all seriousness, "Do you think the churches of the South will ever wake up and do something about this race problem?"

And if it is to be a film on the invisible empire then let the electronic devices turn to the political processes in this country from the capitol dome to the JP courts, the police stations, the banks, the savings and loan companies. They are all run, not by Kluxers, but by people who are of the middle and upper class, respectable and responsible citizens all. And then do not forget the universities (Christian and otherwise), which, at best, insofar as blacks and other minorities are concerned, recruit those whose cultures and manners are already white; and where poor whites are concerned, use their intellect and influence to convince this country's people that those who can't afford to go to qualify for college should be the ones to go and fight this nation's wars. And those who can afford to go to college can remain in the safety and security of the ivory towers. Finally, film those rejects of the intellectuals as they are taught to hate and kill and burn, interrogate and torture in the fine art of guerilla warfare. Film them as they come back home and try to get an even break with the college educated. Watch them as they try to get back into "decent society." Document it with some words of President Johnson a few years ago when he pointed his long, bony finger at the millions in his television audience and said to the Klan, "Get out of the Klan and back into decent society while there is still time"—a remark which rings loudly of a police state. Watch the reject as he tries to go back into "decent society," and watch the door as it slams shut in his face. Where else can he go but to the Klan? Who else will have him? Who else wants a boy because he was a big Somebody in uniform but who is nobody's darling now? And yes, give some footage to the church houses which taught him racism in one way or another from the day he was born, all very decent, all very respectable, all for very good reasons—to preserve the harmony (that is, the wealth) of the institution.

Then let us talk about those who run this invisible empire, and who created the Klan, Harlem, Watts, and Southside Chicago. We will show you an invisible empire that intervenes in an Asian civil war; an invisible empire which calculates exactly the amount of civil rights legislation that can be passed in this country without the white voting backlash becoming a reality; an invisible empire which deprives this country of an adequate health program and a guaranteed annual income so that no child in this rich land, be he Kluxer or Black Nationalist, must go hungry, uneducated, uncared for medically.

We are not talking about hating the rich. We are simply saying that the invisible empire in this country is far more subtle, far more insidious, cunning, and treacherous than a few hundred people gathered in a cow pasture around a burning cross. It has always been against the law to dynamite churches and burn houses and shoot housewives on public highways. Why then all the HUAC [House Un-American Activities Committee] investigations of a group of folks in the deep South? Why indeed: because what HUAC represents has always been pitted against Southern rednecks. Because we like to simplify problems. We like to find the Jonah and throw him overboard, assured that everything will then be all right.

7

"The World of the Redneck"*

CONTEXT: *For years Campbell has asked, "Why are rednecks the last minority of derision?" When an ethnic group becomes a popular epithet for an "uncouth, rude, vulgar, illiberal, and especially obnoxious racist" class of people, what is revealed about American society? How is the facile identification of the poorer white ethnic group as a collection of "trashy bigots" any different than the historic racism directed at African Americans? Is it not yet another convenient diversionary tactic, another example of the elite powerbrokers transferring fear and contempt onto a convenient and largely powerless minority? As Campbell told a meeting of the Interdenominational Ministerial Fellowship—Nashville's most influential organization of African-American clergy—we "need the Klan" because we use these "rednecks" to make us feel better about ourselves. So long as we have "a scapegoat, someone to blame, ridicule and look down our self-righteous nose upon," we can escape our own guilt and avoid scrutinizing ourselves, Campbell warned.*

In this essay Campbell charts the history of the "redneck," arguing that they are among the most marginalized of peoples in American history. Initially the rich brought them to this continent as indentured servants, only to ignore them once their labor had been exploited. During the secession crisis leading up to the Civil War, the southern aristocracy took a renewed interest in the poor whites because the planter elite needed the plebeians' numbers as cannon fodder for the war. The elite, moreover, created Southern white evangelicalism as a means to their desired ends. By portraying Dixie as God's cause, they hoped that common whites would fight to protect the South's peculiar institution. In the twentieth century the rednecks were again disenfranchised, this time by the New Dealers who bailed-out landowners at the expense of the tenant farmers.

---

* From *Katallagete*, Spring 1974, 34–40. Reprinted with permission.

The fingerprints of Howard Fast's Freedom Road *and Howard "Buck" Kester's* Southern Tenant Farmers Union *are evident on this piece, as Campbell calls for the unity of society's disinherited against the manipulative and divisive powers that be.*

Not long ago I was on a program at a leading Southern university where journalists were gathered to discuss the South and its people, their religion, their racial attitudes. The morning was given over to the subject, "The Black Church Today." The speaker was a black man, a former professor of philosophy, holder of earned and honorary degrees, author of several books, a man highly respected in the academic world. His presentation was brilliant and entertaining. It was also filled with the dialect of his heritage and numerous racial anecdotes. (Perhaps this was what made it so entertaining to his all-white audience.) Whatever the reason, he was well received.

The afternoon topic was "Redneck Religion." I was to be the leader of that discussion. I began by noting that the two titles ranged from one of extreme sophistication to one of extreme vulgarity.

"The Black Church Today" was a title filled with dignity, intellectual sophistication and liberal, academic acceptance. But the other title, "Redneck Religion," was just the opposite. I wondered aloud what the response would have been if the morning subject had been "Nigger Religion," and the afternoon had been given over to a discussion of "The Church of the Culturally Deprived and Increasingly Alienated Caucasian Minority." Of course, I knew already that the response would have been one of offense at this poor taste, this uncouth verbiage, this insult to a struggling minority, despite the fact that the term "redneck" is as filled with emotional intensity as the word "nigger"—though originally "redneck" was used in all good sport. Likewise, the term "nigger" was used originally in all good sport, with no harm meant at all. No harm, except that in both cases the words were, and are, used to describe a powerless, and to the user, unattractive group. Nevertheless, I had accepted the title assigned to me and proceeded with the discussion.

Like the morning speaker, I spoke often in the idiom of *my* people, the rednecks. But instead of being applauded, I was roundly attacked by the chairman as a fraud, posing as a "know-nothing" because he knew that I had graduated from an Ivy League school and "knows better than to use that kind of grammar." Needless to say, he also knew that the morning speaker had attended some of the world's finest universities and that his degrees and academic accomplishments far exceeded my own.

More recently someone I know quite well was doing a coffee house performance before a refined, ecclesiastical group of Episcopalians. He opened the gig with a currently popular country song called "Rednecks, White Socks, and Blue Ribbon Beer." It was received with much hand clapping, foot stomping, and cheering. But the house grew silent with hostility when he announced that his next song would be, "Niggers, Mudguards, and Red Ripple Wine." *Let's don't make fun of one another's favorite minorities.*

The point of the anecdotes is that both subjects in the symposium and both song titles had to do with two proud and tragic peoples. To argue now as to which is the more proud or tragic—redneck or nigger—would be futile. But a discussion of the origins of the tragedy of each is appropriate.

Much has been said and written of the origin of the tragedy of black people. Serious consideration of the origin of the tragedy of the "redneck" is both lacking and long overdue. . . .

I am proud of my people. I am proud because I know that historically they too were the victims of the seeds of time, seeds which they did not plant, but the harvest of which has been thrust upon them and that they could have done worse. And because I know that without the incessant manipulation by the politics of the privileged they would have done better. . . .

As one who has been through the romance and drama of participation in the civil rights movement of the fifties and sixties I know how easy it was, and is, to identify with the most obvious minority—in this case the Blacks—and dismiss a less obvious minority—the rednecks, woolhats, peckerwoods, po' white—as "The Enemy." But there is a real sense in which the redneck has been victimized one step beyond the Black.

It is bad to have your back and your blood taken as happened to the Blacks. But there is a sense in which it is worse to have your *head* taken away. Through it all the Blacks knew what was happening, that they were suffering, and why, and who was causing it. And early in the game they set about the task of doing something about it. But we whites never got their head. The job on the redneck was more extensive because he had his *head* taken away. He still hasn't identified his "enemy."

Perhaps one reason why he hasn't identified the enemy is that he too, historically, was a slave. It was a more sneaky kind of slavery, so the redneck never had to acknowledge it. His was an indentured slavery: "Serve me for seven years and I will set you free." But freedom to what and in what context? Most often it was a freedom to founder, to drift, to wander westward in frustrating search of what had been promised him but never delivered—a secure life in a land of plenty.

Certainly I am not saying that all redneck history can be traced back to an indentured servanthood. The fact is that today very little of it can be so traced historically, because white scholars have never dwelt on it. By contrast, blacks created a culture out of their slavery, a history, art, music, literature. The white servant, ashamed to admit that his progenitors had been brought to these shores in almost the same fashion as the Blacks, would be more apt to tell his grandchild that his fathers landed at Plymouth Rock. Such deception was bound to result in a schizophrenia which may account for more of the deepest hostilities, bigotries, and prejudices of the redneck than any other historical factor. . . .

For the most part, politics has been seeped in his [the redneck's] bones and sinew by those whose "politics" brought him over to the "new world" as indentured servants, and so his hopes have been pinned on many stars—from Shiloh to Tom Watson, from Robert E. Lee to Huey Long, and from General Nathan Bedford Forest to General MacArthur, Franklin Roosevelt, and George Wallace. But each time his hopes have been appropriated by the gentry class and his has been left yet again stranded. . . .

I believe that the South stands where she stands today—neither integrated nor segregated, neither bussed nor unbussed, neither an integral part of the nation nor a nation unto herself—because the redneck has never been a party to any of the alliances which have been formed or the truces which have been written. Maybe this is because he steadfastly clings to the Baal worship of Politics as Messiah to deliver him from his infirmities, or maybe it is because he has been deliberately manipulated and used by the very persons upon whom he has depended for deliverance. But whatever the reason, the redneck, not the Black, has been largely the unseen and unacknowledged factor when it comes to the solution of what we seem to believe is our most pressing social problem: poverty/race/war. Moreover, he has been used by us all as a whipping post. When we think *bigot* it comes out *redneck*. When we think *racist* we think *redneck*.

Yet it is my bias that the redneck is probably the least racist of any group in white American society. This is so because racism is not an attitude, a prejudice, a matter of bigotry. . . . *Yet if we are white we are racist.* For racism is the condition in and under which we live. It is the structures in which we live and move and have our being. And we are, or seem to be, powerless to change them. . . . Yet there continues to be less real racism in redneckism because the redneck participates in the society from a base of considerably less power than the rest of us. . . .

True, many alliances have been formed. First comes to mind the old paternalism, the *noblesse oblige*. . . . It was a working relationship between two groups, the aristocratic whites and Blacks. But it failed. The alleged religion of the South was Judeo-Christian, but the alliance between the upper-class white and the Black failed because the ethics of the Southern aristocracy was not Judeo-Christian, but Greek and Roman; their politics was not democratic, but Stoic. By that is meant that among the Stoics ran the political conviction that sovereignty inheres *naturally* in the best man. . . . The nobility and graciousness which James McBride Dabbs so likes to describe in the "manners" of the South, had its roots, not in Christianity, says [Walker] Percy, but in the Stoic notion of a hierarchy of creation whereby those at the top behaved justly, decently, and gentlemanly toward those at the bottom they ruled. . . .

The Christian doctrine is that God is sovereign, creates no hierarchy and that original sin will not allow those who grab the reigns of governorship and power to rule very long without doing it sooner or later for their own sake. But in the Stoic notion of a hierarchy there was no place for the rednecks. The Blacks had been owned as property. The obligation to them was apparent to the noble Stoic. The upper-class white took care of his own as duty demanded. . . .

But the poor white was not even needed and thus there was no Stoic obligation toward him. So several things happened. The white masses got restless. They stood in their cabin doors and watched [Faulkner's] Colonel Sartoris as he passed out the necessities of life to the Blacks, a house to live in, food, medicine, churches, a piece of land to farm, run money to make the year's crop, help when he got in trouble, while he was left destitute and alone, despite the fact that he might have been on the front lines at Chickamauga, and he resented what he saw. He had no one to help him with his physical needs, no one to help him meet his psychological needs. So he turned to hating. And it was a religious hate. His religion was not the educated and well-tutored Stoicism of the aristocracy. His was a vague, varying an ill-defined folk religion, a combination of old wives tales, Indian lore, and half-remembered biblical passages passed around between visits from the circuit riding Methodist or Baptist preachers who came through on their way from Philadelphia to Natchez. Added to this was what he learned during the Civil War years.

The gentry still had a problem. . . . Since the Black could not vote, he did not need to be feared. Because the redneck could vote he was always a potential threat to the alliance between the Colonel and Uncle Lewis. A trump card was needed. There was one available and it was freely used.

The trump card was the black male, the poll tax, and disenfranchised women. . . . It was an easy matter to figure out a system whereby the voting redneck could be convinced that if he insisted on the egalitarian activities of the Populist movement or the Farmer's Alliance, his daughters would be ravished, in mass, by Black Bucks. In that wise the one advantage the poor white had, the vote, was negated and turned against him, by his own markings at the ballot box. . . .

What does all this have to do with the religion of the redneck? Everything. His religion has been and still is virtually synonymous with his politics and economics. There seems to be little doubt that it was "Christian" leadership which provided the morale which sustained the Civil War. . . . And one of the most tragic things about the institutional religion of the redneck is that it developed as an institution during the years of a defensive self-consciousness about slavery when the South was living under the cloud of the threat and then the reality of war. Previously, the aristocracy possessed the ever so respectable steeples of Calvin and Henry VIII to preside over their altar fires and tea parties. . . .

I would insist upon a distinction between my honest-to-God poverty-stricken brothers and sisters in the boondocks and hollers, and the "successful Snopes" described by William Faulkner, and I am willing to admit that not all rednecks are financially poor. But the religion of both groups has the same basic root. And that root which provided the branch and arose to steepled heights went deeply into the soil of slavery and war. In short, it was a religion founded on violence.

Because the South had limited industrial resources the success of the Confederacy depended on the degree of intestinal fortitude developed by the man up the creek from the plantation owner's mansion, or by the overseer who was raising a regiment—that is, the poor white. For the first time since indentured servanthood, the redneck was needed. But he had first to be convinced that he was a member of God's chosen people. So the church of the aristocracy went to work.

Already that church had settled the rightness of slavery. Now they had to create a religious community based on war in order to keep that war going. . . .

The cause of the Confederacy would have soon crumbled without the united and ecumenical efforts of its clergy providing the needed morale. Almost unanimously they identified Abraham Lincoln with the king of Egypt and Jefferson Davis was another Moses, leading his people to certain triumph. . . .

A new religious community had been born which had received its theological training from some of the finest, most educated, minds of the day, when, during the war, the redneck had tasted a close association with the gentry for the first time since his fathers were brought over as indentured servants in the colonies. The gentry had left their religious markings on him as they had not bothered to do when their fathers had been indentured. Now [post-war] the redneck was left to do with those markings what he would. And he would do much. He would span the breadth of Dixie with one of the most powerful religious machines ever known in the history of Christianity. He would build church houses, form congregations, split congregations to form new ones. Hundreds of denominations and sects were founded, then split with each division becoming even larger than the original. He would develop an evangelistic method with a fervor and zeal which even the hardest of hearts could not resist. He would take the antics of the aristocracy—card playing, dancing, drinking whiskey, fiddling and frolicking, and messing around on Saturday night—and make of them cardinal sins. He would build the biggest and most expensive theological schools with a tithe exacted from a people who often could not afford bread. He would demand the most rigid fundamentalist teachings of his young preachers and missionaries. He would become the most patriotic of all Americans, fighting her wars, defending her most reactionary political values and institutions, shunning the new, clinging to everything old. He would become the champion of The Faith and The Nation for he would virtually equate the two. . . .

It was and is a pietistic, individualistic, literalist kind of Biblicism. But let us make one thing strong and clear: he *believed* it. . . .

And then, just as he had been driven *to* the land by the bad faith of the rich, thousands, and then millions of his number were driven *off* the land by those who came to *help* him. Dressed in the sheep's clothing of T.V.A., A.A.A., and other New Deal agricultural programs which might have been spawned with good intentions for him but which were soon appropriated by the gentry and almost as soon exploited to the point that the end result was the current curse of agri-business with no place nor need for him. So yet again he was left stranded, this time without the hoe to lean on, only the automobile factories, the steel mills, the shipyards, the welfare lines. And as he was driven off the land with the increase of industrialism, the rise of the technological era and the parallel growth of agri-business, he took his religion with him. In Pittsburgh and Gary, Chicago, Detroit, and Dayton he would harbor a deep suspicion of Yankee Baptists and Methodists and would desert their names and join the overnight sects. . . .

The religious expression of our redneck historically was mingled with piety and with hate. The two have gone hand in hand, piety and hate. The same thing is true of a large segment of Old Testament Judaism. And there were adequate historical reasons in both cases. [Campbell here compares such imprecatory Psalms as 137 with some of the harsh KKK rhetoric.]

The subject under discussion at this point is not right, wrong; justice, injustice; good, bad. The subject under discussion is human tragedy. . . .

The point is important enough to repeat that in both cases, the redneck of Israel and the redneck of Dixie, there was adequate historical reason for their discontent. They believed something enough to hate and kill about. They were not lukewarm, a quality described by the writer of Revelation as being worthy only of being spewed out of the mouth of God.

But a more important point still is that it was from them came the Messiah. It was through the likes of them, the most unlikely of all, that God brought forth the Christ. We think, "how interesting it is that our Lord was born in poverty, in such humble circumstances, not in a motif befitting a king!" A more interesting thing is that he was born among this family of haters.

Most of us suspect that if Christ came back today he would once again be born among the lowly—Black or hippie. But wouldn't it shake us up a bit if he came today and was born into a Klan family!

"Hey man, Jesus is back."

"Yeah? Who'd he look like? Ralph Abernathy or Abbie Hoffman?"

"He looked like Robert Shelton [Grand Wizard of the United Klans of America]. He's wearing a robe and a hood!"

Surely now, you are not reading words glorifying the Ku Klux Klan. What you are reading is an affirmation of the absolute sovereignty of God.

How quickly we make heroes. And how quickly we choose enemies. And how slow we are to see the tragedy of history and come to terms with that part of it which is ours.

We are again in a time of ridicule against the redneck for starting what he calls his "Christian academies" in the South—the little frame buildings dotted about the countryside or located in church houses to avoid integration. How we look down our liberal noses at such blatant bigotry! But dare we liberal, educated, cultured whites—dare we, talk about Christian academies? Who founded Emory and Vanderbilt and Mercer and Duke and Sewanee, or Yale and Harvard? Here are the *Christian* academies. And what have they stood for historically? It is they who have trained and *educated* the managers, the owners, the soldiers, and the rulers of this present world. If there is any logic and any truth at all in the earlier paragraph of this essay which says the redneck is less racist because he operates from a base of little power, then it takes no genius to see that these Christians academies are more racist, teach and carry out more violence and repression in one day than all the pitiful little "Christian academies" springing up in cow-pastures will in a generation.

What then shall we say of our redneck brothers and sisters? Again, I hope that you do not judge this a simple glorification or romanticizing of either the redneck or the Klan. What I am trying to say is that the alleged redneck is a crucial factor to the social problem of race/poverty/war. I am trying to say that he, too, has been manipulated, used, and abused, and that what makes a man like George Wallace so dangerous is that about ninety percent of what he says is true, factually and historically accurate. I am also trying to say that the redneck, even in this post-industrial, technological age, has hung on to a scrap of individualism. In this commitment, this dogged determination, this recalcitrant, complaining, murmuring, seething hostility, and seeming helplessness, there may yet emerge deliverance from that body of death in the race and poverty which talks and haunts and infects our land. If not, not; and death's shroud will blanket us all. What form the potential deliverance could take I have no notion. No predictions. Only the sign of Jonah. . . .

8

Letter to McGeorge Bundy*

CONTEXT: *Defining the Committee of Southern Churchmen [COSC] was always a difficult task—even for those closest to it. Campbell once acknowledged, "We are, I suppose, a weird group. We are sometimes called fundamentalist, but our chief contributors could hardly qualify as such. We are sometimes referred to as antinomian—and maybe so—for our phones are tapped and we are questioned by the FBI." Then there is the journalist Elliott Wright, who, after interviewing Campbell and James Holloway, unsuccessfully tried to explain to his Religious News Service editor that the two were "left of liberal." Or this "reference" from Campbell's long-time Ole Miss friend, Jim Silver, who explained to the executive editor at Random House that Campbell was "an intellectual (he doesn't look the part) do-gooder among the church people in the South, trying to get them to see the light about race. He edits some screwy church magazine [Katallagete] which I am sure is a non-profit outfit. I don't know who subsidizes it, but certainly someone."*

Then imagine Campbell and the Committee of Southern Churchmen trying to connect with McGeorge Bundy. In 1961, Bundy resigned a Harvard dean's position to become special assistant on foreign affairs to President John Kennedy. Continuing on after Kennedy's assassination, Bundy is often "credited" with shaping the Johnson Administration's Vietnam policy—especially the practice of "sustained reprisals" against the Vietcong. In 1966, Bundy became the president of the Ford Foundation, and it was in this capacity that Campbell addressed him.

In this letter, Campbell explains the "weird" reconciling mission of COSC—the effort to serve "the lepers" of American society. As such, the COSC was neither a civil rights organization, nor part of "the Movement."

---

* Dated December 7, 1966, James Holloway Papers, University of Mississippi.

Forcing change on the South through legislation might be understand-
able, and even to a degree necessary, Campbell admitted. Until the racists
are, however, (a) appreciated and included in the conversation as equals,
and (b) lovingly mentored and converted from their error, the real goals
for which any such legislation might be drafted could never be achieved.
Instead of turning to such an "amoral and a-ethical instrument" as the civil
government and its law, people of faith could authentically partner with the
society's disinherited and incarnate reconciliation. The letter is not only an
interesting illustration of COSC trying to explain itself, but also an expres-
sion of Campbell's views on reconciliation.

Dear Mr. Bundy:

If presumption can be defined as the little going directly to the big, this is
an act of pure presumption.

The Committee of Southern Churchmen is a group of men and
women in the South who for the past three years have worked at the task
of putting some ethical meat on the dry bones of Southern folk religion.
Our charter limits us to one hundred board members. These board members are staff of this office. That means they work in their own communities and states on their own time to try to bring about a more democratic
system in the South. We are interracial and our number includes Baptists,
Methodists, Roman Catholic, Church of God, Episcopalian, Presbyterians,
and others. We publish a magazine, furnish a weekly column to approxi-
mately a hundred newspapers in the South, have a number of radio programs, do a lot of speaking, help find jobs for those displaced because of
an involvement in the racial crisis, go into the crisis areas of the region
to serve as liaison between the militants and the adamant, and in general
do whatever we can to say to the South that the religion they proclaim is
more than pretty altars and correct liturgical colors.

We came into being for the purpose of working with the recalcitrant
white Southerners. We had no quarrel with those who chose to identify
with the Negro Movement, but we felt that the South was, in a sense,
on the verge of another reconstruction. The white Southerner was seeing
the truce signed by his two traditional enemies, Negroes and the federal
government. It is our feeling that until he is made a party to the truce
there will be no settlement. The white Southerner—especially the low-

income white—stands in the strange position Chesterton spoke of—as a man who will neither come inside the house, nor put it entirely behind him, but stands forever grumbling on the porch. We see our job as getting him to come inside and be a party to the settlement.

The middle- and upper-income groups did become a party to the settlement. It was a very simple matter. They were not converted, and they did not change their minds about anything. They were brought to heel by the dollar sign. With court decisions and national legislation it was no longer profitable, not really possible, to maintain a rigid system of segregation in business and industry.

With that development a large group in the South was pushed into almost total isolation. That group is what some call "the white ghetto." It is what HUAC [the House Un-American Activities Committee] has called a "criminal conspiracy" as it is exemplified by the Ku Klux Klan. I do not believe the Klan is so much a criminal conspiracy as it is a mass movement. It is an abstraction. It is a state of mind and an economic state. Mass movements feed and grow fat on inept police attempts to crush them.

It is with that group that we are now primarily concerned. The mayors and managers who have been brought to the conference tables through economic sanctions cannot do the same with the Klan, the rednecks, the wool hats. They do not have the leverage with the Klan (again as an abstraction, not an organization) that the federal government had with them. There is little or nothing to withhold. They cannot threaten to squeeze the economic life out of a group which has given up ever having any economic life of any consequence.

Whereas at one time the Klan type and mentality was a valuable and desirable thing because it served the system, it is now something to get in the way. Whereas they were once accepted and even loved, they are now shunted aside, ridiculed, investigated—with Southern congressmen doing the job—and pushed more and more into isolation.

What happens to isolated groups? We know from Harlem, from Watts, from Rochester and Chicago. Fortunately for us all other government and private agencies are pouring talent and funds into those areas. Competent social scientists conduct studies and tell us that educational levels, median incomes, degree of unemployment, cultural factors, and many other things go into the making of such behavior as we have witnessed there. It would seem that the nation would have learned from the famous and well-done Appalachian Survey of a few years ago that the same is true of the Klansmen of the Deep South. Some have seen it. But for the most part they are considered a police problem. Of course, they *are* a police problem. But only in the sense that Watts and Harlem are police problems when they erupt.

Society has always had its lepers, its unpardonable sin. We see the Klan (not organization) as the new lepers of our day. The churches do not work with them, government does not to any effective degree. We work with murderers, alcoholics, and schizophrenics, but we seem to shrink back in trembling modesty from any meaningful contact with overt racists.

If I appear in sympathy with the Klan, it is in the same sense that I am in sympathy with any other sick individual or group. But there is a bit more to it than that. If this letter should later become a proposal to the Ford Foundation, I do not want to mislead you. The truth is that I do feel a certain empathy with the racist which I do not feel with the average murderer, alcoholic, or schizophrenic. At the head level I can hold him in contempt. Four years at Wake Forest, one at Tulane, three at Yale, three years in the army—or the grace of God—taught me that he his wrong. But at the gut level, I can still hear his anguished cry when the rains didn't come in time to save his cotton. I can still see his agony on Christmas Eve while I, his six-year-old child, feigning sleep, waited for a Santa who would never come; I can still feel the severity of his economic deprivation for I can't forget the drawing of my own little belly in the middle of the Depression on a Mississippi farm. If I had not shared this plight; if I had not lived with him in an atmosphere of suspicion, distrust, ignorance, misinformation, and nefarious political leadership, surely I could condemn with gut as well as head when I see him fomenting mob violence in front of his schoolhouse, or gathering in Neshoba County [MS]. Perhaps any consideration of this memo should be directed elsewhere for one cannot claim to be objective about those from whose loins he sprang.

But I can be objective enough to seek that the jails of this country are not big enough to hold all the Kluxers. And I can doubt, on many grounds, the wisdom and righteousness of a governmental policy which seeks to meet the challenge of the Klan resurgence by measures which are exclusively police in character. The untouchables, the outcasts, the lepers of Watts and Harlem who raged in blind frustration behind the walls of their black ghetto could not be cured in that manner and the new outcasts, the new lepers behind the very real walls of their white ghetto cannot be helped in that manner either.

I am now ready to make my pitch. Society has learned, painfully, to reject the murder but not the murderer; to reject schizophrenia but not the schizophrenic; alcoholism but not the alcoholic. In the same way, and with a painful awareness of our own limitations, we dare to reject racism but not the racist. By definition, there is no one beyond the pale. In the name of all we believe holy, we dare to claim our robbed brothers in the white ghetto; we dare to love them in this critical hour of their need . . . and ours.

We propose to establish a limited program in the heart of the white ghetto. We will hire a young minister—in each community—whose latent racism is under sufficient control so that it will not be precipitated by the overt racism of his parishioners. This young man will operate out of a store-front Social Center on the main street of a rural town. The Social Center will be equipped with second-hand furniture, TV, record player, refrigerator, and simply recreation paraphernalia. He will hire an "indigenous assistant," who will be paid a small salary to assist in various ways. In an atmosphere charged with dangerous paranoia, this "indigenous assistant" offers reassurance to "the boys" that there is nothing being hidden from them.

Certain peripheral advantages will be hoped for in the wake of the program's *limited* objective. Informal contacts will be opened up with both the "jackleg preachers" of the Pentecostal sects and the middle-class ministers of the orthodox Protestant churches. The young minister can be a reassuring liaison between "the boys" and such harsh (to them) institutions as the local recorders' court, the hospital, various CEO programs, county agents, employment offices, and those who come into the region for whatever purpose. . . .

We could romanticize and add a great deal more that we hope for. All-night sessions in a effort to dissuade someone from burning a church house or joining a lynch mob may be more than actually will happen. But who knows? We do not suggest in any way that this program will "change" the overt racists of the white ghetto. We claim that here is a group which has been too long neglected and that sooner or later all of us will have to pay for that neglect.

We are already paying for it. Georgia will pay for it for four years. Mississippi will go on paying. Alabama. California? Most of our members worked hard for the passage of the recent civil rights legislation. We have long recognized the need and urgency of political measures to remedy the political, social, and economic abuses and inequities that are a part of our nation. But in recent events we have seen the signs of the tragic consequences of the illusion that political nostrums would cure everything that was wrong with us. We see being exacerbated the very situations the maneuvers sought to remedy. There is no substitute, we believe, for a continuing personal relationship with people, based on a solid moral commitment. Most of us liberals scoffed when a former president said, "You can't legislate morality." But there is a germ of truth in that cliché which, it seems to me, we are now forced to examine. . . .

Cordially yours,

Will D. Campbell

9

Letter to Walker Percy*

CONTEXT: *For a time the renowned Southern author Walker Percy served on the board of the Committee of Southern Churchmen [COSC]. In this excerpt from a handwritten letter, Campbell explains to Percy his appreciation for his brothers and sisters in the Ku Klux Klan. As such, this undated personal letter both conveys the private side of Campbell's commitment to reconciliation, and his concern to "wash the wounds" of our social lepers.*

Walker Percy later broke ranks with the COSC when the Committee publicly condemned the Vietnam War and supported Dan and Phil Berrgian's raid on the Catonsville, MD, Selective Service office in May 1968.

Dear Walker:

As you know, I don't submit annual reports to board members of the Committee of Southern Churchmen. Instead I try occasionally to write a letter to different ones when I have been involved in something which I think will be of interest to him. Since you are a writer, I decided you may have some interest in an experience I had last week.

As you know, I spend a considerable amount of time with some of the Klan units. I do so for several reasons. One, I believe that here is the real tragic figure of the South for us today. We have always had an unpardonable sin in this culture. It has ranged from drinking liquor, to saying ugly words at the Holy Spirit. Today the unpardonable sin is the avowed (honest) nigger hater. He is the new leper. Time was when the Klan was desirable and useful to the Colonel in the big house. Politically and economically, it was an asset. Now the Colonel has discovered better ways. We need industry, we need federal grants. But this large pocket of

---

* Undated, James Holloway Papers, University of Mississippi.

deprived and depraved souls which we have created remains. They have been produced by the same socio-economic forces that have produced the black ghettos—the same brokenness, social rejection and isolation, ignorance, under and unemployment, poor schools, working mothers, broken homes, and all the rest. And they are as potentially as violent and explosive as the inhabitants of the black ghettos. While we have finally awakened to the need of understanding why the black poor behave as they sometimes do, we continue to see the Klan Movement (and it *is* a social movement, not an organization) as simply a police problem. So the HUAC has a hearing, isolates a Jonah, exposes the corrupt (and thus vulnerable) leadership, puts them in prison, and we assume our race problem is going to be solved.

Last week the whole scene came into sharp focus for me when I was called upon to bury one of them in Greene County, North Carolina. . . .

I have never tried to learn the secrets of their crimes. A few have related some, but I prefer that they didn't. This is something your priests have that we do not. I do not know how to live with the seal of confession. I know that no matter what they tell me, no police chief, FBI, HUAC, or whatever have you would ever pry [it] out of me. But I find it easier not to know. Some of my friends accuse me of romanticizing these people. I don't. I know they are tough and mean, some are killers, all are near incorrigible racists. But all of them are little boys playing war—little boys for whom Christ also died—Raymond Crawford *and* Eldridge Cleaver. That's the scandal of the gospel. . . .

Love,

Will

D. The Incarnation of the Church

CONTEXT: *Throughout his writing, Campbell warns that, seeking to incarnate reconciliation, the church will find the way unpredictable, objectionable, and frustrating. In the pieces that follow, Will encourages the church to persevere, to ignore convention (i.e., "breaking the pavement of countless cultural status quos"), and reclaim its scandalous ministry. The socially disruptive church is incarnated in reconciliation.*

10

"Symposium on Transcending Ideological Conformity"*

CONTEXT: *In 1991, the editors of the* New Oxford Review *selected a dozen individuals whose lives resisted the standard categories of "right," "left," and "moderate," asking the twelve to clarify their respective individual viewpoints. The list of invited "misfits" included: Will Campbell, Robert Coles, Ronda Chevin, John C. Cort, Stanley Hauerwas, James Hanink, Amitai Etzioni, James Seaton, Dale Vree, Jean Bethke Elshtain, Ronald Austin, and Christopher Lasch. Hoping for clarification and explication, the editors asked these nonconformists:*

1. *How did you come to adopt your unusual stance?*

2. *Are you often misunderstood or mistrusted? How difficult is it for you to maintain your stance?*

3. *How do you connect your "leftist" views with your "rightist" views in a way that you find consistent?*

4. *Why is it that so many people fall into rigid left-wing or right-wing ideologies, such that if you know their position on one issue you can usually predict their position on virtually every other issue? Why are so many people prone to be "politically correct," whether Left or Right?*

5. *What are the prospects for getting more people to transcend ideological conformity?*

Respondents were encouraged either to answer each specific question, or to use the questions as a springboard for a comprehensive—albeit brief—

* From the *New Oxford Review*, October 1991, 7–8. Reprinted with permission from New Oxford Review, 1069 Kains Avenue, Berkeley, CA 94706, U.S.A. Online: http://www.newoxfordreview.org.

response. Will chose the latter, illustrating that when reconciliation is incarnated, it is a new politic.

I have never understood who sets the parameters into which we must all fit. I don't trust them and don't acknowledge their lines. I have never tried to be politically correct. (I do not here use that term according to the current controversy in the academy, but rather in the sense of politics as the realm of Caesar.)

To answer your queries runs the risk of sounding as if I am trying to rewrite the Acts of the Apostles. My life has not been that venturesome. At the risk of seeming immodest, I will list a few involvements which others have cataloged as "Right" or "Left."

Early in my life I took a position against racial discrimination, joined Martin Luther King in the formation of the Southern Christian Leadership Conference, walked to school with the Little Rock Nine, and involved myself in the civil rights movement in various ways. In none of this did I think of myself as being on the Left. Others, in the Mississippi of my white rearing, did. The designation was theirs, not mine.

When the Grand Dragon of the North Carolina Ku Klux Klan was indicted and tried for contempt of Congress, I helped raise money for his defense. I was with him the night the marshals came to take him away. I kept in touch with his family, visited him in Danbury prison. I should not have been surprised when some considered that a move to the far Right, even though I also visited others there for crimes of war resistance. I saw no inconsistency since neither Isaiah nor Jesus said anything about ideology. Prisoners are prisoners and it is our vocation to set them free.

I harbored deserters and draft dodgers and took some of them to Canada during the Vietnam War. Was that of the Left or Right? To me it was neither. Though seen by most as politically left, again, someone else was drawing the boundaries.

I have written, spoken, stood in vigils against the death penalty. Liberal? If others wish to categorize, they are free to do so.

I see the fashion in which abortion is practiced as the greatest American shame since slavery. Does that mean I am in league with the Reagan-Bush syndrome and am now a right-wing Republican? God forbid! For I believe the economic policies of those administrations have resulted in far more abortions than their rhetoric or gestures have prevented.

So what does it all mean? If these are not political acts, are not to be categorized by someone's scheme as "Left" or "Right," then what? Are we talking of anarchy when we suggest that Caesar's, and society's, nomenclature is irrelevant to us? Perhaps so. But let it be the Christian anarchy Vernard Eller and Jacques Ellul so ably describe, not the anarchy which simply becomes another political position to be campaigned for. In Christian anarchy there is no Left, Right, or Center. Christian anarchy has to do with grace and human freedom. And it is human freedom which seems to me to be the essential message of Jesus. Thus my seeming contradictions, in a life which has spanned almost 70 years, reflect an effort to survive as a human being, free of other archies which inevitably define a channel in which its adherents must swim or be excluded, and which, by nature, are enslaving, for they claim ultimate allegiance.

11

"Last Act in a Tragedy: Where to Sit in Scottsboro"*

CONTEXT: *An example of reconciliation's social nonconformity comes in Will's essay on the last of the trials associated with the "Scottsboro Nine." By most accounts the Scottsboro Nine trials are a low point in American jurisprudence, pitting racist, reactionary conservatives against vigorous progressives. In 1931, Ruby Bates and Victoria Price accused nine African-American men of rape. The nine were arrested and initially tried in Scottsboro, Alabama. Although the testimony of Ms. Price and Ms. Bates (both white women) proved utterly inconsistent and often implausible, the jury convicted and sentenced the nine defendants to death. Higher courts repeatedly threw out the convictions, but the state of Alabama worked for twenty years to execute the defendants. Eventually all were acquitted, but enduring years in fetid prisons and an unjust legal system had ruined their lives.*

Initially the accused had been the social pariahs, but by the late twentieth century society had reassigned that role to the accusers. In 1976, for example, a low budget NBC docu-drama retold the Scottsboro case, portraying Ms. Price as the face of racism and injustice. For NBC's depiction, Ms. Price leveled a $6 million suit against the network.

Entering the courtroom in Winchester, Tennessee, for this trial, Campbell could not decide where to sit. Where was his allegiance, and who was deserving of condemnation? Would he sit with Ms. Price, the odious plaintiff who incited the original injustice—who still clung to her disproven story nearly a half century later? Would he sit with the major TV network, the journalistic principality that depicted Ms. Price as a racist buffoon. Ms. Price was, Campbell notes, one of the economically disenfranchised, who, like so many in that time and region, had been a pawn of "the system."

* From *Christianity and Crisis*, July 1977, 189–91. Reprinted with permission.

Was it fair, Campbell puzzles, to condemn the pawn without holding the system itself culpable? Was it fair to fix the blame on one or two damaged characters, without holding society itself responsible for the exploitation of individuals like Ms. Price in the first place?

In this essay, Campbell both exposes a system that meets out justice by honoring one side by shaming the other, and illustrates a Christian ethic that labors to reconcile. Campbell also illustrates that reconciliation does not mean "living happily ever after." In this case, reconciliation can leave matters uncertain and ambiguous.

In a nearly deserted courtroom in Winchester, Tenn., what will probably be the last legal proceedings in the case of the "Scottsboro Boys" came to an end shortly after noon on July 13. To some it seemed the coming of slow but sure justice, the final acquittal of the innocent. Others were not sure what it meant. Whatever it was we were watching, it had been 46 years and 4 months in coming.

I couldn't decide where to sit. I recognized five different and distinguishable groupings, all small, all with plenty of room around them. I walked around the modest federal courtroom for a few minutes and then sat on one of the long benches as far from the other groups as I could get. It was not that any of the groups were hostile. I would have been welcome to join any one of them. And it was not that I would have problems identifying, at least in part, with any of them. Each had a right and reason to be there. Each reason had something to be said for it. I like to take sides. But I couldn't decide where to sit.

The story which was coming to a probable conclusion began on a freight train between Chattanooga, Tennessee, and Paint Rock, Alabama, on a cool March morning in 1931. The awful weight of economic depression was apparent as dozens of hobos boarded and left the freight trains of America at every stop, some going some place for a purpose, most going nowhere and for no purpose at all. The trains were home for a quarter of a million people and most railroad officials ignored company directives to report any trespassing on the cars. That is what Conductor Robert Turner did on that windy morning as he watched 20 or so pitiful souls scramble for a position on his train as it left the Chattanooga station.

Normally most of them would have stayed on the rails until they reached Memphis, some leaving along with way at stops like South Pittsburg, Scottsboro, Huntsville, or Decatur if that was where they had purpose, or if Hobo Intelligence indicated there was a "jungle" to serve as their hostel for the night, or that there was the possibility of a handout or some small job there. But on this train and on this day things would not proceed so smoothly. The station master at Stevenson heard a little group of bruised and sometimes bloody white boys telling him that a "bunch of niggers" had started a fight and had thrown them off the train, and that they wanted to press charges against them. It did not seem serious or unusual but he notified the local law.

When the train reached Paint Rock, not more than an hour away, it was greeted by a deputized posse consisting of every white male in the little town who owned a gun. Their orders were to search the train, capture every Negro on it and bring them all to Scottsboro. Their mission was soon accomplished with neither resistance nor undue force. But as the search was ending the posse found something amongst the freight they were not looking for—two young white women.

It was the beginning of one of the most infamous chapters in American jurisprudence—the case of the Scottsboro Boys.

Charlie Weems. Ozie Powell. Clarence Norris. Willie Roberson. Haywood Patterson. Eugene Williams. Olen Montgomery. Andrew and Leroy Wright. Nine nobodies. Within the following decade they would become black names as well known as Joe Louis and Jesse Owens. But sooner forgotten. The term "boys" might have been a racist designation at the time. But it was also a fact. Only one was not a teenager. One was 13 and one was thought to be 12.

The two young white women identified themselves as Ruby Bates and Victoria Price. They would be as well known.

Quick Verdict, Slow Justice

The days and years to follow, the weeks and months of testimony, convinced most people—Judge James Horton among them—that when the women saw the deputies they feared they would be arrested and charged with violation of the Mann ("White Slavery") Act. (A man had traveled with them across the state line.) After a delay of 20 minutes or so, one of the women indicated to the posse that she wanted to report something to an elected official. When one was brought she told him that they had been raped by the nine Negroes. After a series of near-lynchings the nine were quickly put to trial, defended by a court-appointed attorney. All were found guilty and were all sentenced to death in the electric chair.

The litigation and the political and ideological warfare that followed for two decades have carefully documented by Dan Carter in his book *Scottsboro: A Tragedy of the American South.*

It was to be the South's Sacco and Vanzetti, and a case which would give more notoriety and public exposure to the Communist Party in the United States than it had ever known.

Entering the case with their International Labor Defense, through the most unbelievable machinations the Communists wrested the defense of the nine from the NAACP and several ad hoc defense committees; the response made the party a strong factor in Alabama politics for more than 10 years. Though eventually compromising and permitting the noted jurist Samuel Leibowitz to handle the actual courtroom proceedings in later trials, the Communist Party became a force to be reckoned with.

It was a day when no faction could claim to be free of bigotry and acrimony. Even the generally mild-mannered Leibowitz, after a stinging courtroom defeat during which the county solicitor had advised the jury to "show them that Alabama cannot be bought or sold with Jew money from New York," would say of the Southern jury, ". . . those bigots whose mouths are slits in their faces, whose eyes pop out like frogs whose chins drip tobacco juice, bewhiskered and filthy." Neither prosecutor nor defense; neither North nor South was temperate with its rhetoric and ethnic slurs. And the Scottsboro Boys remained in jail.

With the passing of time, and after the involvement of such calmer heads as Allen Knight Chalmers, Grover Cleveland Hall of the Montgomery *Advertiser*, Will Alexander of the Southern Interracial Commission and numerous others, the last of the Nine was released. But that was 19 years and 2 months later. And by then the Nine had served a total of 130 years in prison for a crime which was never committed. Few now, whatever their regional and racial bias, doubt that there were for a fact two crimes committed on that train—the Mann Act had been violated and there was a fight between the young blacks and white hobos. But those violations were totally lost in the allegations of rape of white by black.

Now, 46 years later, I was confused as to where I should sit as I entered the courtroom to watch a final chapter. The occasion was a lawsuit against a large and wealthy American corporation, the National Broadcasting Company. The plaintiff was a pathetic countrywoman of 70 years, overweight, dressed in loud purple, teeth in bad need of repair, head-shaking with palsy, black, stringy hair very much in need of washing. Ordinarily I would have had no trouble in taking a seat beside her. But the woman was Victoria Price, now known as Victoria Price Street. (I wondered where I would have sat if Clarence Norris, the last survivor of the Scottsboro Boys, had been present. But he wasn't.) So I didn't know where to sit.

The stage had been set several months earlier when NBC showed a TV movie called *Judge Horton and the Scottsboro Boys*. It was based on Carter's book and though his research was thorough and the writing excellent throughout, on the last page of the book he had reported that both Ruby Bates and Victoria Price were dead. Now I was sitting three rows behind Victory and she was very much alive. Flanked by two lawyers and facing a federal judge who was about to give the final legal judgment in the Scottsboro case, Victory was suing NBC because of some of the things the movie had said about her. She had been, she said, libeled, slandered: her privacy had been invaded. Everyone in the courtroom knew that what was really at stake was whether a Southern judge and jury would still agree that she was telling the truth. This time the stakes were $6 million.

Six million dollars for a poor country woman. The money to come from a big, rich corporation. Normally it would have been a natural for my glands. And even then I wasn't sure that I didn't want her to have it. Still I remembered the sickening accounts of the horrors of Scottsboro, the Decatur and Birmingham jails, the years at Kilby and Atmore prisons. I remembered nine children, confused, ignorant, most having to make a mark for a name, one almost blind at the time of the alleged crime, another so sored and cankered with syphilis that he could walk only with the help of a stick, physically incapable of the act of which he was accused. Nine captured, caged, tortured, broken, battered, and destroyed human beings. All on the testimony of a woman whose reputation for veracity was not defended by even the most friendly witnesses the State could produce.

I remembered another woman of questionable morality, already convicted and at the point of being killed by stoning. And a man who stopped her execution, forgave her, and sent her on her way. Would his "good news" have reached this far? My god! Of course! And *I* didn't know where to sit down.

Court transcripts, stories, articles, books, judges, lawyers on both sides, even the later testimony of her companion and co-accuser, Ruby

Bates, all scream through the years that Victory Price was a lying woman. Who was she? Who is she now? What put her on that train? What put the Scottsboro Boys on that train? What forces produced this accident of history? Anyone who would look for answers in the Southern juries Leibowitz described, or the Northern money spoken of by the county solicitor, or the Communists who became whipping boys of liberal and conservative alike, had best look again.

Systemic Sin

It was no accident at all. It was what we now call "the system." (We used to call it original sin and probably should have stuck to that explanation.) Of Victory Price we know that at 13 she had gone to work in a cotton mill in Huntsville, working 12 hours a night for 20 cents an hour. By the time of the train ride the mill in which she worked had cut working time to three shifts every other week. That is $1.80 a week. Victory insisted, rightly, that neither she nor anyone else could live on that amount. But she never acknowledged publicly the means by which she had supplemented her income. She didn't have to; others did it for her.

Against defendants of her own race this woman's testimony would have been considered (rightly or wrongly) of no value at all—the more so when she had every reason to lie and when everything else in the circumstances affirms she was indeed lying. But she lived in a certain time and place, and she told the kind of story that society of that time and place wanted to hear. And so she was rewarded with her freedom; at the price of nine wasted lives.

Now nearly half a century later, she sat facing a Kennedy-appointed federal judge, his court convened by a black bailiff, not far from the two courthouses where she had told her story so many times before. But this time all her aiders and abettors were gone. Beside her was her husband, his coriaceous face so deeply lined, so nearly black from the years of accumulated grime, baked in by the years of toil in the Southern sun that he could have passed for one of the original Scottsboro Boys.

The judge explained to the jury of four men and two women why he could not let them decide the verdict on the basis of evidence. "It is now," he said, "just a matter of law. And the law is not for a jury to decide. You can only decide guilt or innocence within the law." Judge Horton, in reversing a jury decision in one of the trials, had said some similar words. And paid heavily for them. But his words had freed no one. Judge Neese was saying that he was ruling against the plaintiff, the effect being a directed verdict of not guilty for NBC.

The tired old woman would not get the money and would return to the little farm where she and her husband live and work.

Though I had not chosen to sit beside her I did want to say something, anything, to her. I settled for words with which many neighbors still greet one another, not meaning to refer to the outcome of the trial. "How you feeling?" She answered quickly and emphatically. "I feel like ain't no justice been done. I didn't lie in Scottsboro. I didn't lie in Decatur and I ain't lied here. I've told the truth all the way through and I'm a'gonna go on fighting 'til my dying day or 'til justice is done." I had not the slightest doubt that she was totally convinced that she *had* told the truth. And she had probably been so convinced almost from the very day she whispered to her companion as the posse approached that they should say they had been raped in order to avert charges being placed against themselves.

I mumbled something that made no sense to either of us and walked away from Victory Price. As I left I had the feeling that Victory Price stood no more of a chance in that courtroom in 1977 against NBC than the Scottsboro Boys had stood in another one nearby against the state of Alabama in 1931. And I had the feeling that there was something wrong in both years and places. In 1931 it would not have been difficult to figure out what it was. (That is, if we had had our present enlightenment and sophistication.) In 1977 it was not so simple. (Even with our enlightenment and sophistication.)

I knew only that Victory didn't get the money from NBC. I knew that I had not known where to sit. I felt a little confused. And a little sad for Victory Price, for the Scottsboro Boys, and for us all.

12

Interview with *The Wittenburg Door**

CONTEXT: *If reconciliation can be uncertain and ambiguous, it is hardly surprising that the church incarnating such an ethic can be hard to pin down.*

"Will Campbell is weird—a good kind of weird, but weird, nonetheless. He's ornery. Will usually says what he thinks . . . when he thinks it. He has been known to sip a Jack Daniels or two, and his language is . . . well . . . spicy." Not a bad endorsement from the editors of the notoriously irreverent Wittenburg Door. *In this interview, Bill McNabb begins by asking Will what "the Church" is, and Campbell maintains that he doesn't know. Campbell, of course, has quite a strong working definition of "the Church." It is diametrically opposed to what he calls "the steeples" (or what most people believe "the Church" to be).*

In this iconoclastic piece, Campbell challenges traditional definitions of "the Church," and sets the ground for an alternative description.

To capture the flow of Campbell's thoughts, his responses to McNabb have been woven together in a more seamless design (i.e., rather than the question-and-answer dialogue format that appeared in the article).

Hell, I don't know what the church is. Jesus said something about the fact that He was going to *build* the church. He did say that nothing would prevail over it . . . even the gates of Hell, but He didn't ask me to build it. And He certainly didn't ask me to define it. I *believe* the church *is* at work in the world only because of my faith in this Jesus person. Trouble is, I

* From Bill McNabb, "The Futility of Fighting Over What We Believe: An Interview with Will Campbell," *The Wittenburg Door*, March–April 1990, 12–15. Copyright ©1990 The Wittenburg Door. Reprinted with permission.

don't know what Jesus is up to or where His church is. That's good because if I found the church then I'd give it a name and start running it.

Running the church is not ministry, it's not just running an office, visiting the sick, preparing sermons, and working with the sacramental chores. That's just administration. Nothing wrong with it, you know, but it ain't ministry. I think the word "ministry" is rather presumptuous anyway. Sounds kind of imperialistic to me—you know, I can do something for you better than you can do yourself.

I think I'm more like a preacher without a steeple. Kind of like a bootleg preacher. That means I don't minister for the institutional church—the steeple. *No* institution can be trusted, including the steeple. They are all after our souls—*all* of them. It means that I refuse to let any institution or ideology tell me how to do my ministry. There are no conditions, *ever*, in the New Testament. No ideology in the New Testament, either. Second Corinthians 5 makes it very clear that when one is in Christ he/she is a new creature. No longer do we consider anyone by human standards or human categories. That is an exceedingly radical bit of news. When one is in Christ, human categories are no longer applicable. But an institution is a human category and every institution is self-loving, self-regarding, and self-protecting, and anything bad for the institution it proclaims as unchristian.

I say "Don't trust it [the institutional church]." **Don't trust it.** That doesn't mean God doesn't work wherever God chooses, so I wouldn't rule out the stained glass and the mahogany pews and the silver chalices. I don't rule *any* of that out. I am just trying to say that if God is the God of the universe, don't try to put God in this pigeonhole and say "If you want to be with God, come to this edifice or this steeple or serve this particular cause."

I know that if we could abolish all institutions today, tomorrow we would start rebuilding them. Institutions are inevitable, I know that. *I* work within them all the time, I don't claim not to. But I try and say, "I'm working *within* this particular institution . . . *but I don't trust you.* I bend over to put the pinch of incense on the pagan altars all the time, but I try to remember to snicker a little bit when I do." I'm bending over, yes, but if I can snicker, then I maintain a little of my humanity, which is what to be "in Christ" means, near as I can tell.

I'm saying that in my judgment the institutional church is standing today where the rich young ruler stood—both are rich, powerful, and good. I never say the church is bad. Obviously, it's not a bad outfit; the institutional church—structure—is a good outfit. It is also very powerful. It is also very, very rich. So rich that if the structure did what the rich young ruler was told to do, then we could lick the problem of poverty in this country overnight. Let's suppose the structured church *did* sell all of their buildings, parking lots, computers, Betty Crocker kitchens, skating rinks, and gymnasiums. What would happen? I have some hunches about what would happen. We might sing the Psalms for the first time in our lives. An unemployed preacher might come by wanting something to eat, and we might experience the Supper of our Lord for the first time in our lives.

The evil of institutional religion is the result of two confusions. The first confusion is to confuse belief with faith. Belief is not faith. The devils believe. The inquisitions, the holy wars, and the modern-day internal warfare within denominations like the Southern Baptists are never about faith. They're always about belief. Belief is always passive. That's why we kill people—because of what they believe, not because of what they do. But faith is *active*. Faith implies doubt. Paul had doubts at the end of his life—"What if I, after having preached the way to others, have missed the way myself?" Today we are bombarded with the theology of certitude which says, "I've found it. I've got it. If you don't *believe* the way *I* believe, then you are out." That kind of theology has nothing to do with faith. Actually, we confuse the things we wish for with the things we hope in. We confuse wish and hope.

I wish for a world without nuclear bombs. I wish for a world where everyone would have a home, a place to sleep at night. I wish for a world where children are not abused. I wish for a world that is drug free. But none of those wishes are what my hope is in. I may or may not see my wishes come true, but my hope is in eternal things. God will have the last word. I have to admit, if I had been God I would not have made us quite as free as He created us. I wouldn't have made us puppets, but I would have created a little string so if some cat was on the verge of blowing up the universe I could jerk the string and say, "Nope, you're not going to do that." But no. We're just as free as God. We can blow this universe up. *Even so, that is not the last word.*

But you know what troubles me? What troubles me is what an emphasis on belief does to discipleship. It negates discipleship, really. Discipleship is the struggle to be like Christ, even though I know I am not Christ and that I am not going to be like Christ perfectly. But I am expected to try. Once I make what I *believe* the issue, then I'm off the hook. I either believe your particular creed or I don't. So, I don't care about how you live, what I care about is what you believe.

[Take the infallibility of Scripture, for example.] To be quite honest with you, I never have understood that issue. *No one* believes the Bible literally. No one. Pat Robertson, Judge [Paul] Pressler, Billy Graham—*no one* believes the Bible literally.

A fellow came by my house a few years ago and I asked him, "Do you believe the Bible literally?" He responded, "Yes, sir, my brother, word for word." I said, "Well, fantastic." I stood up, gave him a courtly bow and ceremoniously got my hat and cane, extended my hand and said, "I didn't know there was anyone else in the world who believed the way I do. The Bible says that the day has come to proclaim the opening of the doors of the prison and letting the captives go free. I've been looking for years to find someone who agreed with the literal interpretation of that scripture 'cause there's this prison in west Nashville and I can't tear the thing down by myself, but if there's 15 million folks out there who believe in the literal interpretation of Scripture, we can get them all together and raze that prison to the ground." He looked at me kind of funny and said, "Well, now, what Jesus meant by that was . . ." I shouted, "Don't you go exegeting on *me*." He said he believed in Scripture literally. But the prison's still standing.

It all gets back to what we've been talking about. The futility of fighting over what we believe. What does it matter what someone believes? If you are bringing good news to the poor and restoring sight to the blind and healing the brokenhearted and releasing the captives, but you happen to believe that a whale swallowed Jonah or you happen not to believe that a whale swallowed Jonah, what difference does it make "as long as Christ is preached"?

13

"Where's the Church?"*

CONTEXT: *In the South, asking "Where's the church?" may seem like a silly question. In Nashville alone (sometimes referred to as the "Buckle of the Bible Belt"), church buildings outnumber all other types of public-use edifices. Yet Campbell asks a vital question. Whether in middle Tennessee or anywhere else, where does one find the people of God living out the kind of commission described in* The Wittenburg Door *interview above? His answer: "Look for the unstructured, ad hoc communities actually incarnating the reconciling love of God—especially toward those individuals that the so-called good 'steepled' folks discard as 'the least of these.'*

In this undated essay, Campbell takes Nashville's religious community to task for failing to be the church. His critique, however, is easily transferable to other geographical locations.

"Here's the church. Here's the steeple. Open the door and here're the people." All of us remember lacing our fingers, the two index ones formed into a spire, saying those words. It was something we did as children. It is easy enough, now that we are older, to locate the steeple and the people. But it is a bit more difficult to locate the *church*. That is if we define "church" as that one great fellowship of love throughout the whole wide earth. Everywhere there is brokenness and alienation, exclusiveness and hostility, death and destruction. This column will be talking about some of those arenas in the months to come.

Perhaps enough has been said already about the topless waitress and the Scarlet O'Hara Club over in Madison [TN]. I followed the controversy as it was reported in the daily press with mounting interest. Not because another topless bar had come to town, but because of the response of

---

* Undated manuscript, Will Campbell Papers, University of Southern Mississippi.

a sizable segment of the religious community in opposition to it. Then when those who had flexed their political and ecclesiastical muscles were commended and congratulated editorially by my favorite morning newspaper for their success in putting the Scarlet O'Hara out of business, I felt a dismay bordering on horror.

It is not my purpose here to champion the cause of topless bars. Perhaps it is my declining years but even in my younger days I was never particularly excited by the public display of a stranger's anatomy. I see nothing in their existence which would strengthen the moral fiber of a given community. Not so much because they cause men to lust in their hearts—the same thing can be accomplished on a breezy afternoon in Madison Plaza—but because they are demeaning to women. They reinforce the stereotypical notion that the female body is just so much flesh. While my own understanding of Christianity leads me to believe that there are more deplorable dangers to the moral complexion of Nashville than topless bars, let's just agree without judging, without comparing their morality to our own, that we wish they wouldn't go around waiting on tables half nude. (Incidentally, waiting on tables was the first thing folks were ordained to do in the early church. Though it is not stated, one assumes that they were fully clad.)

But whatever became of the Jesus who went to the wedding feast— quite similar to nightclubs in first-century Galilee—apparently enjoyed Himself and when there was no booze simply made some? (I know that we can take our own cultural assumptions and argue that the wine Jesus made from the pots of water was not really booze as we understand the term. But that argument does not pass the test of Scripture. The Bible says Jesus turned water into wine. And wine is wine. I believe that if He had turned the water into Welch's grape juice the text would have so stated.)

Whatever happened to the Jesus who went where the sinners were, fraternizing with a woman who had been married five times and was then cohabiting with another man? Where is the Jesus who stopped the execution of a convicted and admitted adulteress and said if any of you are sinless, then you throw the first rock? Whatever became of the Jesus who forgave even a man who worked for the IRS and became his dearest friend? And have we forgotten that He seldom, if ever, had anything good to say on behalf of the alleged righteous folks of His day? Look out!

Where's the church? Whatever became of the church which saw itself as the leavening of the lump, the yeast of the loaf? How can we be the salt of the earth if we forbid the earthy ones from settling long enough in our midst to get a glimpse of what we are about?

"Go down to lower Broadway and go half-naked all you want to," the righteous seemed to be saying. "Just don't do it close to us." How strange. And how unlike the Jesus who ate and drank with sinners, constantly surrounded Himself with the unseemly. As I understand the gospel He came proclaiming it would have been more appropriate to go over and tell the folk at the Scarlet O'Hara that we love them and God loves them, that although we don't serve tables half dressed, we are nonetheless wretched sinners for whom Christ died, and that we want them as close to us as they can get, and together we may be able to hear the Story.

"We really don't care about you," the righteous seemed to be saying. "We care about ourselves. And we aren't willing to risk being contaminated by your presence." Go back to your own little ghetto of vice. Leave us to our glistening towers of American wholesomeness." On one occasion Jesus, speaking to us all, said that we were blind guides, straining at a gnat, and swallowing a camel. He said that we wash the outside of the cup, but inside it is full of extortion and excess, that we were like white-washed tombs which are pretty to look at on the outside but inside they are full of dead man's bones, and all uncleanness. Those were strong words for so gentle a man. And a lot of folks didn't bear up too well under them.

As I understand the Event of Christ, it is that He died and was raised from the dead because there is not one good among us, because we are all sinners. Habited nuns and topless waitresses, down-and-out musicians and top-level executives, murderers, thieves, least of these. Moss pickers, truck drivers, and Belle Meade ladies. Drunks, addicts, city councilmen, pastors of rich churches. Every last one of us. And we cannot act out the drama by shunting some off to their reservations, pretending that we are more righteous than they.

Nashville, like ancient Rome, is a very religious city. Seven hundred and eighty church houses. But religion is a dangerous thing.

14

Speech to the Southern Baptist Theological Seminary*

CONTEXT: *In 1983, Campbell could have only the slightest notion that this presentation might be one of his last to a large, formal Southern Baptist gathering. The internal gears of Southern Baptist polity were already turning, and the fundamentalists would soon assume the power of the denominational bureaucracy. Even had Campbell been aware, it is doubtful that he could have made a better, more prophetic, on-target presentation.*

This sermon to the Southern Baptist seminarians could appear in numerous places in this collection, but it appears here because Campbell challenges this next generation of clergy to rethink their ecclesiology. Being the church means being outrageously irresponsible with the reconciliation we have received.

The committee which invited me here said that they were the spiritual life committee. I inquired into exactly what that meant, and in true Baptist fashion I got several different answers, with a near consensus. Certainly in a real sense, for the Christian, *spiritual* life is a redundancy. There is simply a life. If God is omniscient, though I have nothing whatsoever against formal prayer, if God is omniscient then every thought is a prayer. Perhaps that is why Jesus said, "Pray without ceasing," so that we are involved in a spiritual life. My understanding of "the gospel," and that is what I want to reflect upon for a little while this morning, is that the spiritual life has something to do with the words which were read from the Bible. It has something to do with the manner in which we relate, as

---

* Delivered at Southern Baptist Theological Seminary, Louisville, Kentucky, March 9, 1983. The transcription, by Richard C. Goode, begins with Campbell's sermon already in progress.

our Lord said, "to the least of these." Now the question though becomes who exactly are the "least of these"?

What's the least thing you can think of this morning? Maybe I'm the least thing some of you can think of. If so, we have it on good authority that you relate to our Lord as you relate to me, and I to you if I should think, "Well, if you think I'm the least, then I think you're the least."

I was reminded this morning when I was getting dressed to come over here, while watching the news, how soon we forget. It was just exactly eighteen years ago today that some of us watched in Selma, Alabama, as hundreds of our brothers and sisters were run down by armed men on horseback and clubbed to the ground—gassed. Some of them left bleeding and bruised, for dead. As I watched this sight in shame, it crossed my mind, "Am I watching the least of these? Is John Lewis, my black brother lying there with his head beaten, for about the thirtieth time in his short life, is that the least of these?" If so, I have it on good authority that as I relate to him, I relate to my Savior. Or, is the least of these, the men on horseback with the clubs and throwing the gas canisters? If they are the least, I have it on good authority that I relate to my Savior as I relate to them. *That*, is scandalous.

Twenty-three years ago this past fall, I sat one night in a modest house in Arkansas. Some of you know where Arkansas is. One of you knows better than others. I sat with a man, an old man. He was black. Some of us had gone down to the schoolhouse that day with his daughter, who had been turned away by troops. He spoke of his seventeen-year-old daughter as his "baby." He said, "I am an old man. My life is over. I've heard Dr. King speak. I am not a violent person, but I am armed. If someone harms my baby, I will kill them." That anecdote to say, that twenty-three years ago, as a relatively young Christian preacher from Mississippi, I suddenly knew that civilization, as we know it, would not survive, and had no right to survive—though even at the time I did not revel in hearing my own epitaph.

About ten years ago, I was spending a week with another friend of mine who heads up what I call the Maoist wing of the Ku Klux Klan. I called it the Maoist wing because he had split with the larger United Klans of America because, he said, they were too moderate. They were revisionists. This man was considered by the authorities to be potentially the most violent man in his state. My purpose in being there was that his wife was seriously ill, and had recently been released from the hospital, and finding nothing in the Scripture about ideology, nothing about political views, nothing about visit the sick and nurse the sick *if* they are morally sound, and because I had been in the medics during the Second World War and was supposed to know something about taking care of sick folks, as they say, I was there. I asked him one evening, "What does the Ku Klux Klan stand for?" He said, "It stands for peace, and harmony, and freedom."

I've never been accused of being too bright, but [with] normal intelligence I wasn't quite ready for that one. So, I decided to play that little Socratic game that they teach us in college, and university, and seminary, when we don't know what else to say. We say, "And what do you mean by that ('peace, and harmony, and freedom')?" Where upon he said, "I mean what you mean. If you don't know what the words mean, look them up. They are in the dictionary." Which I thought was a bit pushy. Look, I'm educated, and he wasn't. I was going to set this little trap, and then spring it and push him in it. In other words I said, "You define the words." Sure, I define the words, just as you define the words you use. That to say that words are a symbol, and nothing else. When we use them they are our words. Alright, you define the words, "peace," "harmony," and "freedom." "What means are you willing to use to accomplish those glorious ends?"

"Oh, murder, threats, blackmail, intimidation, guerilla warfare, burning, whatever it takes."

I stopped as he stopped, because I had set the neat little trap and had cleverly let him snap the trigger, until he began speaking again. He said, "Now preacher, you tell me what we stand for in Vietnam?" It took no genius to know who had fallen into the trap. We all know that what we stood for there, and stand for there, and in Central America today, is peace, and harmony, and freedom. But we don't bother to ask other people to define those words. We define them, and the methods we are willing to use are, by now, well known to us all.

Later in the evening, my friend was showing me his new Klan robe. [He was] very proud of it, as most people who wear robes are proud of them—whatever the occasion might be. He said to me, "Preacher, what do I look like?" And I said, "You look like a Harvard professor," which he denied with considerable embellishment. I said, "I am not a gambler, but I would make you a modest wager that the next time there is a convocation near you, preferably one that has a divinity school" . . . I won't tell you which one I named because some of you might have gone to Duke for all I know . . . "you go at the last minute and get in the procession. Nobody will know the difference." He said something that has stuck with me for a long time. On this beautiful satin, crimson robe, his wife had sewn a gaudy little felt, yellow cross. He said, "Yeah, Preacher, them people would know the difference because my robe has a cross on it." That to say whatever you might want it to say.

It says different things to me at different times. This morning it raises certain questions in my mind about the manner in which we have intellectualized the gospel, theologized it, complicated it with the trappings of academe to make it intellectually respectable in the company of the learned—namely ourselves—rather than letting it remain the scandal, the stumbling block, and laughing stock it was and is.

A couple of years ago I sat in a tiny little courtroom in Newport, Tennessee. Two of my friends had been arrested and sentenced to thirty and sixty days in prison for handling rattlesnakes in a religious service. My purpose in being there was again, Jesus did not say, quoting from Isaiah, "I have come to proclaim release to captives, unless they pick up snakes in church." If somebody is in jail, they're in jail. After the judge had found them guilty, he said to them, "Now fellas, I know this thing is going to be appealed, and if you will promise not to pick up any more snakes . . ." They interrupted him, [and said] "Judge, we don't pick up snakes. We handle serpents. The Bible doesn't mention snakes."

"Alright," [the Judge said], "if you promise you won't handle any more serpents, then I will release you on your own recognizance." They were no more conversant with the finer points of law than the Judge was of the Scripture, and he explained to them, "Well, you just won't have to pay any more bond."

They looked a bit confused at one another, and one of them said, "But Judge, we can't promise you that. We don't know when we're going to lift up serpents. You see it's not like it is in your church. We don't have this written down on a piece of paper a week in advance, where it says: 'Procession, Invocation, Scripture, Sermon, Offering, Lift up Serpents, [etc.].'"

By then the old Judge was a bit confused and said, "Well, when do you do this?"

They said, "When we're anointed by the Spirit."

So he sent the bailiff out to get a dictionary to see what "anoint" means, although he couldn't remember if "anoint" was spelled with one "n" or two. [Once he found it he said,] "Alright, boys, here's what 'anoint' means. It means to pour oil on. To consecrate as if to heal. Now that's what Mr. Webster says 'anoint' means."

They looked confused again, and one of them said, "But, Judge, we don't live by Mr. Webster. We live by the Bible. We already know what 'anoint' means."

Despite the fact that most of us would agree that there are, from time to time, some unpleasant side effects from drinking strychnine and picking up rattlesnakes, whether in or out of church, it occurred to me that I was hearing the best lecture on the problem of authority—and I had sat through a couple of seminaries hearing this [topic discussed]—that I had ever heard.

"Who says Mr. Webster defines every word?"

"Well, the world does. That's who."

"But we are not of this world."

"Well, then you will go to prison."

"Okay."

Isn't it too bad, or perhaps it isn't, that it is the primitive, largely illiterate snake handlers who say, "There is a power higher than you. We must obey God. Lock us up if you will, but you really cannot control us. That is all you can do."

Now I wondered, again, have I happened upon the "least of these" that Jesus was talking about? If I'm going to relate to him, I want to find out who are the "least of these." Am I the least thing you can think of?

Sometimes the least thing I can think of is church bureaucrats, presiding over their altar fires and tea parties, in the midst of suffering and death. Big spires and steeples costing millions upon millions upon millions of dollars, casting their physical shadow, to say nothing of their spiritual life, upon slums and whores and addicts and drunks and thieves and rat-infested tenements, with the fingers and toes being gnawed off the young and the elderly. Investments and holdings in agencies whose profits are made from the manufacture of instruments of death. Could that be "the least of these?" Well, if they are, then we have it on good authority that I relate to my Lord as I relate to them.

That is a scandal, and I don't like it. I want somebody to be left out. I want somebody to be beyond the pale. So do we all.

I like it, Mr. St. Paul, when you say "God was in Christ no longer holding our misdeeds, our sins, our unceasing evil against us." I like it, except I would have said, "Unless, they murder civil rights workers in Mississippi, or club demonstrators in Alabama, or whatever, or lock people up."

Is the Judge the least of these?

I like it when you say I am reconciled to old black men with daughters who are facing hostile troops. I like it when you say I'm reconciled to poor whites and Kluxers and people whose ideology may differ from my own. I kind of like that. But I have trouble being reconciled to religious wealth, and I'm *not* reconciled to those structures. But I am reconciled to every last person within them.

That is the scandal. God was in Christ no longer holding our misdeeds against us. With no exceptions. That's the scandal. That's the good news. It is me and the church bureaucrats, who my guts may tell me are living in heresy.

Cheap grace, somebody is going to say. Well, what's the going rate of grace in Louisville these days? What's a pound of grace worth? If there's a price on it, it isn't grace—it's a commodity, and we ought to go back to selling it. Or, have we?

It is not cheap. It's the price of a lowly Galilean, hanging on a cross, outside a city, looking much like our own. Amen.

15

Foreword to Randolph Loney's *A Dream of the Tattered Man**

CONTEXT: *For Will, reconciliation inspires resistance. We are reconciled. Therefore, we will resist—especially on behalf of the most vulnerable and marginalized—the institutions that exile or seek to eradicate. The dangerous reconciliation incarnated by an authentic church attracts a motley community.*

In this foreword to Randolph Loney's book, Will outlines an understanding of the church as a somewhat haphazard fusion of forebearing, loving, individuals who together serve society's disinherited. In some ways this introduction is a summary of what Campbell developed more fully in The Glad River.

One January day a little group sat around a stone fireplace in a remote cabin in a Southern wilderness. The cabin is just off the Little Lazar Creek and a few miles from the place where Franklin Delano Roosevelt spent many hours and days trying to conquer a power called poliomyelitis that had left him unable to walk.

One who sat with us, [Randolph Loney], was about to battle a power and principality on a journey he was called to walk. It was a journey to be with those held captive. He had read and believed the words of Isaiah and Jesus about proclaiming release to the prisoners. He had sung the Psalm of David:

* From Will D. Campbell, foreword in Randolph Loney, *A Dream of the Tattered Man: Stories from Georgia's Death Row* (Grand Rapids: Eerdmans, 2001), viii–x. Copyright ©2001 Wm. B. Eerdmans Publishing Company, Grand Rapids, Michigan. Reprinted with permission, all rights reserved.

> Let the sighing of the prisoner come before thee:
>
> According to the greatness of they power preserve thou
>
> Those that are appointed to die . . .

Those so appointed were his flock; the place called "death row" the tabernacle in which he would witness to the truth and power of the gospel.

We who had gathered were bold to say, "We are church. In witness to the Word, we call ourselves the Glad River Congregation. And we are here on a holy mission: to ordain Randolph Loney, to set him apart as a minister of Jesus Christ."

Some would have considered us a motley crew, sitting there in that Georgia cabin. And in a sense, although we were physician, college professor, farmer, carpenter, high school teacher, nurse, writer, and unemployed, we were a motley crew. We were not dressed in Sunday finery; no steeple towered over us; no melodious pipes called; no offering was lifted. We were Southern Baptists, United Methodists, Presbyterians, Episcopalians, and no certain declension. At the core of the group were a few folk from Mercer University, where Randy was teaching; they had been meeting together, praying together, singing together for years. The antecedents of us all had once been small and random. My mind drifted back to my own people: the Anabaptists of Europe. They once gathered in similar fashion.

Our preacher that day was Murphy Davis, a Presbyterian of unusual gifts, grit, training, and determination. . . . She talked of spitting in the Devil's eye. . . .

Over fifteen years . . . Randy has gone out as we intended. With the biblical mandate of neither cloak nor script. Without stipend he goes to death row, where he visits, listens, hopes, or just sits. Outside the cell he waits with families and loved ones of those appointed to die. His is not a message of believing this or that creed, affiliating with this or that denomination. His is a mission to *be with*. And when the state has done all that it can do to its captives, he and his colleagues bury them.

Just as Franklin Roosevelt turned to the warm waters of Meriwether County to gain strength to continue his journey, so does Randolph Loney turn to his motley crew, his ordaining council, for sustenance in his own journey. Randy turns especially to the little band of mostly Mercer University community members who continue to gather together, week after week, as the Glad River Congregation. They help sustain him as he contends with the powers and principalities that would bring death to his imprisoned friends, many of whom have made that cursed walk. . . .

This is an important book. Important because it is painfully apparent that our nation's heart, from the Oval Office to the offices of local prosecuting attorneys, has been hardened toward captives everywhere. In the pages that follow there is firm evidence that our Lord's inaugural proclamation to release the captives and let the oppressed go free is still a viable alternative to the nonsense that death at the hand of the state will put an end to killings among the citizenry.

This is an important book because it is rooted in the radical gospel. It is about what the Reverend Murphy Davis talked about at Randy's uncommon ordination. Grace. Forgiveness. Reconciliation.

And spitting in the Devil's eye.

RESISTANCE

A. To the Steeples

CONTEXT: *The church, for Campbell, can be not only an expression of our hope, but can also be a manifestation of our heresy. When authentically incarnating reconciliation, the motley, scandalous church can bring life to a divided world. When mimicking the politics of the principalities and powers, however, the institutional church is but another agent of division and death in the world. Campbell has, therefore, frequently written against the institutional church, precisely because he is for the anarchical church.*

As seen in his writings on reconciliation, Will refuses to be classified with the "left" simply because he was against the "right" on matters of racial reconciliation. In the four pieces that follow, Campbell resists the progressive, liberal, mainstream, institutional church (i.e., "the steeples"). In particular he opposes the presumption that the only way the church can effectively suppress racism is either to align itself with humanitarian agencies and more stringently apply the wisdom of social science, or to acquire political power and more rigorously enforce U.S. constitutional law. The gist of Campbell's diagnosis, in other words, is that liberal/progressive institutional churches are not particularly different from the conservative/racist ones. Both are "pagan" insofar as they trust politics and/or social science, rather that the Gospel, to achieve their understanding of the reconciled, beloved community.

Moreover, Campbell includes a notable warning. To the extent that Christians actually forego striving to be "relevant" and "influential," and instead privilege the peculiar teachings of Christ over culture's political and sociological sense, the church will no longer fit well anywhere in society. To play off a quote by Flannery O'Connor, "You will know the reconciling truth, and that reconciling truth will make you odd." Such, however, is the social and political fate of a church resisting the principalities and powers.

16

"Heresy in Our Time"*

I do not happen to be among those who see the white Southerner as dishonest and insincere. Having lived all my life in the South, I know that there are many, many people who have not been touched by the recent growth of racial discrimination and prejudice. But of those who have been so influenced, I do not share the feeling that they do not honestly believe what they say. I further believe that many of the rabid racists sincerely believe that when they defend segregation they are defending the faith and are witnessing to the will of God.

When we consider that many of these have their reading materials limited to what some of the hate groups stuff in every mail box along the RFD and who have not heard other interpretations of various Scripture passages used to justify the position of the racist, then we can understand why this is so. Nothing could be more natural to such a person than to believe that if God had wanted the races to mix, he would not have made some of us white and some of us dark.

Now the Klan no longer exists in my community, but it has left its stamp in the minds and hearts of generations yet unborn. The White Councils will also be forgotten. But the seedlings they are planting will grow and thrive for a long, long time.

And what are these seedlings? They are essentially religious. Most of what is written and distributed by the White Councils today has a religious theme. Their sermons have a text, poem, and three points, and nothing could be more heretical than this. They are packed with Scripture, so persuasive to the region not ashamed to call itself the Bible Belt.

And because the stamps of his culture have become a part of his religious heritage, it is next to impossible to reach him. If the segregationist

* Undated manuscript, Will Campbell Papers, University of Southern Mississippi.

said, "Down with God and away with Jesus Christ," the job of the church would be cut out. The myriad missionary boards and organizations could begin to function and home missions would go into action and this great evil would be recognized and stamped out in our time. But when he says it is in defense of the faith and in the name of God that he is determined to keep the races apart, the churches in Protestantism are virtually helpless. We can tell the "Black Monday" enthusiasts [anti-*Brown v. Board* segregationists] to pray and they reply that they have prayed all night. We can remind him of the world of the Holy Spirit and he reminds us that Protestantism teaches that every man has direct access to God. We can quote him Scripture and before we can add "even the devil uses Scripture" he has said it to us. We can point him to statements of his denomination, convention, conference, or assembly and he says we believe in the autonomy of the local congregation. . . .

I agree that the Christian faith can be changed at many points that would make it more to my liking, more easily acceptable, more in keeping with my culture and my way of life; but the question we much always ask, "Is it Christian when we have finished with it?"

This you see is what has made heresy so serious in the Christian church throughout its history. It is not that people will say, "I don't like what the church says even if it is right, so I will not believe it and follow it." Rather it is that people insist that the changes they make are actually an improvement. It may be a matter of expediency to meet a given crisis situation and we say, "We will take this bit out of the church and put something else in its place, but just until the crisis is over and then we will go back to the original doctrine."

Professor William Muehl has said,

> Until the present generation, the church has regarded heresy as a far worse evil than theft, murder, or adultery. The heretic has been shunned and persecuted for more diligently than the most brutal criminal. And for what seems to me an excellent reason. The crimes of desperation and passion have a way of lashing back upon their perpetrator in such a way as to create moods of self-accusations and guilt in which redemption is more than ordinarily possible. Far from escaping the judgment of his fate, the murderer finds himself sucked by conscience into the very vortex of its power. The breach of God's love more often than not increases one's awareness of God's presence in an almost geometric ratio. But the heretic, here is a far different case. The heretic's great danger to

himself and to those about him is that in the name of God he begins to move out of the more immediate presence of God. Heresy,
far from creating its own self-destroying sense of guilt, more often
than not, develops a protective pride. It stops the ears of remorse,
it closes the eyes of penitence. It chokes the voice of conscience.

If the racists would say, "We don't care what God thinks, we want
segregation and will have it forever," there would be some hope. Instead
they say, "We want segregation because it is God's will." And to deny God
in the name of God is heresy.

Agreeing that we might be able to improve the Christian faith, to
make it more savoring and agreeable to the taste, we must also recognize
that there is only so much we can do before we have done too much. If
enough of that which is un-Christian is added to the Christian church, it
becomes something other than the Christian church, no matter what we
call it and no matter how loudly we proclaim that we have the inside tract
on the voice of God and we have actually made a stark improvement on
the faith. No matter how faithful our attendance, no matter how many
gold stars we pass out—no matter our feasts, assemblies, and burnt offerings. . . .

The heretic of our day is not one to challenge the accepted number
of angels that will go on the point of a needle. Here is not a concern of
whether Jesus was of the essence or substance of God the Father. He does
not care about the circumference of the throat of the whale that swallowed Jonah, nor even where Cain got his wife. No, he has outgrown these
childish and primitive concerns. He, in the name of God, proves that this
country belongs to the white man. He, in the name of faith, defends the
doctrine of white supremacy. He, with the Bible in hand, and chapter and
verse on his lips, shows that people with dark skin are less than children of
God. In the name of God, he denies the brotherhood of man. In the name
of God, he denies our responsibility to our neighbors if they happen to be
beyond our own man-made boundaries, or have skin of a different color.
In the name of God, he denies the love and mercy and justice of God.

And herein lies the duty of the church. For the church to let the
doctrine of white supremacy dominate our culture (and it still dominates
it in every section of the land, not just my native South), this is a tragedy.
But for the church to permit this to be done in the name of the church, in
the name of God, in the name of Christ who redeemed us and to whom

the church belongs—this is heresy and a heresy such as Protestantism has never had to deal before. . . .

Who would deny the demands which our culture makes upon us? Yet we must ever be careful that we do not completely identify our religion with our culture. How easy it might have been for the early Christians to put just a little pinch of incense on the altar and thereby save their lives, recognizing the supreme sovereignty of the state so that they would be around later to do good. But they did not. "We must obey God rather than man," they said. How simple it would have been for Elijah to have bowed to Baal. Instead he proclaimed the faith of Yahweh, "How long will you go on limping with two different opinions? If the Lord is God, follow Him, but if Baal then follow him."

I cannot deny that too often I put the incense on the altar and give my allegiance to some sovereignty other than God. I cannot deny that too often I bow to Baal. Daily I do it. Status affords a certain amount of privilege and comfort. The demands are too much for us! The demands to conform, to do as others do. And we cannot get away from this relationship of man to man. But there is also the relationship of man to his God—the scandalizing, uncompromising demands of God. The words of Peter, "We must obey God rather than man. He is our only sovereign, He is our God, Him will we serve."

A man whom we worship and seek to serve, some two thousand years ago discovered that the intersection of the demands of this world and the demands of his Father formed a cross, and at this intersection he died. How much of his life and teachings and death and resurrection can we deny and still call ourselves the church? How much that is alien to the spirit of this Christ can we put into the church and still have the church at all?

17

"The Power of the Church in Integration"*

Many contemporary prophets decry the fact that the church is "used" by various elements of society for ends that are other than Christian. They insist that there is no real commitment to, or understanding of, the gospel, but simply recognition that the popular thing to do is to involve the church in important issues at least at the level of using the name. They speak of presidents having their picture made going in or out of a religious service or of various political figures affiliating with a mainline church when seeking public office. They see the success of popular revivalists as reflecting the whoredom of Christianity. Preachers with a floristan smile being named man of the year because they were president of the Kiwanis, active in the PTA, Boy Scouts, March of Dimes, 4-H, generally the beloved mascot of the village, and castigated for prostituting themselves and the gospel.

The cult of success, the Madison Avenue techniques to achieve bigness, the accommodation and compromising of the scandalizing demands of the gospel to gain acceptance in society, all these are pointed out as being the tragedy of the church.

And it is so. Permitting one's self, one's being, one's body to be used is certainly tragic. Prostitution by the church is its tragedy. But it is not its pity. There is a difference in something being tragic and something being pitiful. . . .

[Prostitution is a tragedy.] But the cast-off whore—here is a different matter. Here is a pitiful creature, one who having been used by the many in a brief era of popularity and frivolity is now worthless, finished, disposed of. Those who sought her the most now hold her in the most contempt, and the most charitable emotion others can evoke for her is

---

* Undated manuscript, Will Campbell Papers, University of Southern Mississippi.

95

pity. One who might have been a mother and wife in her prime stands now alone with only despair, the cape of death, about her. She has crossed over from being a tragic figure to being simply pitiful.

There is growing evidence that this is where the church finds itself today, where race relations is concerned. . . .

[Society has cast off the church not] because the ministers and churches of that community were uninterested in improving race relations. It cannot be said that it is because they were silent. They weren't. It cannot be said that it is because they had not identified with and were not popular with the power structure of that city. And least of all could it be said that there was disagreement as to what the problem was, and how it must be solved. And therein lies the explanation as to why they were no longer needed. It was precisely because they *were* vocal, *were* popular, *were* in agreement with the power structure, but they were saying too much of the same things and doing too nearly the same things as secular agents of culture. It was not that they were ineffective, but because they were. But when the time came that it was obvious that the only way to solve the problem, at least temporarily, was by economics, power, and humanistic dimensions, they had nothing unique to offer and so they were discarded, cast off.

The tragedy of the church in its era of popularity in culture has not been that it has lied but that it has carefully manipulated and misused the truth. When the clergy insisted that they joined the Rotarians, played golf with the bankers, accepted free memberships in the country club, identified with the main stream of society in order to influence those they joined, they spoke the truth. But the question now is, influence them with and for what?

Our rationale was that if we just proclaimed verbally, "God was in Christ reconciling the world to himself, He was born of a peasant Jewish girl whose boyfriend loved her enough to marry her even though he knew the child she carried within her was not his own; that this baby was God, and that he was crucified, died and buried, and the third day he rose again from the dead for us and for our salvation"; that in all this they are sinners, in need of a Savior, and this is their Savior—tell them this, we reasoned, and they will scoff. It is not their language. They will not understand. So, we must learn of economics, and banking, trade and marketing, be competent to slip in and out of conversations at the Club of the Supreme Court, uphold law and order, good business, integrate our schools, proclaim the Constitution as sacred, and by doing all these we could build a tower of good in our communities because we had influenced the power structure. We spoke the same language they did. And it was not a lie. It was the truth. (I disagree with Dr. Smith. I don't know how necessary it is for preachers to be experts on political science and economics in order to make the gospel relevant. I doubt if Jesus understood too much economic theory when he threw the moneychangers out of the temple. But he threw them out. Didn't even vote on it.)

Those Christians who were concerned, joined and gave leadership to various secular organizations which had as their goal doing good in society. S.O.S. in New Orleans. HOPE in Atlanta, STOP in Little Rock. All sounding like names of body deodorants. Why do we flee to secular pursuits for a witness? Is it because we are afraid of the more radical and daring dimension of the gospel? The message we proclaimed was too often one of humanistic and humanitarian values. Too often we made the considerations of culture our own. We told them what they already knew better than we. . . .

Harmony was perhaps chief among them. Too long we sat about under the sociological spell of folkways and mores, reluctant to advocate that which might be a violation of what people were ready to do, or *wanted* to do. Our witness and influence would be greatly curtailed if we pushed too far. So the cardinal virtues of peace, goodwill, program, standard of excellence, and harmony within the fellowship endured because if they did not we would lose the influential men from our midst. And that was true. . . .

The Christian message on integration is nothing more, nor less, than the Christian message. It has to do with grace, not law, not order. That something has been done for us, something free, something with which we had nothing to do, something undeserved and unearned. It is the mercy and grace of God which has given us newness of life.

Our power then is in the power of the proclamation of the Word— God become flesh, like one of us. If Governor [George] Wallace had truly accepted and believed that God was in Christ reconciling the world to himself, God was in Christ reconciling all men to one another, and thus to himself, God was in Christ breaking down the walls of hostility that separate man from man and all men from God, God furthermore, was in Christ loving him, accepting him, forgiving him, even if he cannot yet love and accept and forgive his brother—if he had truly believed (lived by) this, he would not have appeared in the schoolhouse door.

And yet Governor Wallace repeatedly used the name of God while standing in the door. And here is the greatest failure of the church! By whatever method, he must be made to cease and desist in peddling pagan wares in the name of Christ. No longer do we burn heretics at the stake, but burning at the stake would be a preferable alternative to giving them the chief seats in the name of harmony and institutional growth.

18

"The Basic Problem Involved in Removing Racial and Cultural Discrimination"*

There are no problems. There is *a* problem. That problem is unfaith. . . .

[Because self-identifying Christians do not believe in the power of the Gospel], the likes of us have turned to social science, to group dynamics, to program kits, gimmicks and various types of human engineering. And we have failed. We have failed because these aspirin will not cure segregation and discrimination. We have failed because our assignment was to cure the symptom, but only relative to the status quo. If we are to be realistic . . . we must view segregation relative to the meaning of redemption, relative to the Christian doctrine of reconciliation and relative to the judgment of God upon His people. The religion of segregation is an attempt to negate the creative act of God, to revise what has already been done in Christ Jesus. Integration has already been accomplished. We are already one. There is nothing left for us to *do*. There is only something left for us to be. There are many institutions, movements, and groups working to accomplish integration. Sometimes the Christian church numbers itself among them. When it does it is engaging in pagan practices for we are already integrated. The problem is not how we are going to build a kingdom. The problem is how we are going to bid humanity enter the kingdom already established. We are integrated by Jesus Christ and we accepted it in baptism. Segregation is the effort to make all of this a lie. But it is not a lie. It is a fact. . . .

The gospel: "What I mean is that God was in Christ reconciling the world to himself, no longer holding men's misdeeds against them. . ." Now I am well aware that you can stand up in any pulpit in the Deep South and

* Undated manuscript, Will Campbell Papers, University of Southern Mississippi.

99

read that every Sunday morning. And as long as you keep it in the first century, there will not be a ripple. I am also aware that if you read it and add: "Now, brethren, what this means is that integration has already been accomplished by Jesus Christ, you are in trouble. What this means is that it isn't important who your shop foreman is, your next door neighbor or your next of kin, for St. Paul continued, if you are in the new creation "With us . . . worldly standards have ceased to count in our estimate of any man; even if once they counted they do so now no longer." . . . The sentimental liberals have considered race as a part of the majestic scheme of God for the beauty of the world—like black and white keys playing in harmony on a piano board, but the truth is, according to Scripture, God did not have anything to do with creating races. It is a worldly standard entirely.

But more important in the gospel message is the often neglected "not holding men's misdeeds against them." That is the hardest part to take for those of us who consider ourselves children of light.

On Monday, we read of an alleged eyewitness account of the slaying of the three civil rights workers in Mississippi [Goodman, Schwerner, and Chaney]. We read of one [Chaney] being tied to a tree and beaten with a trace chain until his bones were broken, his blood flowed out on the ground and his piercing screams no longer filled the night. When his two colleagues tried to break away, they were restrained and similarly beaten. Finally bullets were fired into all three of them to make sure no life was left. The thought that God would let the perpetrators of such an act go scot-free, is almost more than we can accept. But if it is not true then there is no gospel. That is the good news we have to offer. That is the gift of grace. Our sin is that we have not told the segregationist of his. And we have not told him his misdeeds are not held against him, that he doesn't have to go on fearing, hating, and killing. . . .

Our problem is not that we live in this kind of [fallen] world. Our problem is: what distinctive message, what particular and peculiar word do we have to offer the world we live in?

19

"Witnessing When the Cultural Landmarks Are Down"*

Frankly, I don't know what a cultural landmark is. But we are supposed to talk about it and then you are supposed to answer. I am supposed to apply the topic to the specific area of race relations. There was a time when I hesitated to speak to a national gathering on what appeared to me then to be largely a regional issue. But after moving about the North, it didn't take me long to learn that Yankees, being fully human, are bastards too. Hopefully, I believe that despite their being little different from Southerners, God still loves them just like he does those of us of the basement states.

Now if we are talking about how the *churches* might witness when the cultural landmarks are down, we are engaged in a ludicrous pursuit and the question might better be phrased, not, "How may we witness when the cultural landmarks are down?" but rather, "When in God's name will we stop being the *first* cultural landmark to go down when a crisis comes?" . . .

I am assuming that we are talking about how can the individual Christian witness in a crisis situation when the chamber of commerce, the merchants association, the PTA, the League of Women Voters, and such other cultural landmarks as the Daughters of the American Revolution and the Sons of the Confederacy have fallen, and I belong to all of them. . . .

Quite often we feel that we have failed when all the cultural landmarks are down and the reason is that we have identified ourselves with them. IT IS NOT THAT OUR TASK IS GREATEST when the cultural landmarks are down. It is then that our task can begin. Our message is

* Dated November 30, 1960, Will Campbell Papers, University of Southern Mississippi.

that those landmarks are irrelevant. Let 'em crumble. Quit trying to prop them up. The quicker they fall the sooner the Christian message might get a hearing. . . .

Although most of us in this room would be critical of the mass revivalist and their use of Madison Avenue techniques to achieve bigness, many of us in this room commit an even more dangerous act by using intellectually respectable methods to make the gospel intellectually respectable. The sophisticates *should* ride herd on the mass religionists because the mass religionists *do* reflect the symbol of bigness and success. But when we disagree we had better disagree on our knees because in adopting intellectually respectable methods we "touch up" the gospel too, and this is one more effort to make it more palatable to those we are trying to reach. . . .

Well, we *are* a bunch of squares. The gospel *isn't* intellectually respectable and shrouding it in respectable art forms isn't going to make it intellectually respectable. . . .

But we must *communicate this gospel*, mustn't we?

[By attempting to communicate the gospel, however,] we find that we are no different from the mass evangelist because he has employed the symbols of success of those he would win, those with whom he would *communicate*, and we have used the acceptable forms and symbols to *communicate* those to whom we would witness.

Out job isn't to communicate the gospel. Our job is to proclaim it. . . .

In short, our failure has to do not with the cultural landmark, the Fourteenth Amendment, but with the biblical landmark, the first commandment; it has not to do with the Constitution but with idolatry. . . .

The failure of the Protestant faith in America is not a failure to ask and answer the anthropological question, "What is race?" This question has been answered effectively and efficiently. Our failure, it seems to me, is that we have not succeeded in answering the theological question, "What is the church, and what is the nature of the Christian faith?" It is more than an academic question to be considered in seminary halls and faith and order conferences. It is a question to be asked by anyone wearing the sign of the cross. . . .

It is troubling that we who consider ourselves the children of light in regard to race in the South are being much better humanists than we are Christians. Examine our resolutions, our statements, our actions. They speak most often of *law* and *order*, of *human* dignity, of man's rights, of democracy, of constitution, and at best of the principle of the brotherhood of man and the fatherhood of God. Instead of moving in with the message of a savior when all these landmarks go down, we panic and busy ourselves in propping them up. . . .

[We must tell the segregationist] that the Christian gospel was and is a message of redemption; that it was and is "God was in Christ, reconciling the world to himself["] . . . God was in Christ reconciling us to one another and thus to Himself . . . God was in Christ breaking down the walls of hostility that separate man from man and thus man from his God . . . God was in Christ loving man, accepting him, forgiving him . . . even if he cannot love and accept his brother yet . . . tell him this and if he hears it, believes it, and accepts it, he is a lot closer to an integrated church in an integrated society than if he is told that he "ought" to be a good boy and obey the courts. . . .

All our resolutions, petitions, strategies, all our human engineering, all our propping up of the landmarks, will fail if we miss one simple point. We are the *tertium genus*—the third race. The Christian message on race is that race is irrelevant. . . .

Well, all I have tried to say is that we have failed in our message on race insofar as we have failed our message on redemption, and insofar as we have relied upon our culture to supply the landmarks.

20

"Footwashing or the New Hermeneutic?"*

CONTEXT: *Thomas Merton reminded readers ("Events and Pseudo-Events: Letter to a Southern Churchman," Katallagete, Summer 1966, 10–17), that Christians must operate from the belief that disciples have something to offer the world that the world cannot know apart from the Christian community. The distinctive way of the cross is not something the world can figure out on its own—if only humans were smarter, more perceptive, or thought about things more rigorously. Given the norms from which society operates, the Christian* kerygma *will never make sense to the world. Stated differently, the "good news" is absurd and nonsensical when abstracted from the Christian narrative. Consequently, Christians must not strive to explain the difference, so much as to incarnate the gospel's unique alternative to social conventions.*

And yet this is precisely the calling the church fails to honor. Despite confessions and pledges, the church allows the principalities and powers to do its thinking. The quest for social relevance and political effectiveness allows the principalities the privilege of determining the church's priorities and paradigms. Concession to this temptation is, according to Merton, a form of idolatry in which the church substitutes society's simulacrum *(i.e., superficial likeness or cheap knockoff) for God's way. Political activism, in other words, can replace God with a façade, a projection, or an idol created by nations, institutions, and their social and political science. We believe we must do something so utterly extraordinary and awesome, so historically stunning, that society's "movers and shakers" will validate our existence and reward our importance with their accolades. So we spend our energies and resources striving to be newsmakers of, and powerbrokers in, pseudo-events.*

* From Will D. Campbell, "Which Way for Southern Churches: Footwashing or the New Herneneutic?" *Katallagete*, Summer 1966, 1–6. Reprinted with permission.

In the process, however, we judge people according to human categories, e.g., income brackets, professional titles, offices held, or votes delivered.

Presuming the simulacrum to be real, practical, relevant, and success- ful, the church lives according to it, and opposed to God's alternative way and will. We look for "moments" and entrepreneurial opportunities to make our individual and institutional lives exceptional, noteworthy, or otherwise meaningful. We presume that once we bear the badge of power—society's imprimatur—we will prove the merits and relevance of our supposed "good news." Merton, Campbell, and the Committee of Southern Churchmen ar- gue that such "steeple" thinking is a modern form of idolatry.

In this piece, Campbell asserts that if anyone in the Christian fold is getting it right—resisting the steeple's simulacrum—it is the religious sects. Unlike the steeples, the sects embrace vulnerability—marginalization, poverty, and social impotence—to follow Christ. Sects don't worry about branding, image maintenance, or public reputation. The sects will sacrifice institutional well-being to live the scandalous, the socially deadly voca- tion of discipleship. Sects, in other words, are ready to take a bullet for the cause—not in some imaginary future, but today. In good Christian tradi- tion they will be zealous martyrs, and it is precisely that social and political martyrdom that the steeples refuse to accept. "Think sect!"

What will the racial situation be in the churches of the South when the Yankees have all gone home? They said they came because we had done so little. We may question the conjunction, but not the assertion on either side of it. They *did* come. And we *had* done so little.

How short a time ago it was that they came! We had heard the talk of the long, hot summer. Then they came. Several of them we killed. Then the rest went away. At least most of them went away, though none to our knowledge went away because we killed several of them. Most stayed lon- ger because of that.

How short a time ago it was that the Ivy League doctors—mostly the teaching, preaching doctors, but a few of the doctoring doctors— were here. There were the calls to take them bail or to visit them. Was it Birmingham, Montgomery, Albany, or Jackson? Was it freedom ride, voter registration, or sit-in? Anyway, they were here and we were glad, and now they are gone. Sometimes one hears that they are a part of the Clergy Concerned [about] Vietnam [later named Clergy and Laymen

Concerned about Vietnam, CALCAV], a worthy cause, God knows, but how fickle they are, our Yankee brothers.

They came to be our conscience because we let expectant citizens be shot down in the streets and little girls be slaughtered at their prayers. But conscience is not a thing of the moment. It is a thing of generations. It could not be remade in one summer or two.

There was the Mississippi Project, the FDP [Freedom Democratic Party], and COFO [Council of Federated Organizations], baptized in Oxford, Ohio, and confirmed somewhere between there and Neshoba County, where three at once were buried in the red clay of a government dam.

Surely such an offspring would last for a long time. But it didn't. It is true that a law was passed, and then another; and now a third is proposed after Lurleen [in a later version Campbell uses the name Wallace] showed us what we should have known about the South while [Sen. Everett] Dirksen tells us what we should have known about the North—"any further legislation is clearly unconstitutional on its face." (Southern rednecks are one thing. Northern rentals are another.)

Meanwhile there were more than twenty race-related murders in the South in a one-year period following the Civil Rights Act of 1964, making that the bloodiest since the movement began.

And yet they have all gone away. At least almost all of them. And surely their dream is gone. The dream that the Mississippi Project, the FDP, and COFO would arouse that latent goodness supposed to be in all men, Southern and federal, and that we would rise up to stay the evil passion of racism is gone. From that we have awakened. The dream of a degree of justice remains, and thank God. That is an important dream. But the dream of reconciliation based on the coming of the Yankees is gone. If one does not believe it, then let him go to a tavern in Tennessee and hear the manager say, following the visit of a thirsty black man, "Yes, we have to serve them, but we break every glass they drink out of. There's no law against that." That may be justice, but it is not reconciliation. Or let him go into a truck stop with a black friend and watch the waitress stroll casually to the jukebox. Hear her dime produce the words, sung to well-composed and equally well-played music:

> *Move them niggers north. Move them niggers north.*
> *If they don't like our Southern ways,*

Move them niggers north.

There is no law against playing the jukebox. Not yet. To say nothing about the dangers of having one.

Where is the reconciliation? In fact, where is the justice? Is there really any justice in a hamburger? Or does the jukebox negate even the hamburger, for who could hold it down? Anyway, most of them are gone. SNCC [Student Nonviolent Coordinating Committee]—though not really North—remained, but after they declared their intention of becoming all black, their dream of "beloved community" became a spasm—at least for white churchly folk. And the Delta Ministry remains in name, but days after their Poor People's Conference sought to take over the Greenville air base, a faction of that conference sought to take over the leased property of the Delta Ministry at gunpoint! Folks don't like such ingrates as that. Especially if the enthusiasm and financial support from back home are on the wane. The Freedman's Bureau, one of the more promising programs to come South following the Civil War, folded after six years. It did so because the lack of financial support discouraged its advocates to the point of giving up. A very similar thing is happening now, and we may anticipate an early departure of those whom some saw as hostile invaders and others regarded as our last hope. Who then will remain?

We will. We who were born here, who partly created and partly fell heir to what we have come to call "the race problem." Negro and white, Christian, Jew, and pagan, we remain. And we will remain. If anyone does.

And what hope is there among *us*? There are indigenous Negro groups and inter-racial organizations to which we can still look for help. Help, but not Messiah. SNCC, even with its all-black policy, may be at once judgment and long-range hope. Those individuals now involved, however, may see the promised land of true reconciliation (which they verbally reject but still yearn to see) only from an isolated mountain, standing there alone, with neither leader nor follower. And SCLC [Southern Christian Leadership Conference], though wrought with so many internal problems that the sophisticated liberal sees little hope, they may yet be the tailor for the sackcloth and ashes which we continue to shun, but which remains the only acceptable garment for an audience with the Almighty.

But what hope is there among us, within us, the church? If by that one means the institution, after forty years within it we sadly conclude—

none. For there is little to indicate that we are any different today from what we were in 1954, in 1964, in 1965. While we see the all-black policy of SNCC as the hardened heart which God uses as his judgment upon a segment, we the churches may be the hardened heart which He uses as judgment upon us all.

If we are to be honest, we must admit that at the congregational level the white church in the South has not yet had the slightest involvement in the racial crisis. A few pastors have joined an occasional march. A few more have signed statements. Nearly all of these neither march, sign statements, nor serve as pastors any longer, for their flocks not only did not follow them to street and parchment, but did not tolerate the resulting controversy of their shepherds' strange behavior. But if the drought of direct action has been acute during the past few years, the drought of preaching is chronic. Embarrassed with the "Bible Belt" label, the fundamentalists have given rise to, most of us have shied away from a doctrine of man rooted deeply in Scripture, which rejects race as a category, and have turned to more sophisticated documentation for such preaching as we have done on the subject. Rejecting such arguments as none of the preacher's business—as they should have done—our congregations have been left to flounder in the mire of religion—that curse of man Christ sought to dispel, but which continues to dominate us in such proportion as to approach anti-Christ.

But let us not speak now of the churches. Let us speak now of churchmen. If we had admitted the nature of institutions from the beginning, we would not now sink into despair about the inadequacies of the institutional church. Nor is it enough to talk now of "para-church." Whatever ways for witness we may find as Christians will be the witness of the church, or it will not be witness at all.

And there are at least two embarrassments which we must overcome. The first is the embarrassment of biblicism. The second is the embarrassment of the sects. They may well be treated together.

Partly because we rejected fundamentalism as adolescents (and the seminaries gave us higher criticism to sustain the rejection), and partly because we saw the evils of institutionalized biblical literalism, we turned away from seeking answers in the Scriptures. While the religious racists indoctrinated the region with biblical distortions, we have retreated into the sophistication of the New Hermeneutic. No one will deny that a hook and ladder is better equipment for fighting a fire than a garden hose. But the house is on fire. There is no time to send to Detroit for hooks and ladders. There is not time to await scholarly research. Unless, of course, we will enjoy the stoic satisfaction of knowing how the fire might have been put out long after the embers are dead.

The point to be made is a simple one. Everything else has failed. There has not been reconciliation. There has been social change. But do you remember how we used to scoff at the "moderates" when they said, "What they are doing will set race relations back fifty years!" We should still be dubious of this and all other clichés. But it is becoming more and more obvious that the social changes have not seen a corresponding change in the basic human relationships of one man to another—Negro to white and white to Negro. Such interpersonal relationships are not considered important by those who see the change of the structures as our greatest hope. But structures are persons, groups of persons, who lean in the same direction at a given point in history, and presidents, senators, and Supreme Court justices read the morning paper to learn the direction in which their followers are leaning.

And although it is denied by both groups, white liberals are cooling off at a rapid pace, and a considerable element of the civil rights movement is moving pell-mell into the yawning lap of Black Nationalism. Thousands who referred to the justice, rightness, and necessity of the Selma March are now referring to the Mississippi March as a civil rights williwaw without meaning or purpose. Somehow I fail to see the difference if either had to do with injustice, for there was a much of that on the road from Memphis to Jackson in 1966 as there was from Selma to Montgomery in 1965.

And the religious commissions on race are roughly back where they were four years ago—passing resolutions deploring this or that, and urging individual church members to wire the president.

Great God Almighty!

What does, what could, what will *ever* the president of the United States ever have to do with the witness of the church? And when will we quit seeing him as our spiritual head?

But why are we back where we were after three exciting years of more or less active participation in the movement? The answer again is simple. More and more white folks are seeing that the movement is not about coffee and hamburgers, or black and white together, but a more equitable distribution of the goods and opportunities that whites have by being white. And more and more movement leaders don't want whites involved because they don't, they can't trust them. One year ago all the established church groups were issuing nationwide appeals for marchers to go to Selma. There were no such appeals for participation in the Mississippi marches. There were some tactical reasons offered, but the real, the big reason was that those appeals of a year ago resulted in too many white marchers. (If there is one prophetic role the national church commissions and departments of Christian social relations can play now, it is to tell white Christians the truth, however painful and unpopular it might be). Anyone who was surprised with the Black Power development must never have read the Bible or history, for the development began when the first slave ship departed the shores of Africa.

But enough of saying things are worse. Actually things are not worse for everyone. We are not saying that. Things are better for a fairly large number of Negroes. Things are also better for a fairly large number of whites, for *they* are better. The recent civil rights legislation and the economic opportunity programs have had some effect within the culture. Not much, but some.

When we speak of things being worse, we are talking of institutionalized Christianity being worse. It is worse simply because it is not better. It is not better because it remained where it was twenty, ten, two years ago, protective of its own, self-loving and largely self-worshiping, while the world whirled by.

So. Where do we turn? One thing that all other institutions have learned from the civil rights movement is that their own structures which they assumed to be sacred were not sacred after all. Restaurant owners learned that there was nothing sacred about property rights as they had thought. School boards are learning that there is nothing sacred about neighborhood schools as they had thought. ("If you can go to the moon, you can bus our children across town.") Only the churches continue to contend that their structures are sacred. As long as they are sacred, they will be stagnant and sterile. For a sacred tool is one not to be used but to be fondled and polished. Howard Moody says the church is an instrument of God literally to be used up in his service, a service to those not even within it. There is little evidence at this point in God's economy that the church is about to go out of business through such usefulness.

But there has been a segment of the church whose idols have been less secure than mainline white Protestantism. These have been what we call the fringe sects. And what do they do that we don't? Well, they wash one another's feet, they shout, they sing jazzed-up songs to guitar music, they handle snakes. They do all sorts of things. But *what* they do is not so important for our concern as the zeal with which they do it. They do it with zeal because they really believe it. Because they really believe in what they do, the tools they employ are not so important for them. A silver basin is fine for washing feet, but a galvanized foot tub is just as good. A brick, air-conditioned building is all right for handling snakes, but a brush arbor is just as good. Acoustical tile would be dandy for shouting, but an unpainted frame ceiling is just as good.

But aside from those things they do, a case can be made that they were more faithful in the racial crisis all along than the established church.

Consider Horace Germany. Horace, a white man, had lived all his life in rural Neshoba County, Mississippi. He made his living by farming. He was also a Church of God preacher. Nearly ten years ago I saw him for the first time. He was lying on his side, his back purple and sore from a beating he had just received from his neighbors. He told this story only after a letter of introduction was shown to him, written by a Church of God preacher in another state.

He had wanted to build a school for Church of God young people who wanted to preach. He would teach them tent making, of whatever variety they chose. They would study the Bible, and they would do it without regard to race, for he said he believed that the gospel was a "universal gospel to all men, as given by Christ in the Great Commission. All men are made one in Jesus Christ."

To reach his school, it was necessary to drive down a country dirt road which came very near the scene where some years later three civil rights workers were to be murdered and buried. About three miles down that recently graded, winding and sloping dirt road, hardly wide enough for two cars to pass, there was an open gate at the top of the slope. Through the wooded area there was a clearing and a large pond, the kind the US Department of Agriculture builds for farmers to water cattle. Beside the pond was a long shed with lumber stacked almost to the tin roof. Outside the shed was more lumber and concrete blocks, some with black mildew and spider webs, indicating that this building material had been accumulated over an extended period of time. In the center of the clearing there was the foundation and part of the first story of a large building. This was the beginning of the school.

And it was the beginning of his troubles. A week earlier a large crowd had gathered at one of the mainline churches in the area. Some two hundred could be accommodated inside, and another estimated five hundred formed a sea of solemn faces on the dry, dusty lawn and pressed as closely as possible to open doors and windows in order not to miss the important proceedings inside.

There were the customary prayers that must precede any event in church, but a minimum of preliminaries. They were there to discuss the school going up down the road. A resolution was presented, discussed, and then adopted with a voice vote consisting of shouts—shouts not generally heard in the services of that denomination. The resolution asserted that the school was seeking to destroy harmony between the white and colored races of the area. "The college is purportedly a Christian educational institution," the resolution stated, but "we are convinced that the purpose of this college is to promote, foster, and encourage violence and to disrupt goodwill between the races."

Following the meeting at the church a committee of two hundred waited upon Brother Germany and delivered this message: "Preacher, this is it! We mean, this is it! You get your family and them imported niggers (he already had several students) away from here within forty-eight hours, or we will not be responsible for what happens." Horace reported wryly that "Liquor and tobacco smelled strongly, and some of them talked rough."

Brother Germany announced that construction of the school would continue.

He gave me a copy of the newsletter which they mailed regularly to friends and supporters.

> On Friday, August 26, Pres. Germany, Vice Pres. Burns, and three of our brethren drove into Union where we had bought part of a school building. They were loading material onto the truck when a mob of five or six carloads came, drove the Colored brethren away at the threat of their lives, and set into beating Bro. Germany in a most unmerciful manner with blackjacks, fists, clubs, and while he was on the ground they would kick him. It was one of the most outrageous things that has happened since the establishment of any form of law and order in the United States, especially in connection with the activity of the Church. At this writing Bro. Germany is still in the hospital.

He talked sadly of his shattered dream. I asked him what he planned to do. He said that he wasn't afraid. "Jesus died for me, and I will die for him. I could finish the school all right. People from all over the country have said they would bring their trailers and tents and stand guard until the school is finished. But all I would prove is that I am not afraid. I could build the buildings, but it wouldn't be a school. There would be no students. A school is not a school without students."

"And what will you do with what you have built?"

He turned slowly away and gazed steadily at the wall. A plaster of Paris plaque, looking at once like those won at county fair carnivals and the kind made by children at vacation Bible schools, hung on the wall with the inscription: "In all thy ways acknowledge him, and he will direct thy path."

"Yesterday morning one of the biggest bootleggers in the county sent word that he wanted to buy the property. I know what he wants with it. He wants to make a dance hall out of my school and sell whiskey."

"And will you sell it to him?"

"Yes," he said. "Yes, I'm going to sell it to him. I told these people that if they won't let God do his work in this county, the Devil will sure move in and do his. There's a lot more to this race problem than just segregation."

And how right he was. Maybe those who killed Mickey [Schwerner] and James [Chaney] and Andy [Goodman] in Neshoba County that night got the courage to do it from a bottle from what began as the Bay Ridge Christian College.

There were numerous others from the sects who were both prophetic and courageous in the racial crisis. There was James Willis Vaughn, a tall, raw-boned preacher from one of the most rigidly fundamentalistic sects, who preached a revival at Bethlehem Temple in Jackson, [Mississippi], and because the host under whose roof he slept was a Negro, he was fined five hundred dollars, and he and his wife spent sixty days in jail.

But the point for us is not who they were and what they did, but what we can learn from them.

We are not suggesting that we all turn to handling copperheads and washing one another's feet—though if Aubrey Norvel would wash James Meredith's feet, and Meredith would let him do it, I would be for setting him [Norvel] free.

The real point is that the idols of the sects are not as secure as those of the established church. When the Yankees have all gone home here may be the hope for renewal if we in the establishment can learn to . . .

"Think sect!"

POSTSCRIPT: *In a 1972 version of this essay Campbell continues at this point:*

And what does "think sect" mean? It means brush arbors and communion on a kitchen table. It means preaching on street corners and baptizing in a mill pond or out of a coffee cup. It means Clarence Jordan buried in a pine box in southern Georgia. It means Tom Merton's Masses at his hermitage in Nelson County, Kentucky, and the Berrigans' Masses and baptisms in living rooms and in the corners of Protestant chapels and in the streets.

It means poverty. The institutional church stands today exactly where the rich young ruler stood in Matthew 19 (and it stands before the same Lord). He was rich, he was powerful, he was good. The church is rich. It is powerful. And it is good. No one ever calls it bad. It is high on the list of agencies to do good in the community when the need arises. The United Fund, the Boy Scouts, the Lions International, the Red Cross, the church—each will accept its quota of responsibility. Yet the reply of our Lord was to get rid of all that and then come and be a disciple.

Think sect means carrying a cyanide capsule in your navel against the day the enemy is so strong against you that the only way you can preserve that with which you have been entrusted is to kill yourself. [Here Campbell may be drawing upon Howard "Buck" Kester's habit of carrying a cyanide pill with him while he traveled throughout the South to organize the disenfranchised. Expecting, at any time, to be "captured," Kester was ready to swallow the capsule rather than allowing thugs to torture him.] The enemy is now that strong against us. The enemy has made us rich, powerful, and good, knowing that when there was a racial crisis or a Vietnam War, the best we would risk would be debates and resolutions and petitions. The cyanide capsule tucked in our navel is Matthew 19. Let us now swallow it with a joyful gulp. Sell the steeple, the organs, the gold cups, the silver hats, the mahogany pews, and the valuable downtown property, and give the money away. Give it to BEDC [Black Economic Development Conference?], to the Fentress Low Income People (FLIP), to the poor in the Ku Klux Klan, or simply to those of the poor who happen to be nigh. Don't ask if they are from the deserving or the undeserving poor. Just give it away.

And think sect. Then shout Hallelujah! Then sing the psalms. Then follow! But above all, remember that with that one act, Jesus did not offer to the rich young ruler the end of discipleship. That act only qualified him to approach the starting line of discipleship.

Think sect.

After shaking the Neshoba County, Mississippi, dust off his feet, Horace Germany settled in Kendleton, Texas, where he successfully launched the Bay Ridge Christian College. In 1979, Germany invited Campbell to serve as the graduating class's commencement speaker.

21

"Which Is the Real Evil—Snake-Handling or the Establishment Church?"*

CONTEXT: *On one level, Campbell appreciates and elevates the status of sects because, unlike their steepled counterparts, the sects avoid the addiction to cultural respectability that would keep them—as it has the steeples—from publicly incarnating the radical gospel. Here, in this brief excerpt, Campbell again stresses that point.*

The rationale for the cultist in lifting up serpents is not to venerate them, but to conquer the evil which they represent. The rationale of the institutional steeples for lifting up the serpents of culture is that they are sacred and should be celebrated.

I have known for a long time now that each time I participate in an organized, structured, institutionalized, big-steepled religious service I have a far more deadly reptile by the tail than my unlettered brothers and sisters have in handling their rattlers and copperheads. And I have known for a long time that my record in conquering that evil is not so impressive as theirs.

Any study of Appalachian, or American, folk religion should not begin in a brush arbor or mountain cabin. The real folk religion begins at the registrar's office of the so-called Christian liberal arts colleges, the schools of theology and divinity, and seminaries, for here is where the serpents of the cultural and political majority of "folk" are housed, nurtured, fattened up, passed on as sacred and consecrated, ready to preside over the folk religion of the rulers of this present age. . . .

---

* From *Southern Voices*, March–April 1974, 41–48. Reprinted with permission.

Which Is the Real Evil—Snake-Handling or the Establishment Church?

The myth is that the cults and sects of folk religionists contain the ignoramuses, the biblically illiterate, and we must go convert them, change them. And the imperialistic church of this and the last century has done much to do just that—convert and change. The reality is that even in their errors and misinterpretation they are closer to the truth of the gospel than mainline Christianity and should be left alone.

22

"Values and Hazards of Theological Preaching"*

CONTEXT: *In 1987, the coordinators of the Parker Memorial Lectures in Theology and Ministry invited Campbell (along with Albert C. Outler, Max Stackhouse, Gayraud Wilmore, and others) to speak on the vocation of pastors as theologians. Although most presenters highlighted the need for pastors to be intentional, practicing theologians, Campbell, not surprisingly takes another approach. Far from encouraging theological preaching, Campbell questions the very assumptions underlying such an enterprise. He probes the assumptions of power and control inherent in theological pronouncements—lumping together everyone from Augustine, Luther, and Calvin, to Pat Robertson, Jerry Falwell, Paige Patterson, and Paul Pressler (the latter two functioning as the vanguard of Southern Baptist fundamentalism in the 1980s).*

According to Campbell, the more the church organizes, systematizes, and codifies its message, the less scandalous it becomes. He pleas, therefore, for an undomesticated church, one resistant to models of efficiency and effectiveness that would give it social power and political control.

Theological preaching? Never thought about it! If I did think about it, the thought pattern was a garbled montage. Words like uppity, doctrinal, creedal, ethereal—who the Sam Hill thinks about it?

If we take the word theological in the classic sense—study or knowledge of God—I am fearful to begin thinking about it now. How does one *study* God? And is it not a presumption to assert that we have *knowledge*

---

* From Will D. Campbell, "Values and Hazards of Theological Preaching," in *The Pastor as Theologian*, edited by Earl Shelp and Ronald Sunderland (New York: Pilgrim, 1988), 68–87. Reprinted with permission.

of God? I have so little *knowledge* of God that it strikes me as a sacrilege to claim any at all.

But now that I have committed myself not only to think theological thoughts, but also to write them down, I must overcome the timidity and begin. Though still jarred. I am a sculptor. I make things. I dream them up. I am the architect. I design plans and then I create something. I take the manifold and rocker arms from an abandoned Allis-Chalmers C Model tractor, weld them together to fashion a cross, fasten that to a stand that was the oil pan, and give the piece of sculpture a name. I call it *The General Confession*. "We acknowledge and bewail our manifold sins and wickedness . . ." (That's from the 1928 *Book of Common Prayer*. I haven't bothered to check the newest new one.) I take a big earth auger and five drill bits ranging in size from two feet to a few inches and weld them in a zigzag pattern reaching twelve feet in the air. I name this piece of sculpture *Tower of Babel*. It represents sin in my mind. I take a rusty old farm pump and place it in concrete so that it seems to flow into a large sugar pot filled with water and goldfish. It is, of course, *The Fountain of Life*.

So without really meaning to do so I have constructed a theological system. There is sin, confession, and redemption. All these can be found beyond and behind the little log house that is my office. (I suppose real preachers would call it a study.) I tell you about them for several reasons.

First, these icons suggest the inevitability of theology.

Second, most and perhaps the best—theological systems come about without the intention of really meaning to create them. Those who create them generally don't take them as seriously as the generations that follow. And sometimes the creators are not aware of what they are doing. I was not aware of what I had done until a young friend exclaimed, "My God, you have your whole belief system here in three pieces of junk!"

In the third place—and most important in my mind—I tell you about them because they represent the presumption and foolishness of theologizing. You see, I said I was the architect, as well as the builder, the creator, of the sculptures. I made them and they are mine. I am their god. I know everything about them. Do they, can they, know anything about me? Do they even *need* to know anything about me? And what would I do if I discovered that they were even *trying* to learn something about me. *Studying* me? ["]You, *thing*, desire knowledge of me?["] I'll tell you one thing, those objects would be in a heap of trouble. Just as Adam and Eve were in a heap of trouble when they "theologized," when they sought to have "knowledge of God." They were not equipped to deal with knowledge of good and evil. . . .

In partial preparation for this essay, I gave a video cassette of Jerry Falwell, Jimmy Swaggart, Pat Robertson, Ernest Angley, and Jim Bakker to Tom T. Hall, a country picker, storyteller, novelist, philosopher, friend, and neighbor. I asked him to view the tape straight through and give me a bottom-line appraisal of what he had seen. He called on Monday morning with his report: "My God can whip your God." That is, to be sure, a theological statement. But it is a dangerous theological statement.

But wait a minute! Is it possible that *all* theological statements are dangerous? Potentially explosive and violent? Where did the notions I have been describing come from? How do they differ essentially from our own notions? What are Falwell and Robertson trying to do that Calvin and Luther did not try to do? We might argue that Calvin advocated a religious commonwealth, and not a theocracy, but I'm not sure we can draw that line. However, please note that at this point I am asking questions, not attempting to answer them. So I continue to ask them. What is the difference between the First Mainline Church by the Bank and the 700 Club? To ask it more harshly, what's the difference between Oral Roberts' Tower of Power and the pope's jewels? Certainly we can make a qualitative distinction between the beauty of the Sistine Chapel and the crassness of a satellite. But as we do, should we not try to be sure we are not drawing lines of sophistication, lines of elitism? It is permissible for the governors and managers to build that which is aesthetically pleasing to us, but it is unacceptable for the pulpwood haulers, the plebeians, to contribute their collective offerings to build what is aesthetically pleasing to them. Whatever else we might say, on this we can agree: The price of all these things can be traced to the backs of the poor. Great fortunes are made from men, women, and children going into mines, fields, and mills. Whether or not we can establish a theological, cultural, or qualitative difference, all of us, at one time or another, have sung the song "Praise the Lord, and Send Me the Money."

Whether we can distinguish between St. John's by the Bank and the electronic church is not our task. Our task is to talk of the hazards and values of theological preaching. The main thing that makes me fearful of theology, and thus theological preaching, is that theology so often leads to violence. Nothing is so dangerous as religion when it gets out of hand. When it got out of hand, and slingshots and hand-cast spears were the weapons for settling disagreements, it wasn't so bad. But that day is surely gone forever. No longer is it David against Goliath, Ephrathites against Philistines. Today we talk of settling our differences, even religious differences, with nuclear weapons. Too often we use a theology designed for slingshots and spears and apply it to a nuclear age. . . .

Exactly who Christ was and is continues to be the tough one. CHRIST IS THE ANSWER. We affirm it and put it on Cadillac bumpers. Is that itself not the old dualism? The we/them. If the world is ruled by two antagonistic forces, good and evil, we assume that *we* are the advocates, custodians, practitioners, and defenders of the good and that *they* (whoever the *they* may be) are the advocates and exponents of evil. We can justify anything under the sun, for this is an awesome responsibility.

Would not a better slogan be: Christ lived the answer, showed us the answer, and it was so radical that we did all we knew how to do—we killed him. If Christ is the answer, license is a by-product, license rooted in dependency. Christ showed the answer, lived the answer, leads to discipleship, to developing of the potential we all have, to righteousness, to "Be ye perfect," as he, whoever we might think he was, told us to do.

In an important but little-known book called *Witness to the Truth*, Edith Hamilton, a scholar best known for her work in Antiquities, made a statement in 1948 that addresses our subject in a fine fashion.

> So the great Church of Christ came into being by ignoring the life of Christ. . . . The Fathers of the church were good men, often saintly men, sometimes men who cared enough for Christ to die for him, but they did not trust him. They could not trust the safety of his church to his way of doing things.
>
> So they set out to make the church safe in their own way. Creeds and theologies protected it from individual vagaries; riches and power [protected it] against outside attacks.
>
> The church was safe. But one thing its ardent builders and defenders failed to see. Nothing that lives can be safe. Life means danger. The more the church was hedged about with Confessions of Faith and defended by the mighty of the earth, the feebler its life grew.[1]

What this wise woman was saying, it seems to me, or is saying to us in our current context, is what I tried to say earlier: all theological

1. Edith Hamilton, *Witness to the Truth: Christ and His Interpreters* (New York: Norton, 1948), 204–5.

statements, all creeds are potentially dangerous—theology becomes the enemy of Theology. The management mode, leading in our day to media management mode, came early. Christianity would never be made to work efficiently by following Christ literally, Edith Hamilton said. "He had no methods people could adopt and put to definite use." He never laid down that matter of fundamental importance to an organization, clearly formulated conditions on which one could enter it. He never demanded of the people who wanted to follow him that they must first know this or that, the nature of the Trinity or the plan of salvation. He had not insisted on conviction of sin or consciousness of forgiveness or on any belief whatsoever. He talked of such things as a cup of cold water. Ah, but we must build a global sprinkler system.

But you could not build a steeple on that any more than you can build one on the notion of unconditional grace. So enter creeds and theologies to contain, to systematize. Enter violence to protect and propagate the creeds and theologies. Enter Augustine, Luther, Calvin, Pat Robertson. Jesus did say, "Love your enemies, bless them that curse you, do good to them that hate you, and pray for them which despitefully use you, and persecute you [Matt. 5:44]." In defense of church and doctrine the great Luther said of the Anabaptists, "They should be put to death." And they were. Among other reasons he listed were that, one, they had no definite doctrine and, two, they suppressed true doctrine. It was *doctrine*, you see, that was paramount and had to be defended, not the *Way* of the lowly Galilean.

The point to be made is that Christ offered no creed or particular theology. And shortly after his earthly life ended, creeds and theologies began to appear and violence began to be committed in its defense. And always with a theological rationale. In *The City of God* Augustine said, "He to whom authority is delegated . . . is but the sword in the hand of he who uses it . . . [and] is not himself responsible for the death he deals." On that basis Eichmann was innocent. Would you agree that essentially Augustine lays the foundation for the Lutheran position that there is an earthly authority and we shouldn't mess with it? And did Lutheranism pave the way for Hitler's holy war? (Still just asking.) And was not Augustine paving the way to make a moral distinction, not on the basis of conduct, but on the basis of creed? Or belief? But belief is not faith. And faith is not belief. I mentioned earlier those who have not faith, but certitude. Belief is passive. Faith is active. There is but one definition of faith in the New Testament and it has nothing to do with belief, but entirely with action. The one in Hebrews. "Faith is the substance of things hoped for, the evidence of things not seen [Heb. 11:1]." That is, Abraham going out not knowing whither he went. The Christian going out, not because of some narrow body of doctrine, not because of belief, but in the Spirit of the Way. The way the early builders of the church did not, could not, trust because it wouldn't work in the construction of a mammoth institution. And so, as Hamilton pointed out, there was the gradual trivialization of the church until it had become hardly distinguishable from the society in which it finds itself at a given moment in history.

When Calvin began to formulate a positive conception of the use of law as a guide to the Christian, even under grace, he was opening once again the floodgate of violence. Dualism, we/they again. Whether it is Calvin and Luther against the Anabaptists, or Pat Robertson, and yes, [Paige] Patterson, [Paul] Pressler, and the others against the secular humanists. I asked earlier how these differ. I ask it again. And yes, even throw in Augustine. Are not all of them seeking to make Caesar the adjudicator? Luther's church would find the Anabaptists guilty. The state would execute them. Pat Robertson and the others would find the secular humanists guilty and then turn them over to the state to deal with. How? you ask. Correct them in the public schools. That's how. Can we not all see that to place the Bible in the academic mode, to permit it to be taught, let alone to require that it be taught, is to deny the very claim that is made: that the Bible is the inspired word of God. And can we not see that to ask the academy to teach our children to pray is to make the academy Lord? "Lord, you teach us to pray," the disciples asked. They did not ask Herod to do it.

Theological preaching? Never thought about it. Now that I have I am convinced that it can only be the living of a life in community, based on faith, not certitude. I don't like the word ministry. It is arrogant, presumptuous, condescending, maybe even imperialistic. I don't have a ministry, I have a life. As to how well I have conducted it, I will leave for God to be the judge, a God about whom I know little, but whom I seek to honor.

23

"An Open Letter to Dr. Billy Graham"*

CONTEXT: *Efficiency? Effectiveness? Respectability? Influence? By the late 1960s, Billy Graham was the face of religious success. In 1972, for example, the incumbent president, Richard Nixon, coveted Graham's endorsement, which Graham gave.*

If Graham was the popular icon of so-called "relevant Christianity," Campbell, by contrast, was often dismissed as an irrelevant dissenter. Nonetheless, the intentionally marginal Campbell (and James Holloway) publicly challenged the mastermind of religious organization. Graham was a near perfect foil for Campbell's resistance to the steeples.

The chief function of institutions now is to perpetuate themselves by perpetuating myths. Illusion is reality! Form is substance! Current "events" are crises! Style is performance! Doing is being! "Direct" action is the only action.

Institutions institute inhumanity. They can only dehumanize the relationship between those they were instituted to serve. . . .

Nothing is novel about the foregoing assertions. Radicals and reactionaries alike will assert that it has "always been that way with institutions!" That "by definition" an institution can only rationalize and systematize the relationship between men, and thereby dehumanize what previously was a more humane relationship. No doubt they are right. But that is not our point. Our point concerns today, and us: our point is that because of the linking of politics and technique, what defines the technological era is the capacity of its institutions to complete the dehumanizing of mankind. . . .

---

* By Will D. Campbell and James Y. Holloway, from *Katallagete*, Winter 1971, 1–4.

We are not talking about a "conspiracy" among the leaders of these institutions, but of something more serious—of the fact that in our day, institutions move only in one direction, and their principal energies digest, assimilate, rationalize, dehumanize any and all "reform." What does it mean, therefore, to "pray" to get the "good" men in control of institutions which, in the words of Hosea, make all men "detestable like the thing they love"?

And do not think we are saying that no "good" can come within institutions. We know that "there is *no* limit to God's grace!" But we are saying that the "good" that occurs is incidental to, a by-product of, the service institutions are "instituted" to render. . . . True, some are "led to *Christ*" in the instituted church today, but it is done against the stream of five-point grading programs, censors hovering over "Sunday school" literature or "evangelistic crusades" planned and executed more like the Pentagon than St. Paul.

Where is the "gospel" in all this? If Jesus' account of why the Samaritan is good means anything, it means that those who call Him Lord! Lord! are themselves called only to serve *men*, not offices, committees, colleges, sacraments, complexes, faculties, agencies. Maybe they work there. Maybe not. But it seems clear to us Jesus is saying that to follow Him one must be known by who he *is*, not by what institution he belongs to. Indeed, he serves the institution by refusing to serve it.

There is no Christian social strategy. And that means that there is no Christian "vocation" the way our bourgeoisie civilization tried to enforce—having to do with "making a living." These are simple points in our sophisticated and complicated culture, but they have the power to make radical—in Jesus' name—who individuals *are*.

To say it another way, who spread all those lies about Jesus? Who said that we can serve Him only through the agency of institution and ordination, given their authority not by Christ but by Caesar? Who said that we serve only where the churches, their theologians, the Supreme Court, and the president of the United States in their desperation, tell us to serve? Who spread the lie about Jesus that "the church" is a thing, a name, a physical setting: consecrated water, pews, altar cloths, smoke, budgets, computers, bricks, grape juice, bowling alleys, key cards, ordained men (only men), air conditioning, Sunday school boards, parking lots, and the American Association of Theological Schools? Who spread such a lie that denies what the church of Jesus is about, and so lied about the church being a relationship, say, like the one between the man in the ditch and the Samaritan? Or between Jesus and Peter, whose confession that Jesus is Lord is the rock upon which *Jesus* says *He* builds *His* church? . . .

We are not talking about "blowing up" institutions any more than we are talking about putting the axe to the computer. . . . Rather, we suggest as a minimum and starting point that the real "cop-out" today may be those who worship in zeal and dedication "their" institutions (and "their" place in them), who may even on scheduled occasion try to reform them, all the while cursing as "cop-outs" those who see such carryings-on as exercises in idolatry as well as futility.

Who cops out? The reformer and activist who is hostile and intolerant of those who fail to accept his definition of "cop-out," "reform," and "action"? Or those who try to call attention to the quality of institutional failure? Who cops out? Those who seek to serve their Lord by reforming the unreformable? Or those who seek to serve their Lord by being a neighbor to them who are nigh, even those who like themselves are part of institutions?

Who cops out? The men whose service to their institutions found them so committed elsewhere that they were unable to serve the man their very commitments had helped to throw in the ditch? Or the Samaritan? Who cops out? The men who rejected the story of the Samaritan as individualistic, lacking in social sensitivity and undermining the positive programs for good the institutions were following? Or, the Man who told the story of the Samaritan, and who lived it?

Who cops out? The one who despairs of American totalitarianism and imperialism and heists the banner of Hanoi, Moscow, Peking, or Havana? Or the one who sees that the same technique of principalities and powers is at work in all governments and that it is God who sits above the circle of the earth, God who brings the princes of the earth to nothing and judges our governments as He judges us, by what we do to the children, the prisoners, the whores, the addicts, the scared and bewildered, the poor, the hungry—to "the least of them" who is the one we call Lord! Lord!?

Who cops out? The Institute of the Prophets of the King of Israel? Or, Micaiah, son of Imlah?

But why do we address ourselves to you, Dr. Graham? Maybe it is because you are our Baptist brother and we love you. . . . Maybe we are now just a little hurt and peeved to see a man we once tried to stand up for become more and more a man of tremendous power and influence. Maybe we cannot accept your use of that power and influence, in Christ's name, to become a court prophet in the tradition of Zedekiah son of Kenaanah, adding your blessing (and power) to the current Kings of Israel and Judah—whether in the semi-secrecy of a political convention corridor in California, the pages of *Life* magazine, the records of your innermost prayers about political maneuvering on the national level, or on the golf course, in Neyland Stadium at the University of Tennessee, at the East Room of the White House. And whether it is Lyndon Johnson, Richard Nixon, George Wallace, or Edmund Muskie you press to your bosom. . . .

Maybe it is all or any of these things.

But we believe it is something else. We believe that the connection between your power and influence and what you say to and about the Kings of Israel and Judah must be broken. For the best example of what we mean, we believe that the only way you, or any of us, can *minister* to the troops and inhabitants of Vietnam is to prophesy to the Pentagon and White House—in the tradition of Micaiah, son of Imlah.

24

"Can There Be a Crusade for Christ?"*

CONTEXT: *Even as the Watergate crisis exposed the dangers of any alliance with the principalities, Katallagete visited yet again the problem of the "steeples'" quest for power. Beyond the collapse of the Nixon Administration, Campbell and Holloway were undoubtedly goaded into response by such ballyhooed projects as Expo '72 in Dallas and "Key 73." Billy Graham's organization administered the former, creating a gospel music festival that drew significant media exposure. Managers of the latter (i.e., Key 73), touted it as an ecumenical triumph, with some 150 different churches and denominations dedicating the year 1973 to an all-out evangelistic blitz, or crusade. Their cause was to "call our continent to Christ." Campbell and Holloway lamented the tendency of the steeples to appropriate the marketing means of "civilization as we know it."*

Through initiatives like Expo '72 and Key 73, the well-intentioned institutional church yet again bore false witness to the very gospel it proclaimed to propagate. Instead of enabling individuals to live the reconciled relationships they already have with one another in Christ, the steeples promoted a chauvinistic, conquering ethic that only divided and further alienated God's children from one another.

Fundamentalists and evangelicals were not the only ones capitulating to "civilization as we know it." Liberals were just as inclined to uncritically baptize the progressive civilization as they knew it. Campbell once again called both the Right and the Left to stop trying to administer the gospel according to successful managerial models, and start appreciating, accepting, and living according to the accomplished fact of reconciliation.

---

* By Will D. Campbell and James Y. Holloway, from *Katallagete*, Summer 1973, 2–6. Reprinted with permission.

No doubt the title is overworked.

We have heard it in other times and places. Yet the crusades go on and on. And in His name. Not just the circus barker, sawdust-trail, tent-pitching successors of Marjoe, or the hundred thousand Expo '72ers in Dallas, shouting slogans, pointing upward with the index finger, declaring their independence and alienation from the adult culture, then adulating a few, select elders who then admonish them to go on back home, join the local Steeples, and repeat what has been repeated for centuries. And not just the [Oral] Robertses, the [Billy] Grahams, or even just the Key 73ers, who make a crusade sound and be, so smooth, so sophisticated and respectable that one dare not put it in the same category as any other crusade.

Not just those. But all of *us*. The others have been analyzed, dissected, and diagnosed—so often declared by the rest of us to have nothing what-soever to do with gospel—that there is no point in covering that ground again. Except those "crusades" go on, too: mainline, structured, organized Christianity carry them on. So, once again, we have something to say about them. And also about ourselves, who so often have stood aside as the ministerial alliances organized and bled their people for enough of their coin to rent Braves Stadium, or Neyland Stadium, or Cobo Hall. Stood aside, and scoffed that Jesus was not a crusader and that what was happening there was something less than, other than, Christian.

It is one thing to scoff, to be embarrassed by the taste or style of the Bible-thumping, biblical-quarterbacking fundamentalist. But it is quite another to examine our own crusades, also in His name, and so false witness, containing no "good news" and reflecting even more of the "civilization as we know it" (as the president of these United States likes to put it). . . .

False witness is a temptation ever-present to the Christian. But do we even grant *that*? Are we not instead at ease in Zion in word and deed—that is, in Nashville, Rome, Canterbury, Geneva, New York City, and wherever brick and mortar reach into the skies throughout "Christendom"? At ease we are. We no longer see the contradiction, nay the *lie*, in the witness to Jesus in crusades—be they against Muslims or Albigenses blessed by popes and saints; against the natives (the "Indians") of our "new" world by Catholic and Protestant conquistadores; against blacks and Asians by political missionaries; against an anxious middle class and totalitarian youth culture by the media evangelists. Where in the Gospel account of

Jesus do we find crusade on the agenda? It is just not there. Yet it *is*, today, as it was yesterday, the main item on the agenda of our civilization's witness about Jesus. So that must be the heart of the matter about true and false witness: the difference between the Jesus of the Gospels, and the Christ of the institutional church allied with "civilization as we know it."

Gospel as we know it today is not just influenced by, not just tainted or weakened by "civilization as we know it," but defined and interpreted by "civilization as we know it." Consider the Quaker president of the United States [Richard Nixon] and the self-confessed *Christian* social science administrators and bureaucrats, Graham and the myriad other mass evangelists, political preachers and theologians, Key 73, Christian "social action" against racism, poverty, Vietnam, pollution; and, (alas) consider even the "ecumenical" movement. Each is an instance of the transformation, and therefore perversion, of the earliest confessions about Jesus into the ideologies of their particular crusade—all of which are an inextricable part of the history of western civilization since the "fall" of the Roman Empire.

What we are saying here is that crusades are crusades: their means *are* their ends; their *means* are what crusades—*all* crusades—are all about. Politics and culture are the "Christ" for all crusades. . . . Christ is *our* crusader, for our *causes*. . . . There can be no "decisions" for Christ in crusades. There can only be *enlistments* by individuals, institutions, structures, and movements into ideological causes, into the political maneuverings.

. . . Consider Paul. And Jesus. Why no urgent correspondence from Paul about a Jesus-directed duty to subvert an empire as the base for worldwide crusades for Christ? And where was there ever anything about Jesus to provoke the imperative to crusade? He turned down the proposition Satan made. And it was a proposition both Jesus and Satan agreed was Satan's to make. The proposition was to bring all peoples to their knees, politically. He also turned away offers of guerilla warfare. The cross-ties he carried up the hill were not used as clubs or hooks, weapon or subtle inducement, forcing a "decision" for Him.

When did Jesus pray for civilization and political order? He didn't. But when we are enjoined by crusaders to "pray for me" (your "leader"), and to "pray for civilization as we know it," our witness in His name is as if He lived and prayed only about that deadly idol, "civilization as *we* know it." And that is precisely the point of false witness: Jesus for us Christians today is not the Jew scorned and rejected by culture, politics, religion. He is not for us the One judged criminal by "civilization as we know it."

Kierkegaard had it right: Jesus today is a Christ exalted not by God, but by civilization. He is Crusader in our causes because we believe that it is *we* who have authenticated Him, that our civilization's programs, and not *God's* deed, resurrects Him from death at the hands of society. . . .

Or maybe it is all just a "failure of communication." But the people in the New Testament also know about the problem of "communication." They knew it on several levels. Sometimes they became stumbling blocks and offenses when they confessed "Jesus is Lord." And sometimes—especially when they did communicate—they were stoned, thrown into jail or, when they were lucky, out of town. Jesus also knew about the problem of communication; it is a central part of the Gospel story. Toward the end, when things began to come into focus about Him in his civilization, popularity sagged, attendance fell off sharply, friends looked the other way, denied or betrayed him, and he was tried and executed by the legal and religious authorities of "civilization as *they* knew it."

[The communication of the gospel is further obscured by the way] most of the language, symbols, images, rites, and testimonies about Jesus in the Gospels have been appropriated by and are the property of the institutional church and "civilization as we know it." The language is not devoid of meaning. The words are full of power—not the power of God, but the kind of power that comes from the age-old alliance of the institutional church with "civilization as we know it."

Now if the agenda of the gospel is not crusade, then what is it? . . . The answer might well begin with the unequivocal *minus-sign* Jesus is when placed alongside that deadly equation of the gospel with the crusades of "civilization as we know it." Begin with this: crusades are just what the good news *is not*. The good news *is* just what crusades are not. . . . The good news is *not* an enlistment on behalf of Christ to conquer anyone, or anything. It is *not* "Onward Christian Soldiers! Marching as to War!" It is *not* a call to *do* something. It is a call to *be*—*in* Christ, to *be* Jesus. . . .

The good news *is*. The good news does not call for anything to be "done"—by religions, doctrines, programs, politics, movements, education, institutions, philosophies, or causes. . . . These doings are the very gods which have lured us, in Jesus' name, away from Him and where He *is*: namely, *with us*.

Immanuel! God with us in Jesus. That *is* the agenda of the gospel. Movements, education, politics, culture, and the rest may be ever so legitimate and preserving. But they are not redeeming. And when, and if, they presume to save us—from anything—they lie about Jesus if they use His name, and lose their legitimacy for everyone, Christian and non-Christian, because in so doing they become as gods.

The ideology of Watergate is supplied by the language of the Bible. That is why Watergate is the essence, not an accident, of politics and economics as crusade. Watergate sought to save us, not destroy us. There is "Watergate" in all institutions and causes today—political, religious, educational, economic, social. It is so because they all presume to save us, to be as God. . . .

The good news can never be the advancement of cultural values or political arrangements. It is about *us*, *where we are*, in bedrooms and bars, jails and supper tables, gatherings of faith hoping to confess Jesus is Lord. The gospel is the trust that makes neighbor, brother. It is the trust that makes each one free with and for the other as Jesus is with and for us: *the gift of God.* Crusades dehumanize, abstract, use, and institutionalize us. They do *things*. They carry on programs, make golden calves, build temples, turn the coss into art forms of gold and paint. Crusades are the things we *do*, the *gods* of those of us who do them. . . .

The gospel is not interpretation. It is truth between people. It is not theology and teachings, religious good works or political advancements. It is *event*: the gift of faith and trust that men and women, girls and men, boys and women, *be with* the other as Jesus is with us, as God is with Jesus, with no questions as to whether the "other" is Kluxer or liberal, black or white, deserving or undeserving poor, prisoner for incest or prisoner for burning draft records. . . .

Thus, the gospel does not concern what most of us want to hear about good news, namely, something advancing our causes. Rather it concerns *us*, where we *are*, *now*, and has nothing to do with our programs or movements whose aims are the advancement of our culture and politics. Yet we eagerly, scholarly, and enthusiastically dismiss the gospel as being sentimental, pious, unrealistic, irrelevant, and so powerless to oppose as Jesus did the starvation and slaughter of innocents. Or the guilty. How often we oppose war and poverty for political reasons only, justifying war and poverty on political grounds when it suits our causes!

So the good news is God's gift, not civilization's doings. It is this: if I am love to you as Jesus is love to me—even unto the place called The Skull—there is no hate, suspicion, resentment, hunger, murder, violence, alienation. And the news is good, for even when hate, resentment, suspicion abound, Jesus is still love *to us*. . . . The good news is the kingdom of God where *we* are, *now*. Jesus likened it to the trust, that is, the joy, freedom, spontaneity, excitement of the little children.

Of course it turns the world upside down!—no rules, movements, programs, or crusades just the gift of resurrection against the deaths of "civilization as we know it." Just the *minus-sign* of Jesus, outside that grotesque equation of the gospel with "civilization as we know it," those massive conquests and deaths seeking to liberate humanity from the evils of hunger, war, violence, ignorance, poverty, alienation, and hatred by crusades—crusades which in turn breed hunger, war, violence, ignorance, poverty, alienation, and hatred. And the necessity of more crusades.

The minus-sign of the good news is in truth the *plus-sign*, the sign of Jesus, the way to death which leads to eternal life. The cross.

We believe that the New Testament is straightforward when it confesses Jesus is Lord. That confession does not take us out of "the world" and on to crusades, but leads us into "the world" defined not by civilization as we know it, but *re-defined* by the confession about the gospel of God.

To repeat. We speak not only about and to the crusading of Graham, Hargis, Roberts, Humbard, and the others in their commerce of media evangelism. We speak also about and to ourselves, we who have spawned all those crusades of false witness to our Lord by our identification of Jesus with our social, political, and cultural ambitions and conquests.

Is Christ a crusader? The question itself is the question of false witness. The good news is Jesus struggling up the hill, cross-ties strapped to his back and, before the eyes of those who loved yet betrayed him, undergoing the agony of death by the spikes driven into his body by the religion and politics of "civilization as we know it." The good news describes Jesus' resurrection as God's doing, then and now—not as our programs, politics, accomplishments. . . . "Jesus is Lord" is not a crusade conquering our brothers to "civilization as we know it." It is the confession God gives us the power to *be*.

25

Excerpts from *Forty Acres and a Goat**

CONTEXT: *Concluding a presentation on "Religion and Violence in Southern Culture," Campbell told the audience, "in preparing for this occasion I paid a visit to the headquarters of the largest Christian denomination in the South and one of the largest in the world [the Southern Baptist Convention headquarters in downtown Nashville]. I lounged in overstuffed swivel chairs behind expensive, and I suppose, beautiful mahogany desks. I conferred with well-paid executives in spacious, thick-carpeted office suites. I sipped coffee in a ceramic-tiled and antiseptically clean refreshment room, and listened to a discussion of a forthcoming Christian golf tournament. I went outside to shake it all and walked through a slum area where night jars are emptied in the backyard and tried to ignore half-clad children gazing at me through hungry eyes. I passed the new Metro jail and heard the prison sounds of mid-afternoon. Through the wino district where the Rescue Mission is threatened with closure because the derelicts empty their bladders in sight of nice people on their way to or from a large downtown church, its steeple casting its shadow on their sin. I thought again of the wretched violence of silence. And it kept running through my mind: Religion is just too nice ever to be trusted with so important a matter as the salvation of our souls."*

In the excerpt that follows, Campbell's imaginary confessor and conscience, T. J. Eaves, helps Will articulate his frustration with the steeples. As a concept, the church might be aesthetically pleasing and psychologically reassuring, but the institutional church merits resistance because it really has nothing to do with the work of Christ and the vocation of discipleship.

---

* From Will D. Campbell, *Forty Acres and a Goat: A Memoir* (Atlanta: Peachtree, 1986). Reprinted with permission.

(pages 148–52)

"Why'd you drop out of the steeples?" T.J. asked one day en route to a meeting. He had asked the question before and I had several stock answers, generally frivolous. "When I accepted the call, I didn't know it was collect," was one of them. "I lost my lease," was another. I had the feeling T. J. was not going to let me off with flippancy this time.

"Don't you miss going to church?" he came back when I tried to be cute.

"I'm not sure I've ever been to church," I answered. "Church is a verb. That's what Carlyle Marney used to say."

"But don't you miss the gatherings? The singing, preaching, dinner on the grounds, the fellowship, support?"

"Sometimes I miss it all so much I think I'm going to bust." He didn't answer, just sat waiting for me to go on. "Some folks say, 'You know, every Sunday morning the old devil tempts me to stay home. Not to go to church.' Well, he tempts me to go. Yeah, old buddy, I miss it. I really do."

"Then why don't you go back?" he asked. I wasn't comfortable with the pressure.

"Well, I guess if the Lord can beckon someone to come underneath the steeples, He can beckon some folks to come out from under them."

"Yeah. Guess so," he said. "Just so we don't miss a beckon."

I motioned to a stack of church bulletins a friend in California had sent me a few days earlier. They were on the back seat with some other mail.

"Read the announcements," I said. "Go ahead." He began to read some of the scheduled events out loud. Marriage Enrichment Seminar. Weight Watchers Club. Mother's Day Out. He shuffled the bulletins like a deck of cards.

"Well now, Brother Will, don't be so cynical. What's wrong with that? A lot of marriages are in trouble, so they tell me. People shouldn't be so fat. And mamma needs some time away from the house too."

"Nothing wrong with it," I said, "but what does any of it have to do with John 3:16?"

"Let's see what the wild card says," he laughed. "We'll make this one the wild card." He flipped one of the bulletins onto the seat between us, leaving it there for a moment like it was cooling off. "Ah yeah. I'll bet you liked this one. Bible Study Ski Trip. That's *January* 3–16. For just $750, any member of the congregation can go to Aspen. Ten full days of skiing, with instructions for beginners. Bible study each evening around a cozy fire."

"Yeah. I really liked that one," I said. "Go on."

"At seven o'clock Thursday this steeple has a workshop." He put both hands to his temples. "Splitting Headaches."

"Yep, I've been there," I said. "I've had some splitting headaches under the steeples. But you're lying to me now. I don't remember that one. Don't make it worse than it is."

He threw his hands up in a gesture of, "Would I lie to you?" He pointed his finger to the line he was reading and held it up so I could see. "Splitting Headaches Seminar," he repeated. "And that's at seven on Thursday. You believe me now? Tai Chi. That's Monday at 5:30. On Wednesday it's Yoga. I thought Wednesday was prayer meeting night. What's Tai Chi, Reverend Campbell?"

"Don't know, Reverend Eaves." He reached over and honked the horn. "Something worthwhile, I'm sure. Something I don't have to go to church to get. To do. Whatever. What else do we have today for the followers of the Way?"

"Well, let's just us see what we can find here for little ole Brother Will. Gotta teach him how to hustle the program. Gotta stroke his madbone." He rummaged through the stack, pretending to pick one at random. "Ah-ha! Here's a dandy. Baptist Open. Excuse me. That's Third Annual Baptist Open Golf Tournament."

"Baptist *Open*?" I asked. "Both?"

"That's what the man says. That's out of the Bayou State. Now, let's hear it for Louisiana!" he shouted, clapping his hands and stomping his feet on the floorboard. He rolled the window down and pretended to push something outside.

"And from the great state of Texas, we have this one. It's a seven o'clock swimming party." He scratched his head from the wrong side and went into his monkey act. "Woops! Afraid I'll have to miss that one. It has an exclusionary clause: designer swimsuits requested. We always went in naked, and everyone knows God didn't design black birthday suits. Anyway, black folks don't get naked." He folded the announcement sheet and put it in his pocket. "They get *neck*-ed."

"R.S.V.P.?" I asked, motioning to the pocket he was buttoning.

"No, I want to read that one again tomorrow. Today I ain't believing it. But let's hear it for Texas. Yeaaa Texas!" he cheered.

"Now who's cynical?" I said. "But you dropped one. See what it says."

"All rightie, Brother Pastor," he said, searching for the place. "Here's a goodie for you. 'Today we are introducing a new member of our church staff. Minister of Puppetry.'" He began quacking, talking like Donald Duck. "'And we have added this week three new buses. That brings the total to ninety-one. And to encourage the kiddies. . . .'" He dropped the Donald Duck routine and read in his own voice. "'. . . to bring a friend to ride the bus to church, a dollar bill will be hidden on each bus on the trip home. Each child who brings a friend to Sunday School will be permitted to join in the search for the treasure.'" He began scrambling around the car, turning things over, jerking the glove compartment open and scattering maps and tissues on the floor, looking for the dollar. "Mamma, get the Clorox," he yelled. "And that's not all, Christian bussing fans," he went on. "'Every child who brings two friends gets to participate in the nickel grabbing.'" He read the rest silently, then paraphrased. "Yep! A big bucket is jam-packed with nickels, and the little kiddies get to keep all the nickels their little hands can come out of there with. Ho boy!"

He sat staring out the window, pretending to count the telephone poles as we zipped past them. I wondered if he might be thinking that his church did none of those things. If that was what he was thinking, he didn't say it. Instead he began talking about that not being the whole story, that there were some good, meaningful, helpful activities listed in the bulletins too. "Not all of it is hustling the program," he said. He mentioned soup kitchens, food banks, and tutoring classes. "What about the R.A.'s and G.A.'s?" he asked, referring to the Royal Ambassadors and Girl's Auxiliaries, church clubs for boys an girls to teach them about evangelism. His voice was like and entreaty, like he wanted very much to hear me say something kind about the steeples. "Don't you believe that's better than the kids being on the streets, taking dope or something?"

"Royal Ambassadors and Girl's Auxiliary," I said, sighing deeply. "I can tell you don't have any little girl babies to think about. The little boys are royalty. The little girls are auxiliaries. That one may be the saddest of all. At least in the long run."

"You're driving too fast," he said. "Sixty-six telephone poles in one minute."

"How many am I supposed to pass?"

"Now, tell me what you really, deep, way down deep in the bottom of your gut miss the most about it," he said, his speech more serious, more probing than it had been before. "So far you've just been trimming around the edges."

"Well," I began, not knowing what he wanted me to say, "I always like it when the service was over and I was standing at the door and the people filed by and said, 'Mighty fine sermon, Brother Campbell.' I guess I always really liked that."

"I'd be much obliged if you would tell me the truth, Reverend Campbell," he answered, leaning back in a gesture of near resignation. Then, sitting straight up, he said, "You're still talking about show business. You didn't give a rip about all that and you know it. Mighty fine sermons, my hind leg. You weren't even listening when they filed by. Someone could have said, 'Your wife just got run over in the parking lot,' and you would have smiled and said, 'Thank you very much. I appreciate it.'"

Something took hold of me. Something strange. Almost overwhelming. For the first time I had no choice but to be serious and honest with my catechist. There was a lump in my throat. Not a sad lump and not a guilt lump. Deeper than that. I shifted nervously, but it wasn't an agitated nervousness. Some mysterious mixture of joy, melancholy, and nostalgia. I didn't try to figure it out. Without thinking, I began to speak. "In obedience to the command of our Lord and Savior Jesus Christ and upon the profession of your faith in Him, I baptize you, my sister, in the name of the Father, the Son, and the Holy Spirit. Amen."

T.J. answered quickly, like he had known what I was going to say. "And that's what you liked most?"

"I didn't say that's what I liked the most. I said that's what I miss the most."

"You still baptize people," he said. "You do it all the time."

"Yeah. But when I put them under the water and look up, there's not a lot of people standing on the creek bank. Or on the river bridge looking down at us. No one is singing, 'Happy day, happy day, when Jesus washed my sins away.'"

"They're not there because you went off and left them," he chided. "You plumb went off and left them standing there on the bank."

Somehow I wasn't offended, just went on feeling what I had been feeling. When I didn't answer, he began to chuckle. "Or maybe they moved inside, huh?" he said. "Say, you ever baptize folks in one of those heated tanks with a picture of the Jordan behind you?"

"Yep. I've done that too."

"You miss those crowds too?"

I didn't answer again and he didn't push me. When he saw I wasn't going to answer, he added, "I'm really sorry, Brother Will. Real sorry."

I thought I knew what he meant but I wasn't sure.

(pages 168–70)

Ordination. Holy Orders. Who is a Reverend and who is more Reverend than whom? There is the Reverend, the Very Reverend, and the Right Reverend. (Why not the Left Reverend? That way me might get along better with Marxist Christians.) All of it gives me trouble, particularly since it had such a trivial beginning. It started back in the New Testament days over who should put food on the tables. Some of the Greek-speaking folks thought their widows were not getting their share. So seven men were chosen to distribute food while the others were left to do the holy things. There was a service, the apostles laid their hands on the heads of the seven, and ordination was born.

Somehow things got complicated and turned around. Nothing seems quite as divisive as determining who can be declared Reverend. Today a lot of Christians spend more time and energy arguing over whether women should be ordained than they do opposing a nuclear end to the world.

I have tried to stay away from it. That's the way new denominations get started, and we have enough of those already. If I believe that all institutions are inherently evil, I cannot then say, "But we're going to start a pure one. We can do what they do better." It is important that no one ever take seriously, or try to perpetuate the Church of Forty Acres and a Goat.

However.... There have been ordinations. Not standardized. Not institutionalized. It has never been done the same way twice, and the name for the body doing the ordaining has never been the same. Generally it has been done to subvert the State. Or expediency to fit our own schemes. Sometimes both at once. A young man who regularly visited hospitals, jails, and skid row got drafted and would have been an unhappy and useless soldier. A few of us got together and declared him a minister by the authority of the Dolan House Fellowship. Caesar asked no questions.

The next time it was a man with a Ph.D. degree in English who was assisting a Presbyterian minister in her ministry to men and women on death row. The authorities said he could not continue unless he was a duly ordained minister. She, along with some others who called ourselves on that occasion the Glad River Congregation, duly ordained him.

J. Andrew Lipscomb was ordained by the United Methodist Church when he was young. That body has what they call special appointments for preacher not serving a local congregation. Chaplains, college teachers, denominational workers, counselors, and the like have no trouble getting a special assignment. The personal advantage is that recipients can enjoy all the fringe benefits from both church and state.

Andrew's wife was the county health nurse in a poor, rural county in South Georgia. He provided his part of the family income as a carpenter. He also did priestly chores for the neighbors. After years of hedging, evasions, and embarrassed discussions, the bishop finally advised Andrew that a carpenter could not be a United Methodist minister in his Conference. Suddenly he had no authority to do the weddings and other things for his neighbors.

The Lazer Creek Congregation provided the unentitled preacher the following portfolio:

GREETINGS:

To all believing brothers and sisters everywhere. On this day, April 7, that being the same day as the anniversary of the resurrection of our Lord from legal execution by the state, or Easter Sunday, we of the LAZER CREEK CONGREGATION, did receive and accept Brother J. Andrew Lipscomb as a minister of that risen Lord.

Brother Lipscomb, having in earlier times passed the doctrinal tests of a sister body of believers, the United Methodist Church, and we being in a fellowship and having no quarrel of essential dogma with that branch of our Lord's tree, accepts the examination as well as laying on of hands of our kindred believers upon him.

We commend him to you, and by the authority vested in us by our common Savior do hereby commission him to do all priestly and prophetic duties in our, and His, name.

Several of us signed the document and Caesar has not questioned what we did. The hierarchy of the United Methodist Church chose not to comment, nor to formally transfer Mr. Lipscomb's orders to the Lazer

Creek Congregation. But then, in fairness to them, it has no known address.

Certainly the structured, steepled, institutionalized church has trouble with such ecclesiastics by subterfuge. I suppose there is something wrong with it, but I haven't had time to try to figure out what it is. What the Founder thinks—well, every day I'm closer to finding out.

26

"A Personal Struggle for Soul Freedom"*

CONTEXT: *In the midst of the Southern Baptist's internecine fights in the late 1980s and early 1990s, a group of moderate Baptists formed the William Whitsitt Heritage Society as a community committed to resist fundamentalist power in the Convention. Among its other activities, the society confers a Courage Award each year, and named Will Campbell the recipient for 1995. The following is an excerpted version of Campbell's no-holes-barred speech to the Whitsitt Society, delivered on July 21, 1995. In keeping with his iconoclastic vocation, Campbell seizes the opportunity to take a jab at even his Moderate admirers and hosts. Although some of his points are specific to the Baptist context, clearly Campbell's "sermon" is directed at, and relevant to, all "steeples."*

When Buddy Shurden called and asked if I would come here today I said that I would. I realized that I had made a mistake as soon as he added that I would have to make a speech and would have an assigned topic. No pocket speech. That is always mildly daunting, even to a bootleg preacher such as I. It was even more troubling when he said that the subject would be, "A Personal Struggle for Soul Freedom." Unsettling because we all know that the most vain of mortals are those who make a career of humility lest their true vanity be unmasked. Exhibitionism is ill-bred, and vainglory is the cardinal sin, another reason to be judicious with superlatives when reporting on one's own pilgrimage. I have perceived over the years, however, that the only way we can truly learn from one another is by being willing to bare as much of our anatomy as our nervous system

* From *Christian Ethics Today* 1:4 (December 1995), online: http://www.christian ethicstoday.com/cetart/index.cfm?fuseaction=Articles.main&ArtID=430. Copyright ©2000–2008 The Christian Ethics Today Foundation. Reprinted with permission.

will permit, always, of course, circumscribed by some bounds of modesty. Generally we are careful to hide our warts and blemishes and thus deny our true humanity.

Well, that's about the extent of any defense I choose to make regarding my remarks here today. Except I will ask you to bear in mind that the subject of those remarks was not my doing. I consider this appearance more of a visit over the fence than a formal lecture. However, if in the course of my remarks I should saunter off into a homiletical mode, please understand that I get exceedingly few opportunities to preach to Baptist audiences. Some of it might be retroactive.

To digress from that assigned topic right off, a geriatric propensity it seems, there are a couple of things I want to say before getting more personal. So rather than bury them deep in the bowels of this palaver after some might have dozed off or made a hasty retreat to more pleasant pastures I will simply get them out of the way early.

The first thing I feel disposed to share is what is apparent to us all, namely that if Jesus Christ had been a Moderate he would never have been crucified. By definition of the word there are too many options. Had he been a Moderate he would have joined Pontius Pilate who gave him ample opportunity to cut a deal, to compromise.

And just to make sure all established camps are alienated forthwith, I hasten to add that it is further obvious that Jesus certainly would not have been crucified had he been a Fundamentalist for it was they who, in their zeal and certitude, clamored for his blood. Had He been a Fundamentalist He would have been one of them and accepted the crown they offered.

Jesus Christ was a RADICAL! And for that he died. Died so that we might be free. Free from religiosity for certainly he was not a religious man. Far from it. Free from the Law. Free from tyranny, especially religious tyranny. Free from piety to save us. Free from certitude and thus free from creedal strife. Jesus was a RADICAL!

I can make no such claim for myself. I'm an old man now and haven't been killed for my radicalism. Always the cock has crowed in time. Sometimes just in time, but nevertheless in time to cut a deal. So in the little anecdotes that follow, do not hear me as boasting of my own faithfulness. Mine has not been the excursion of a martyr. I can claim no heroics. Quite simply, I am a Baptist preacher of the South, but it was determined a long time ago that I was not a Southern Baptist preacher. And I know the difference between the two. I must add, however, that the decision that I was not a Southern Baptist preacher in the conventional sense (make that, Convention sense) was not made under the sovereignty of King Judge and his band of ecclesiastical highwaymen but under the reign of those who, when met with ignominious defeat, dubbed themselves "the Moderates." Please believe me when I add that I report that with neither rancor nor self-righteous gratification. If I didn't love you I wouldn't be standing here today. I would be back in Tennessee tending my crops or sitting before my typewriter. I report it as a matter of history. That's just the way it happened.

The second thing I want to say is that on one occasion when a certain prophecy didn't come to pass Jeremiah said that it was not good to be too sure of God. Today we are bombarded with a theology of certitude, and even cocksureness. A creed that might well begin, "My god can whip your god."

On one occasion Kierkegaard observed that God may take Christianity away as the one way of convincing people of its truth. That is what the prophets called living under judgment. It would seem clear, to any discerning reader of Scripture, that judgment is the only term that can be applied to the absurd, conniving, farcical, nonsensical, mean-spirited schoolyard scuffle that has raged in Southern Baptist circles for more than a decade. Some would prefer to call it Diaspora. But Diaspora infers that there are somewhere the righteous, the faithful, living outside the tribal boundaries. Where do we see the righteous in this depraved imbroglio?

Was Kierkegaard onto something when he said that God may take Christianity away as the one way of convincing people of its truth?

How many of you remember the pulleybone? That delectable little part of the chicken that is no more. Don Tyson doesn't know how to cut up a chicken. I remember one Sunday when my two brothers and I were literally fighting over who would get the pulleybone. Our mother had placed it aside and we had drawn straws for it. Contending that one or another had cheated to draw the shortest straw we had resorted to childish fisticuffs to settle the matter. But while we were fighting the cat jumped on the table and made off with the pulleybone. If you don't mind a pussycat being a metaphor for God, it seems to me that is precisely what has happened.

But judgment? That's a harsh word, an awesome notion to ponder. Are we prepared to consider that the so-called fundamentalist (a misnomer if ever I heard one) takeover may just be God's judgment on the rest of us? We have it on good authority that it has happened in our history. Read the Bible. Not all the kings of Judah and Israel were good kings, righteous, just. Some were despicably evil, yet the Scriptures tell us they were raised up by God's own self as judgment.

If you will permit an aging wordsmith this bit of literary license I will remind you of Manasseh, in the lineage of David, successor to Hezekiah, who ruled in Dixie—well, it was called the Southern Kingdom but you can see where a devious mind is going. He ruled for fifty-four years. Not one word of prophecy was recorded during those years. During the reign the prophets were killed.

A further parallel is the manner in which the Southern Kingdom was influenced by the politics of the day, becoming so subservient to, so at one with, Assyria. Surely we can see what is happening, what has already happened in this country when there is never a SBC gathering without a wall-sized American flag in the background, a George Bush, a Dan Quayle, an Oliver North, people who wouldn't have been able to join the early Baptist movement by virtue of being civil magistrates, spewing forth the most un-Baptistic nationalistic rubbish and receiving frenzied, rabid, fanatical cheers, and foot-stomping from thirty thousand alleged Baptists. Great God Almighty! What's going on here? What happened? The radical gospel is not sixth-grade civics. And American nationalism is not the gospel of the kingdom now. But I don't want to get into that. I've never been one to get involved in any kind of controversy.

An even more frightening parallel between Manasseh's reign and what is happening today is that the Southern Kingdom prospered during that reign. Both church and state prospered and so it was assumed that God was blessing both. Judgment is a tricky thing. It isn't measured by the every-member canvass, the latest Cooperative Program figures coming out of Nashville, or the latest figures out of Atlanta. The implications of that Scripture are in the Book and you are the proclaimers of the Word. I am not suggesting that your exegesis of that text next Sunday refer to Judge Manasseh of Houston or the Reverend Doctor Manasseh of Dallas but that's up to you. I'm not your homiletics coach.

Judgment? But we were better than they are. Were we? Where were we as a denomination in the sixties and seventies when cities were burning, when black Americans were being gunned down for no greater crime than the color of their skin and their quest for freedom? Where were we during those long decades when human beings were denied the ballot,

145

had to drink from designated fountains, could not go to parks, theaters schools? If you don't recall I'll remind you. We were sitting in silence, minding our own altar fires and tea parties, building tall spires and fine steeples, watching God's world crumble around us. Ah, but now we have apologized for all that. Have we now? If we bump our neighbors off the sidewalk and into oncoming traffic and say, "Excuse me," and walk away, we have served the neighbors not at all. It is only when we bind their wounds and see them through the ordeal that true reconciliation is in evidence. Biblically it is called the story of the Good Samaritan. Politically it is called affirmative action. We await some timely word on that currently controversial moral issue called affirmative action from the Christian Life Commission, the Cooperative Baptist Fellowship, or any other Baptist faction.

Where were we as a denomination from our founding in 1845 until 1920 when no woman was allowed even to cast a ballot as to who would rule them? We know very well where we were. And how many female preachers and deacons did we have during those years we look back on with yearning? We know how many. Where were we as a denomination during the long years of carnage in Southeast Asia? What support did we offer those noble youths who refused to participate in that evil and uncivilized scandal? What prophetic resolutions did we pass in our solemn assemblies as thousands of our finest fled to Canada or suffered incarceration in obedience to the very principles that brought the Baptist movement into being? Ah, some day we'll apologize for that also.

And some day we'll apologize for what we are doing to gay and lesbian Christians and non-Christians. But not yet, for we ride the waves of culture. I mention that, not to dramatically inject into the discussion the most explosive issue on so many agendas today—well, that, too—but to suggest that we always take our cue from culture, from Caesar. We discern the signal of culture, rush out and clothe the sight in vague and misinterpreted Scripture, never taking the Bible for what it is, a book about who God is, but as a buttress of the biases of culture. We did it with slavery. We do it with war, gender exclusionism, poverty, and now we're doing it with homophobia. And some day we'll apologize. Some day we'll call the fireman when the fire is out. We joined the civil rights movement when the prophets were safely dead. Jesus was a RADICAL! There comes a time!

The list is long. How does one behave under judgment? Maybe by just not caring about the things that really, after all, just don't matter anymore. If they ever did. By not agonizing over triviality. Jesus, quoting Isaiah, said that he had come to proclaim the opening of the doors of prisons, and letting the prisoners go free, bringing good news—food and housing—to the poor, seeing eye dogs for the blind. Jesus was a radical. So should I care who the next president of some man-made, yes man-made, convention, fellowship, or what have you may be? Does it really matter in the glaring white heat of Isaiah's and Jesus' words? I say you nay. Am I going to alter the course by the latest utterance of some institutional pimp who appears to spend most of his time blow-drying his hair and in his free time dismisses some of his finest teachers and scholars, seeking to make robots and handmaidens of a once-gifted faculty? I say you nay. But again, I don't want to get into that.

I reckon I'm supposed to say something about my own personal quest for soul freedom, painful and pretentious as it may be. I was introduced to the radical Christ I have sought to follow, albeit from afar, sitting around a pine knot fire casting its light upon the pages of my parent's Bible as they read to their four issue in a little frame house in rural Amite County, Mississippi. And then they prayed. Every night. It was in the throes of the Great Depression and sometimes bones were weary from heavy work and stomachs not always full but the ritual was never neglected.

I learned theology from my father's table grace as he said the same words three times a day no matter how meager the fare. The words I heard from the day I was born until I left his table at seventeen summed up his theology, his philosophy, his very life. And after eight years of what we call higher education I never found a more succinct summary of the Christian movement. For his simple words acknowledged the existence of the Deity, they spoke of mercy, of thanksgiving, sin, forgiveness, restoration, and always concluded with the benedictory AMEN. What else is there to our faith? Hear his words and see if anything essential is missing.

> O Lord, look down on us with mercy,
> Pardon and forgive us our sins,
> Make us thankful for these and all other blessings,
> We ask for Christ's sake. Amen.

Those words made a deep impression on me and I began early to take them to heart. As the words took flesh it was in relationship to other human beings. We lived in one of the most rural and presumably most racist counties in the nation. How then did I grow up to give my entire adult life to the struggle for racial equality and reconciliation? I learned lessons, lessons centered around my father's table and hearth. Not mandated prayers in Caesar's schoolroom.

Mercy? I was about five years old. The Campbell families lived in a little cluster adjacent to our Campbell grandparents' house. Grandpa Bunt and Grandma Bettye. On Sunday afternoons we gathered on their yard to play. Twelve or fifteen of us yearling boys at one time. On one occasion an elderly black man was shuffling down the country dirt road. Some of us began to taunt him. "Hey, nigger. Hey, nigger." Grandpa Bunt was sitting on a tree stump whittling. He called us all around him and spoke gently but firmly. "Now, Hon." Grandpa Bunt called everyone Hon. Boys, girls, men, women. We didn't have all those Freudian hang-ups in Amite County in 1929. "Now, Hon. There ain't no niggers in this world. All the niggers died a long time ago."

"Yeah, Grandpa. John Walker. He's a nigger. There he goes on down the road." John Walker was just out of the state penitentiary for stealing a mess of roasting ears. Grandpa Bunt wasn't through with the lesson. "No, Hon. He's not a nigger. He's a colored man. Have mercy, boys. Always have mercy." Colored, of course, was the acceptable term at the time. I never forgot it. Grandpa Bunt would be considered uneducated today. But he knew of mercy. I went away to college and university to study social ethics and race relations. I never heard a more profound lecture on the subject. If I did I forgot them.

I also learned of that radical Jesus in experiences in a little one-room church house called East Fork. One of my earliest recollections is of sitting in that house one night during a summer revival. As coal oil lanterns flickered dimly and the preacher was about to begin, the service was interrupted by a long line of robed and hooded men. We were low-church Baptists not accustomed to vestments in the service so it got our attention. It was the Ku Klux Klan, marching in a somber and ghostly procession. The Grand Dragon presented a large pulpit Bible and an offering of money to the congregation that was politely accepted by the visiting preacher. The men then turned and left as they had come. Only one person stirred during the proceedings. Uncle Jesse, my father's oldest brother, a man not known for personal piety, left his seat, walked out of the church house and never came back. When I preached my first sermon at the age of sixteen, as I read the Scripture my hands moved across those large, embossed letters, KKK, on the back cover of the pulpit Bible. I thought of Uncle Jesse, then dead of a gunshot wound. I hope I thought also of pardon, sin, forgiveness.

I was a little older when a young Negro lad got in Albert Carroll's farm truck one Sunday afternoon and drove it into a tree not far from where it was parked. I was visiting my mother's parents, Grandma Bertha and Grandpa Will Parker. A group of men soon gathered with the lad and a gin belt. Grandma Bertha confronted them, spoke firmly and stood fixed at her picket gate. "I don't care if he's colored. And I don't care if he stole Albert Caroll's ole truck. He's fifteen years old and you ain't gonna beat him." And they didn't. Grandma Bertha died at fifty-nine and I never forgot her. . . .

When I was just turned seventeen I was ordained in that little church house. The ordaining council was my daddy, my Uncle Luther, my Grandpa Bunt, a cousin, and a country preacher. They didn't ask me a lot of doctrinal questions. They understood that I wouldn't know the answers and didn't really need to. They had taught me about church. And what it meant. . . . My daddy knew a lot about personal soul freedom. A lot more than I know.

Now in case you've missed it, the point of my lifting up my progenitors before you is not to suggest that through their influence I, Will D. Campbell, became a courageous man, deserving of the great honor you are now bestowing upon me. I know better than that. I lift them up because they can be duplicated in hundreds of thousands of cases throughout this land. All of you can tell these same stories of those stalwarts who came before you. The point, the only point, is that these are the stuff of Baptist history. And these are the people who have been double-crossed, betrayed, ignored, trampled on like so much chaff in this demonic fight over the pulleybone, a fight of which every last one of us here has been a part. Otherwise we wouldn't be here at all. We would be back in those little communities at the gravesides celebrating the Grandpa Bunts, the Grandma Berthas, those great people who were, and are, our history but are now discounted by the high and mighty whose fight, in the total scheme of human history and Christ's unendable story, won't amount to the crepitation of a flea in a whirlwind. Does it never occur to those doing the fighting that the world is paying not the slightest bit of attention to their sparring? And when they notice at all it is only a chuckle.

To be more immodest, there was a contract out on my life for a time when I was involved in the civil rights movement. The community was much upset about Will Davis's carryings on with the colored people. I had been writing about it, speaking widely, and it was being reported. There was a movement to strip me of my ordination. Two things prevented it. One, they didn't know how to go about it. (One of the beauties of Baptist polity.) And two, a couple of crusty old Navy veterans sent word that if they tried to take Will Davis's ordination away they would come up there and filibuster until hell froze over. At the risk of disharmony within the fellowship the matter was dropped.

What they didn't understand was that my ordination certificate, with misspelled words and the marred grammar of country people, signed by those mentioned above, hangs above my mantle, glued securely and forever on top of my college and university degrees, hiding them from the eyes of the world. That's my marching orders and no one can ever, ever take that away from me. Not ever. Those Baptist people did that to and for me and it can never be undone. Not with anyone's words, resolutions, or actions. That's what it means to be an old-fashioned Baptist. That's what soul freedom is all about. Are you listening, you who wreck schools of learning, who pass absurd resolutions, who place limitations on God Almighty as to what gender He can and can't call to preach His gospel. You don't scare me, you ecclesiastical bullies, you blind guides who strain at a gnat and swallow a camel, who devour widows' houses, who bind heavy burdens and lay them on the shoulders of the poor and lift not a hand, you who for a pretense make long prayers, you who compass sea and land to make one convert and when he is made make him twofold more the child of hell than yourselves. Woe unto you! Whited sepulchers outside; inside full of the bones of the dead, and of all uncleanness. Are you listening to this old man? THERE COMES A TIME!

With that undergirding from a tiny, rural church, with no paved parking lot, no gaudy steeple, no Betty Crocker kitchen nor gymnasium for our own children, and with a half-time preacher, my quest extended into adulthood.

As most of you know my institutional flings didn't work out. None of them. There is not time here to list them nor explain their demise. To do so would serve no purpose. Doubtless part of my failure within the structures had to do with my own intractable genes. Whatever. I was a pastor, a university chaplain, an employee of the allegedly most free religious institution in the world. I didn't keep any job for long. But through it all I discovered one thing. All institutions, every last single one of them, are evil; self-serving, self-preserving, self-loving; and very early in the life of any institution it will exist for its own self. So beware out here this week. True soul freedom cannot be found in any institution. That is the guts of my testimony to you today. True soul freedom can never be found in any institution. If they will pay you, let them. I did it too. But never trust them. Never bow the knee to them. They are all after your soul. Your ultimate, absolute, uncompromising allegiance. Your soul. ALL OF THEM. Jesus was a RADICAL! And His Grace abounds.

As the sands of time run out on me I do not consider that I have had a ministry at all, except in the sense that all believers are priests. I have had a life. As to how well I have conducted it I am willing to leave to the One so mysterious, so elusive and evasive, so hidden as to say to Moses from a burning bush, I AM WHO I AM, to be the sole judge. I can only exult that grace abounds. . . .

27

"There Is Hope"*

CONTEXT: *This speech from October 27, 1994 to the members of the Associated Baptist Press hit many of the same themes and is every bit as blunt with the "Moderates" as Campbell's presentation to the Whitsitt Society. This time, however, Campbell is more direct both in resisting the SBC steeples, and stressing the need for disciples to oppose the principalities and powers. Campbell's iconoclasm, however, is never an end in itself.*

Despite his condemnation of the "steeples," Campbell's stresses a theme of hope. He points to the creative purpose and potential of reconciliation—reconciliation with the marginalized and disinherited of society.

When I was going to school on the G.I. Bill of Rights, right after the Spanish-American War, they told me that the first few minutes of any address or sermon should be given over to sheer foolishness and nonsense. I reckon John Seigenthaler's introduction has pretty well covered that so we can proceed to the subject at hand. Whatever that subject may be. Actually, John, I was born in New York City. In the Soho district. My mother was a dancer at Radio City Music Hall with the Rockettes. My father was with the Secret Service guarding Mr. Garfield, until that terrible accident. Then we moved to Mississippi and started picking cotton for a living. And if you're buying all that I have some choice beachfront property in the Smoky Mountains you might be interested in.

Some of you asked about my walking cane. I'm always glad because that allows me to tell one of my favorite stories. Something that really happened, though perhaps I should be ashamed to tell it. The cane was

* From *Christian Ethics Today* 1:2 (June 1995), online: http://www.christianethics today.com/cetart/index.cfm?fuseaction=Articles.main&ArtID=431. Copyright ©2000–2008 The Christian Ethics Today Foundation. Reprinted with permission.

made for me by a neighbor who was what we would call illiterate. But he knew something abut aesthetics; knew what was pretty; what really, finally mattered. He tore down an old abandoned barn many years ago and discovered that some of the rotting timbers were made of wild cherry. He put them aside and when he was old he made things that were at once beautiful and useful for those he loved. Fortunately, I was one of them. It is, I think, a fine metaphor for the gospel—taking something rotten and making something beautiful of it.

All of you know about security at airports. Well, I walk through the upright sensor and the cane doesn't set off an alarm because there is not a gun in it. Not even a sword. Just a piece of wood. On one occasion the guard—the fellow who had been empowered, had a badge, you know—told me to go back and put my cane on the roller after I had walked through the upright sensor. Well, that didn't make any sense to me but I went back and put it on the roller. And then I stood there. He said, "Now come on through and get your cane."

I said, "No, no. If you don't mind bring it back to me. Now I have done what you asked me to do so will you do what I'm asking you to do?"

He said, "Mister, can you walk without that cane?" By then people were backed up behind me clearing their throats, 'bout to miss their airplane don'cha know.

I said, "We don't pay you to ask medical questions. That's a different specialty. They're called physicians. Just bring the cane back." He was getting mad and I was somewhat out of sorts myself. When I got home and told my wife about it she accused me of being mildly in the grape but I wasn't. Just vexed.

Finally he said, "Mister, if you want your cane you're going to have to come down here and get it."

I said, "All right. Whatever you say." Then I got down on my belly and crawled the length of the roller. With that people were hissing and booing him. ". . . Making that poor old man crawl to get his walking cane." Then, with feigned caducity I pushed myself up and with a palsied hand got the cane, gave it a sassy little twirl and walked on down the corridor, leaving him standing there to face the crowd.

My wife said, "Do you want to get hijacked?"

"Where in the Sam Hill would they take us today? L.A.?"

"Well," she said, "Why do you do things like that?"

"Because," I said, "I'm a Baptist!! I come from a long line of hell-raisers. I was taught that I wasn't a robot; that I was a human being with a mind, capable of reason, entitled to read any book, including the Bible, and interpret it according to the ability of the mind I was given. That's why I do things like that."

What happened to those Baptists? Where are those people who were drowned in the Amstel River, tied on ladders and pushed in burning brushheaps because they believed in and practiced freedom of conscience; because they believed in total, total separation of church and state; because they were so opposed to the death penalty that they wouldn't serve on juries; because they would not go to war, any war, for church or state, would not baptize their babies, not so much for doctrinal reasons but because they saw it as enrollment by the state, a way of the state maintaining control of the faithful. For those offenses they were hunted down like rabbits by armed horsemen. Where are they now? What happened?

It's a long way from that to a civil magistrate standing with a wall-sized American flag in the background—a George Bush, a Dan Quayle, an Oliver North—spewing forth the most un-Baptistic nationalistic rubbish and receiving frenzied, rabid, fanatical cheers and applause from thirty thousand alleged Baptists—Great God Almighty!! What's going on here? What happened?

We know what happened. And if we will be honest we have to admit that it happened long before a Texas judge [Judge Paul Pressler] and his little covey of rich preachers who, where Baptist history and Scripture are concerned, appear to read only until their lips get tired, or until they find a passage that will bolster their political agenda and with that authority go out and wreck the fellowship of one of the nation's largest religious bodies, determined to make robots of its adherents and eunuchs and handmaidens of its finest teachers and scholars.

"Man was first in creation and woman was first in the Edenic Fall" [when Carl F.H. Henry was chairing the Resolutions committee of the Southern Baptist Convention at Kansas City in 1982, this phrase appeared in the Resolution on Women and was approved by the messengers] . . . now ain't that cute! Has such a nice ring to it. But the dialectics of it is overwhelming. Therefore, they reason, women should not be ordained as proclaimers of the Word. That's the kind of logic that makes a fellow crawl through airports on his belly. If woman was first in the Fall she should have priority in ordination. Or so it has always seemed to me. Woman discovered sin first, she has been at it longer and thus should be more adept at identifying sin and casting it out. But then, logic seldom prevails over bigotry.

Surely we are living in the throes of the greatest religious and political heresy ever to blow its chilly winds over this land called America. My yellow dog [Democrat] genes tempt me to say it is a political heresy because it is Republican; and Baptists, in my youth, were Democrats. But that isn't the reason. It is a political heresy because it is espousing a course that is a rollercoaster to a fascist theocracy. To unfreedom. It is a political heresy because it is in direct opposition to our earliest political document.

It is a religious heresy because it is religious, yes, very damnably religious, and the founder of the Christian movement was very, very anti-religious—certainly anti-religious—and came to establish freedom and end religiosity.

But I don't want to talk about what those little people have done. I've never been one to get involved in any kind of controversy. What's the point of talking about what they have done?

They're not here. We're here. And if I may sound a note of warning to this assemblage it is that it strikes me that too much energy is spent bemoaning the fact that the institution known as the SBC—and by that we mean some imagined, romantic SBC of the decades of the 40s, 50s, 60s and 70s—is no more. There was never anything sacred about that institution, nor any other institution, so why lament its demise? It wasn't a true copy of the Baptist birthright in the first place and didn't deserve to survive. So the Associated Baptist Press should not attempt to resuscitate a corpse but espouse the kingdom now. Don't seek the living among the dead nor seek to find a risen Lord in a sepulcher.

I know it is rude to accept an invitation to someone's house and then complain about the decor but one thing on which I always agreed with Robert Taft is that tact is dishonest. So the second warning I would sound is that you tolerate the designation, "Moderate." The original Baptist movement was a radical, revolutionary one, scorned and persecuted by both the established church under Luther and Calvin, as well as Rome, and the established state under whatever prelate was in power. Christian discipleship can never be moderate. Christian discipleship is always radical, and thus costly. The demise of the Baptist movement began long before Judge Pressler and that bunch of ecclesiastical highwaymen began their reign of terror. When did it begin? It began, in my judgment, when a movement began to become an institution, a principality. It began when we went to Baal-Pe'or and became like unto the things we detested.

Institutions, by their very definition, are evil. For their *raison d'être* is always and inevitably self-survival. They, all of them, when they are threatened will go to any length, tell any lie, engage in any program to protect themselves. And justify it as being in defense of Almighty God. That is what Paul was talking about when he spoke of powers and principalities and spiritual wickedness in high places. That is why it is safe to say the things that brought us to this hour began long before the so-called takeover. The takeover, of the Baptist movement, my friends, began on our watch. Nay, long before our watch. It began with the formulation of creeds and theologies. Our Anabaptist ancestors—and Professor Estep is correct to trace our roots back to them—knew that, and that was why they had to be killed. They were dangerous to established institutions, a peril to principalities. Schwarmers, they were called. Radicals who swarm about like bees on the loose. The left-wing of the Reformation they were known as. Yes, Left-wingers. Not Moderates. Where are they now? What happened?

The historic Baptist notion of discipleship over creedalism survived in the new country for a time but now that is no more. The Baptist people, once a movement (or sect if you prefer Troeltsch's understanding) is now a creedalistic institution. And has been for a long time. Oh, when I was a boy in Mississippi we claimed that we weren't. But we were. We said the Bible was our creed, and made a fetish, an idol, of the Bible. Which part of the Bible? Certainly not that part where Ezekiel said, "She lusted after lovers whose genitals were like mule's genitals (That's from chapter 23 of Ezekiel, verse 20. I'm sure some of you will want to grab that Gideon Bible when you get back to your room and check the text.) I cite it here for more than cosmetic or melodramatic effect. The significance of that text for this gathering is that the prophet was addressing a group not too dissimilar to the neo-Baptists of our day. (And neo-Baptist would be a more accurate designation than fundamentalist.) "Your genitals are like mule's genitals." If you grew up in the country as I did you know what God was saying through the prophet Ezekiel. A mule is a hybrid. Sterile. God was saying to that right-wing bunch, "Ha." Well, never mind.

I was speaking to the state annual meeting of the ACLU in Mississippi not long ago. It was not a large gathering which struck me as being odd for Baptist is the state church in Mississippi and the First Amendment was the idea of a couple of Baptist preachers. Anyway, some Baptists were protesting the gathering because the ACLU defends pornographers. It does but it also defends Baptists, if it can find any, which isn't easy to do these days. Anyway, I cited that passage and challenged the censors to burn that book because it contains hundreds of passages equally tempting to the aggressive scissors of censorship. With the Bible as our creed we regularly repented of the bingo games of our Catholic neighbors but I recall no repenting of the sin of whipping black people. Nor even lynching them.

But, I wander. A geriatric propensity I suppose. My point is that the Baptist movement floundered when it became institutionalized, when it became a vessel, not of faith, a faith such as Abraham had, and certainly not a vessel of radical discipleship such as our spiritual ancestors were, but a vessel of certitude, of theologies and creeds. And thence the fighting. "My God can whip your God." Doesn't that about sum it up?

What then are the inherent dangers of creeds, of theologies, of certitude?

In an important but little-known book called *Witness to the Truth*, Edith Hamilton, a scholar best known for her work on antiquities, made a statement almost fifty years ago that addresses that question:

> So the great Church of Christ came into being by ignoring the life of Christ. . . . The Fathers of the church were good men, often saintly men, sometimes men who cared enough for Christ to die for him, but they did not trust him. They could not trust the safety of his church to his way of doing things. So they set out to make the church safe in their own way[. Creeds] and theologies protected it from individual vagaries; riches and power [protected it] against outside attacks. The church was safe. But one thing its ardent builders and defenders failed to see. Nothing that lives can be safe. Life means danger. The more the church was hedged about with Confessions of Faith and defended by the mighty of the earth, the feebler its life grew.[1]

What this wise woman was saying is, to me, highly infuriating. She was saying that the structured, institutional church was a cop-out from the outset. Even as a bootleg Baptist preacher of the South (not a Southern Baptist preacher and I know the difference), and steeple drop-out, I am

1. Edith Hamilton, *Witness to the Truth: Christ and His Interpreters* (New York: Norton, 1948), 204–5.

not ready to go with her that far. Yet she has much evidence on her side. She was saying that no institution could be made to work efficiently by following Christ literally. For He had no system, no rules, no methods people could adopt and put to definite use. Edith Hamilton was correct as she continued that Christ never laid down that matter of fundamental importance to an organization, clearly formulated conditions on which one could enter it. He never demanded of the people who wanted to follow Him that they must first know this or that, this creed, or that catechism, the nature of the Trinity or the plan of salvation, or subscribe to an Abstract of Principles to the satisfaction of the Sanhedrin. He had not insisted on any systematic belief whatsoever. He talked of such things as a cup of cold water. Ah, but we must build a global sprinkler system. And while we are appointing committees and electing boards and creating giant agencies to build the global sprinkler system the one near at hand perishes from dehydration as we pass by on the other side.

The inherent danger in creed over faith, Edith Hamilton said, is that creed is passive. Faith is active and leads to discipleship. Creed simply requires recitation. What's the point in believing a whale swallowed a man unless we understand that it is a story about justice. The problem with biblical literalism is that it is biblical illiteracy. The words are known but not the tune. The Bible is a book. A book about who God is. It is not a scientific dissertation to be required in Caesar's academy. But again, I wander.

Where, then, is there hope? If not in institutions, in bigness, certitude or creed, where is it? In freelance acts of discipleship I believe. Certainly grace abounds and there is hope. I have been accused of being a man without hope in my writings, of being in despair. Not so. There is a difference between perplexity and despair. While it is true that I take no hope in partisan houses, in ideologies, or even theologies, I see hope all around me.

For every soul that groans under the burden of bigotry, ignorance, discrimination, rejection, and violence there is hope.

For every hug and act of kindness extended to one dying of AIDS, there is hope.

For every hand reaching sacrificially to the homeless by offering shelter from the cold and food to ward off starvation, there is hope.

For every man who says to his neighbor, "Your wife is a child of God; you strike her at your own peril," there is hope.

At the risk of toadying to our host tonight, for every organization that stands for freedom over against the tyranny of fools, there is hope.

In a Florida editor with bills and house notes and family to feed who stands tall and says, "My skills you have bought for many years for little pay, but my soul, sirs, is not for sale, goodbye," there is hope.

For every word and story you write and put on the wire containing a message of radical discipleship to a living Christ, there is hope. There is hope, for there the star of Christmas shines again, and there the star of David glows anew, for there is Immanuel:

God with us.

28

Excerpt from *The Convention**

CONTEXT: *At the height of the Fundamentalist-Moderate fight for control of the Southern Baptist Convention in the 1980s, Campbell penned one of his strongest sermons on (and to) the steeples. Presented as fiction, this iconoclastic "parable" is a condemnation of the SBC's use of* realpolitik *to govern the life and work of a community of humble, sacrificial, reconciling faith. Here Campbell calls for an authentic application of the alternative politics of Jesus, instead of the power politics too often used to gain ecclesiastical command and control.*

Campbell's parable describes an imaginary SBC convention in Chicago, where Dorcas Rose McBride, a rural Mississippian, would run for the SBC presidency. The irony, of course, is that the SBC was unlikely to ordain women to the ministry, let alone appoint one to the denomination's highest administrative office.

In this scene, the Moderates, who have been losing ground to the Fundamentalists in recent years, meet with Lilith Harrison-Arney, Miriam Porter, and Maureen Owen, the women planning to nominate Ms. McBride. Moderate party patriarchs, Chuck Bender and Vernon Hedge, appeal to the women's hope for any success, reminding them of behind-the-scenes realities and political machinations. In other words, this scene depicts the Moderates inviting the women to abandon the McBride candidacy, to back their viable candidate. Together their proposed coalition could defeat their common enemy—the Fundamentalist ticket. Campbell's parable is a sharp lampooning not only of the Fundamentalists, but the tendency of steepled Christians—of every denomination—to think and act as savvy political scientists and party hacks rather than powerless disciples of Jesus.

---

* From Will D. Campbell, *The Convention: A Parable* (Macon, GA: Mercer University Press, 2007), 136–44. Reprinted with permission.

"You know, I've always thought that women were *superior* to men in every way," Bender said, opening a packet of Sweet 'N Low and pouring it in his coffee.

"I doubt that," Lilith snapped.

"No, I really mean it. I don't just say that because you live longer. Elephants live longer than any of us. I mean . . . I taught in my seminary for a while, and invariably my best students were women. They had better insights, could write better, preach better. Just superior in every way."

"The staff checks I sign every month don't reflect that," Lilith retorted.

"And that's not right either," Hedge said, munching on a biscuit with no butter. "That's one reason I wanted to talk to y'all." Lilith gave a knowing glance at the other two women. "You know," Hedge continued, "we moderates have a fighting chance to turn this thing around at this convention. We always get forty-odd percent of the votes on every issue."

"The fun-damn-mentalists outfoxed us and got control," Bender said. "There's been a truce for a few years, but it's been an uneasy truce. A seesaw battle. Sometimes we win, especially at the state level. Most of the time, however, they win. But we haven't been sleeping all the time. We've groomed a bright man, Chester Fleming. He's a lay preacher and lawyer from South Carolina. We think he has a fine chance to win. In a fair fight. The [Fundamentalist's] chief of staff—that's what I call Epperson—is worried sick."

"And you want to ask for our votes?" Lilith asked.

"Not exactly," Bender said quickly when Hedge tried to answer first. "Of course, that too. But the main thing . . . well, this is a crucial year. If the fun-damn-mentalists win one more time, the right-thinking people of the church will be history." He had given the same vacuous chuckle every time he had said "fun-damn-mentalists," and he had waited each time for them to laugh with him. None of the women had.

"As a matter of fact," Lilith said, reaching over and picking a slice of bacon from Bender's plate, "we're running a candidate of our own." She said it as if she knew he already knew, as if she knew what the men had come to talk to them about.

"To tell the truth, that rumor is going around the convention," Hedge said. "And to be perfectly candid, that is what we want to talk to y'all about."

"Then talk to us," Maureen said, leaning backward. "Don't you want a *superior* president?"

"Now, Maureen," Hedge said, "you know that I, personally, would be just absolutely, totally tickled pink to have a woman as president—"

"Then you'll help us," Lilith interrupted, reaching across the table to stroke his hair. "We know it's an uphill battle, Vernon, so we'll need all the help we can get."

Hedge sat for a moment, moving the string on his tea bag around the lip of the cup of hot water the waitress had just brought him. Miriam watched him, and somehow, she felt deep pity for the man. She saw sadness in his eyes, which looked to her like those of a young girl, mothered too soon. Miriam also thought of her younger brother telling her about his unsteady conscience as a bombardier not fully committed to the Vietnam War that he had fought. She wanted to tell Hedge that she understood, that she loved him. But she said nothing.

"You know I would want to help," he said, as if sensing Miriam's thoughts, but maintaining his guard. "If I thought it would work, I'd be out there right now, buttonholing every commissioner I could find. But it won't work. You know that as well as I. It would just split the votes. And not only that, it would drive a rift in the church that's wider than the one already here." He could sense that his words were as unconvincing to the women as his silence had been. The words were even unconvincing to himself, but he continued, though less earnestly: "It's healing this church needs—and now. It's terrible for people who are supposed to be followers of Jesus to be forever fighting among themselves. If we can just get it back, if the thinking people can get control again, then we can appoint the right people on boards and trusteeships, and things can be like they used to be."

"That's exactly what we're afraid of," Lilith said. "Things *will* be like they used to be. That wasn't good enough, Doctor Hedge."

"I know it wasn't good enough, my young friend," he said, his blue smile moving Miriam even more deeply. "But at least we were trying. And we were making progress in every area. If the know-nothings hadn't moved in, we would have several hundred women as senior pastors by now. Instead, we have four. You're right, we were moving slowly, but we were moving. Rome wasn't built in a day, and these things take time. They must be done without rancor. They must be done in mutual repentance. And with love."

"I can preach about love, too," Miriam said. "Each morning a young woman walks past our church office window. She leads one child by the hand and carries a baby in her arms. She is taking them to a child-care center. And until she returns for them, she is plying her wares to the downtown *noonsie* crowd. She is called a whore, sir, but she chooses to think of herself as a working single parent—a loving mother."

"I know about such things," Hedge interrupted. "In my work with the Children and Family Services Department, I dealt with it all the time. But there are ways of ministering to . . . ways to go about those cases—"

"And how have we gone about them?" Miriam said. The years of pent-up anger and frustration, now mingling with the love she could not help but feel for Hedge. "Yesterday in this convention center, we gave a standing ovation to the governor of Illinois. A temporal ruler. A man who used to be a senator. A man who was chairman of the congressional Armed Services Committee. A man who daily presided over the ruthless subsidies for arms makers while this mother, this child of God, spread her legs for camouflaged human beings in order to feed her young."

Maureen and Lilith, who had never heard Miriam talk this way, looked at one another as if they wanted to break into a wild cheer. Bender and Hedge were fidgeting, their faces alternating between blushes and chalky blanchings.

"We are weary of the cropped compassion of religious zealots," Miriam resumed, reaching both arms toward Hedge as if to embrace him. In charity and in chastisement. "You say there could have been several hundred women pastors by now, instead of four. But why not several thousand? Why not fifty-one percent of the total? And, no, we women would not be perfect pastors. Many of us would be not better than Blanchard and Johnson's 'one-minute managers,' those mayors of their supersteeples who administer their altar fires and tea parties and call it the Church of the Almighty. Spare me. All we ask is to let us, at least and at last, *try*."

Bender started to say something, but Miriam cut him off. Her voice had been rising. She could feel the blood rushing to her head. "I know I'm being preachy. But indulge me. We women aren't allowed many sermons, and Hedge has already given us his . . . . Or somebody's." Bender ducked his head; guilt was apparent in his veiled expression.

"We are equally weary of being told about our superiority while being treated like dolts," Miriam said. "You, moderates and fundamentalists, go on muttering prayers to the private deities of your choice. You told us of Another, and we believed. Both the moderates and the fundamentalists see the fighting as a great tragedy. We see it as growling over a bone with no meat."

Hedge stared at the floor. Bender stared through the coffee shop window and appeared to be looking at nothing. Maureen and Lilith sat like cypress [trees], absorbed and rejoicing. Meanwhile, the coffee shop had been filling up with commissioners on break from committees and caucuses. Sitting in small groups, they had been whispering among themselves as Miriam's voice grew louder. Some began listening with baffled intentness.

Miriam suddenly became aware of this growing congregation. The years of conditioning. Proscriptions that had denied pulpit access. She no longer felt these restraints. She pushed her chair back, gripped the edge of the table, and stood erect.

She nodded invitingly to the strangers at nearby tables. "Maybe nothing can be salvaged at this convention of a long-dead conscience," she said, looking around, "but let us women try as you say you are trying. Maybe no religion could survive the short journey from the wholesome filth of a stable, the delivery of the little baby with no trained technician to perform the episiotomy or to suture the lacerations of a virgin maiden, to the sterile sickness of spires and the grand ballrooms of McCormick Place on the Lake. Have we so muffled the little bitty baby's cry, the mother's wail that all hope is gone forever? Have we so amplified the steepled rhetoric of doctrine—doctrine without discipleship—that we can do nothing?"

Some of the people nearby began moving to other tables. Others strained to hear, or see, what was going on. Miriam glanced at the retreating patrons in the shop and raised her voice loud enough so that no one could escape her message:

"There are those of us who will neither write nor listen to such demeaning epitaphs. Whatever and wherever it is, this thing called *church* will be renewed. And we will begin here in this body. Not because we are women, but because we are human. And still Christian. At least for now. Though there are other gods panting after us, as we are mightily tempted by their flirtations."

29

Sermon at Riverside Church, NYC*

CONTEXT: *Campbell frequently addressed "the steeples" metaphorically. Here, however, we have Campbell speaking directly to—even in—one of the most influential steeples in the U.S. As one speaker in a series at the Riverside Church in NYC, his assigned topic is that of "race and racism in American culture." Of course, Campbell has consistently resisted racism. Such abuse of power is an issue that Christians cannot extract from its larger social and theological context.*

His message of hope, however, is that we are left neither to our own devices, nor to the agency of institutions to solve the vexing problems of racism. In fact, Will's proclamation this particular Sunday morning is that the problem is resolved, and has been for millennia. The problem is now not so much racism, per se, but the church's unwillingness to change its ways and incarnate the solution. Despite our rhetoric of faith and confidence, we apparently don't believe our own message. Intellectually we seem to know that we are to refuse judging, classifying, or thinking according to human standards, but we are addicted. Instead of imitating the ways of our reconciling Lord, the church and its members choose to conform to the patterns and policies—the conventionalities—of the principalities and powers of this world. We don't practice the message we profess, and then have the audacity to scratch our heads and wonder why injustice is so persistent and resilient. Like addicts, we continue to look anywhere and everywhere for the next fix, but resist altering the behavior that causes (or at least contributes to) the problem.

Campbell's loving, yet pointed, charge to the Riverside steeple, and all other steeples, is to confess our addiction. Acknowledge that we have tried just about every self-righteous, self-interested, self-promoting form of self-

* Delivered May 17, 1984. Transcription by Richard C. Goode.

improvement, but have not yet submitted to the prescription of Christ. Stop trying to invent slick, sophisticated, new remedies for racism, militarism, and economic oppression, Campbell counsels. Live the outrageous remedy taught in Scripture, the one we profess to have faith in. Being reconciled is our form of resistance.

Morning. I've been sitting here trying to spot my people out there, and then Bill [William Sloan] Coffin stands up and reminds me of what I already knew. We're all one another's people. But some of you are from down home, ain't you?

The committee responsible for my being here gave me but two bits of instruction. They instructed me, number one, to talk about race and racism in American culture today. Number two, to talk about twenty minutes. And the truth is that on the second instruction they were considerably more emphatic than on the first.

Talk then no more than twenty minutes on race and racism in American culture. That would be mildly intimidating and overwhelming to say the least if I did not know that Bill Coffin, Maya Angelou, Miles Horton, and Anna Hedgeman had already preceded me and that another will follow. By my calculation, if each of us is given twenty minutes that comes to 120 minutes, or two solid hours, and surely that should be enough time to settle the problem of racism in American culture, once and for all.

When William Sloan Coffin Jr. and I were in divinity schools, shortly after the Spanish American War, our homiletics professors used to advise us to give the first five minutes of any sermon or address over to foolishness and nonsense. Consider that admonition fulfilled. Not by my words, but by the assignment itself. They further led us, Bill, as you may recall, to hope that the time clock would begin at the end of the period of foolishness and nonsense, so let the secondhand now commence.

The truth is, twenty minutes should be quite adequate to say all there is to say on that subject because for those of us who call ourselves "Christian" it was settled 2,000 years ago when St. Paul said God was in Christ, and that because God came into human history we are to no longer consider *anyone* by human standards, human categories, and race is a human category. God didn't create races. The scientists did that. And if the learned doctors had not seen fit to tell us that some of us were to be called Caucasian, some Negroid, some Mongoloid, it probably never would have occurred to us to so designate ourselves. In our ignorance we might have been content simply to look upon ourselves as fellow human beings, upon one of God's planets. No longer, Paul said, do we consider *anyone* by human standards, even though once we did, and God knows we did. We don't do that any longer. That should have settled the matter. But the truth is, further, it didn't. Or for those of us who call ourselves "Christian," it should have been settled at Pentecost, when every known linguistic and ethnic group stood together in one place, integrated, hearing the mighty acts of God and everyone understanding. But 2,000 years later, here we are. And more than 3,000 years ago the matter was settled for the Jews when they were directed in the wilderness to accept the *goy*, the sojourner, the stranger, the different one, as part of themselves. And that if any were held prisoner, or in bondage, or in slavery, every fifty years there was to be a year of Jubilee, when the prisons would be open, the shackles loosened, the slaves freed.

That in itself would go far in solving the problem. But here we are. Once again, after all our seminars and symposia, our wars, our social movements, our legislation, our presidential decrees, our denominational resolutions, our children murdered at their prayers and rotting in their graves, our young buried in red clay dams in Mississippi, or gunned down in Harlem robbing for enough dope to stand for one more night. After all the books have been written and the sermons preached, and the confessions made, here we stand still asking the same question. "What can we do about the problem of race and racism in American culture?" is what your committee asked of me. And it is encouraging that we still ask the question. But it is terribly discouraging that really none of us want the answer. We don't want the answer, for we already know the answer. So the question we are *really* asking is, "What can we do about race and racism in American culture, and keep all this?" And the answer, my brothers and sisters, is *nothing!*

In my judgment the question no longer has to do with race, as race is traditionally defined by the social scientists. In my judgment American culture has almost but not quite, and I repeat, almost but not quite, forgiven people for being black. What we can't forgive them for is being poor. And that's the tough one for us. It's the tough one because the answer is so apparent. Apparent because the institutional, structured, steepled church stands today precisely where the rich young ruler stood. He was not a bad man. He was a good man. And we are not a bad outfit. We are a good outfit. Listen to us sing. See our programs. We are good people. He was a powerful man. And he was a rich man. Not an ignorant man, a well-educated, sophisticated man. And we as an institution are good, powerful, rich, and terribly sophisticated and learned. And yet the man many, if not most of us call "Lord" said, "Never mind all that. Go and sell what you have, and give it to the poor. I have come to proclaim release to captives, turning folks loose, recovery of sight to the blind, seeing-eye dogs, good news to the poor, food, clothing." And that leads to a new question, "How much is Riverside Church worth?" We'll just auction it off.

But before I press you on *that*, before the bidding begins, I must confess that we have the title to 35 acres of geography in middle Tennessee. Land worth more than a $1,000 an acre. And the Scripture does not support me in any place that I can find, and God knows I wish it did, in the notion that because our little farm isn't worth very much by New York real estate standards, we are exempt from the admonition. But the further truth is, that institutions are so cunningly evil, that even if we wanted to follow those words of Jesus, we *couldn't*. Without prior conversation with your trustees, I feel comfortable in saying that there are bylaws and constitutions which would forbid any such act of lunacy. And I can state, and honestly so, also that I cannot sell our little place because it is jointly owned by the family. And then I can say, "Of course, *I* would sell it and buy seeing-eye dogs, and bail bonds, and food for po' folks, but Brenda and the children wouldn't." "He who loves son or daughter more than me is not worthy," He also said.

Well now, I seem to have boxed us in. But maybe not. Maybe for too long we have concentrated our efforts on the assumption that our vocation is to solve all the problems of the world. Rather than trying to determine what we are, who we are, already, here and now, in this present world. And what we are, at least according to St. Paul in the New Testament lesson, we are a people already reconciled, whether we know it or not, whether we live like it or not, we are already brothers and sisters. Not perhaps, maybe someday if we be good boys and girls, but already. It's over. One people, all of us. And then our call, our vocation, becomes to *be*, not to do, but to *be* what we already are. To behave, to live as if the story is true, and to live it out in our lives—in the world, in the streets. And yet there is still the world out there. The world of one gigantic yell that the story is a lie. And what kind of a world is it that we're saying that this news thrusts us into?

I said earlier that, in my judgment, race as it has been commonly defined is no longer valid. I also said that the culture has managed to almost forgive people for being black, but that it cannot forgive them for being poor. And I think it is *true* that race as defined by the social scientists is no longer a valid concept. So perhaps we should redefine race in more meaningful terms. There is the race of the rich, and there is the race of the poor. There would be two to begin with. The rich race in the numerical minority, for we are told that 65 percent of the world's population goes to bed hungry each night. And even *that* is a racist statement. We, the rich, forget now that you are white, or black, or yellow. You are in the numerical minority. You are rich. I am rich. And just to say, "goes to bed hungry," is anti-poor, thus, "racist" under the new categories of what constitutes a race of people. "Goes to bed" makes a false assumption about poverty. A more accurate statement would be that 65 percent of the people in the world go to *sleep* hungry, for they have no bed to go to. That is the luxury of the more affluent. To have a bed, when we the rich say go to bed hungry we most often picture clean sheets and a foam rubber pillow, perhaps even with a little green mint on top of it. I, a few times in my life, have gone to bed hungry. I have never, in my life, gone to *sleep* hungry, with no bed to be hungry on, or even to die on. Certainly there are many other luxuries we the rich enjoy. The luxury of worship is certainly one of them. At least worship as we define "worship."

Last winter I was attending a retreat sponsored by one of the better-known and sophisticated American denominations. I see no need to say which one. Some of you may be Episcopalians, for all I know [laughter]. We decided in the finest democratic tradition that as a part of the retreat, we would observe silence, which would be observed from 10 o'clock at night until 11 o'clock the following morning. I did alright, during the night, particularly that part of the night when I was asleep. But something kept bothering me the following morning, as the sunny-side-up eggs, English muffins, Canadian bacon, and grapefruit halves already sectioned out for our convenience, were passed around the pious and silent tables. I will confess to being well into my second cup of coffee before figuring out what was plaguing me, and before exploding in a fit of rage, "Enough of this nonsense!" Here was a luxury 65 percent of the human beings in the world can't afford, for you cannot yell and scream, and push and shove, for the half a cup of rice for your starving babies, and be piously silent. So there can't be any poor Quakers. The racism of *worship* is what we're talking about now. And there is precedent in the Scripture for what we are talking about. St. Paul, on one occasion, came close to telling the church at Corinth to just simply cut it out! At least the Eucharistic portion of worship. And talking with them about Holy Communion, he said, "For he that eateth and drinketh unworthily, eateth and drinketh damnation (not a blessing but damnation) to himself, not discerning the Lord's body. For this cause, many are weak, and sickly among you, and many sleep." Already dead, because of the luxury of worship.

So in the kind of world we're talking about, it is just remotely possible that the most Eucharistic thing we could do would be to abstain, for the sip of wine and the swallow of wafer in our gullet, contains more calories than a lot of people get all day.

Well, what would some of the other symptoms of racism be, if there were to be the new categories of rich-poor? Well, it's deceptive. One of the most racist things I have heard said recently was by the president of these United States when asked to respond to the problem of the stock market. He said, "It doesn't bother me, I have no stocks." Perhaps that doesn't sound racist on the face of it, but when you think about it, a man who could be that calloused about Wall Street . . . how concerned do we expect him to be when speaking of mothers seeking aid to dependent children? And perhaps his most racist *act*, was the head-busting of the PATCO strikers [the Professional Air Traffic Controllers Organization in 1981]. That doesn't sound racist on the surface. Only a handful of the air controllers were black. None of them poor. And few of us feel great sympathy for people whose wages were already higher than most. But while we are looking the other way, the precedent is set. Start at the top, this time Mr. Caesar. You got in trouble before when you started down here with the sanitation workers. There were still a few people of conscience who would march, and demonstrate, and challenge you on this. So bust the heads of folks up here, and it's a short step from convincing your subjects, Mr. Caesar, that PATCO workers can't strike against the government, to establishing that *any* strike is a strike against the government or national defense, whether miners, garbage collectors, school teachers, whatever.

And while we're on that subject, let it be said, lest we have forgotten, that not all the mighty kings of Judah and Israel, raised up by the Lord, were good and just kings. Some of them were terribly evil. So maybe Ronald Reagan is the judgment of God upon us—a wicked, idolatrous, stiff-necked, racist generation.

The symbols and symptoms of racism in American culture are far more subtle today than they were 15, 10 years ago, and I think even more pernicious. The very things we fought so hard to achieve, have robbed us of clear issues. And what *we* call the years of the civil rights movement, we had flesh and blood issues, and flesh and blood enemies. Lunch counters. Voting booths. Schoolhouses. Theaters. Parks. And we had the [James] Eastlands, [Strom] Thurmans, and [Orval] Faubuses, and [George] Wallaces, and [Ross] Barnetts to do battle with. We did indeed fight with flesh and blood. Today it is the more demonic, deceiving, powers and principalities. In 1960, five thousand people, ten, fifteen [thousand] could surround a courthouse and say, "We're here because you won't let us vote." "We're sitting at these lunch counter stools because you won't serve us." "We're marching around this schoolhouse because you won't let our children in." Those issues are gone now, or at least badly blurred. And I would suggest to you this morning that even things we see as progress may be nothing more than our own naïveté.

Some of you have asked, just since I have been here that I say a word about the resurgence of the Ku Klux Klan in America. Well, how about you tell me about the resurgence of Westchester. We'll swap out horror stories. I know you've read a lot of stories about the rise of the KKK. You read, for instance, about how Mrs. Viola Liuzzo was murdered on the Selma to Montgomery highway. But did you also read that now it comes out that the one who actually pulled the trigger was in the employ of the FBI? You've no doubt read of the massacre of five members of the Communist Workers Party by Klan members in Greensboro, North Carolina. But did you read that one the chief organizers of the violence was a paid informant for the police? You have read that Bill Wilkerson, who heads up out of Denim Springs, Louisiana, the Knights of the Ku Klux Klan, I believe his group is called, considered by all Klan watchers of the media and the intelligence community to be the most violent of all the Klan groups, training women and children in warfare tactics, organizing youth groups in high schools, mass producing hate literature of the most scurrilous nature, but did you happen to see that also Bill Wilkerson has been an informer for the FBI for almost the total history of his Klan group?

There are about 800 people in this country this morning waiting to die at the hands of the state. A disproportionate number of them are black, and *all* of them are poor. None of them were put there by the Ku

Klux Klan. One of them, my friend and brother, it seems now will be the first of that 800 to go, on the fifth day of next month, one minute after midnight. He's a good man now. I was with him just before Christmas last year, and for a Christmas present he wanted a little Waylon Jennings cap I was wearing. But the Warden said it would be setting a precedent to let him have a cap. Cullen would get his cap in two weeks. Unfortunately, it will have been soaked in a vat of acid overnight, and electrodes will be hanging out of it, and he would be led down a corridor to receive his cap, and seated in a chair and who knows how many volts of electricity it would take to curl his hands and send these quivering, shivering motions through his body, and his face contorting, and his heart slowing down, and then the room will be filled with that *nasty*, stinking, goddamn thing called death. And if you don't know when God damned death, then you don't know about Easter, so you're invited to come back next spring. One quarter of a million people in prison, a disproportionate number of them black, virtually *all* of them poor, none of them put there by the Ku Klux Klan.

Six human beings, all of them black, gunned down in my city. One with his hands cuffed in front of his body. To be sure he was a convicted felon, attempting to escape. But occasionally we read that an elephant attempts to escape from the circus, and we can miraculously apprehend the elephant without doing him bodily harm. We cannot do the same for a human being. Another one gunned down; her crime was being in a motel room with someone who was not her husband. If you want to settle the population problem in America, you might make that approach to solving it, and kill everybody who's ever been in a motel room with someone who's not their husband. All *that* to say, that it takes no genius to suspect, and I've suspected for sometime, a "second gun syndrome" here. When we see case after case of what we call resurgence of the Klan going hand in hand with the intelligence community. What's going on here? Is what we're doing organizing hate groups so we can watch them and report on them and get award-wining series and prizes?

And if so, for what purpose? I'll tell you for what purpose. To keep black people and poor white people hating each other. To keep black people as "niggers," and poor white people as "rednecks." And if you don't know it, I'll tell you; those two words mean the same thing. And as one who sprang from the poor whites of the South, I'm getting about as tired of the word "redneck," which I saw recently used in *Newsweek* magazine,

I heard it recently used on public broadcast, I see it constantly in the daily press. I'm getting about as tired of that word as black people got of *that* word. Because I know what's going on. The two words mean the same thing.

The newspaper, a very fine newspaper in our city, infiltrated a Klan group. That's okay, though anybody who's white with $25, the price of a sheet, can get in. You don't have to infiltrate it. But I'm waiting, I'm waiting for the series on the infiltration of the OBM , of the Pentagon, of the State Department, maybe even the Masonic Lodge, and my son's college fraternity. Or are we to assume that none of those are racist?

If you can imagine thousands of black people herded behind barbed-wire fences, guarded and goaded by hood and robed vigilantes burning crosses every midnight, you are in my judgment paranoid. But if you *cannot* imagine constant electronic surveillance and recording of every word of every dissident black or poor white, a file of her or his, of every activity, legislation already existing and more to come whereby they may be prosecuted and imprisoned and neutralized, if you cannot imagine that, then you are in my judgment living under a serious delusion.

We said earlier that the concept of race as defined and described by the social scientists no longer has meaning, but the powers and principalities give it meaning and it does still exist, and because it exists every white person in America is a racist in the same sense that every male person is a sexist. We've got to make a distinction between racism and bigotry. I am not a bigot any longer. I got educated, learned, converted, something out of that. I am still a racist, because I have *always* had that advantage. I could, and did, live where I please, go to school where I pleased. I could have become the president of the United States, by the accident of birth, or even senior minister of Riverside Church. Wouldn't that have been a gas? [laughter]

Well, what are we to do? What are we to do? O, wretched that we are, who will deliver us from this body of death? Let's just suppose now for a few seconds that there is a very effective, popular, well-known, well-publicized evangelist in your city out at Yankee Stadium. How many will that hold, Bill? About 60,000, 75[,000]? Well, it's full. There comes the time for the invitation and the choir is singing "Just as I am, without one plea, but that thou bidst me come to thee. O, Lamb of God," but all of a sudden the choir director stops and changes the word here. And where they had been singing "O, Lamb of God, I come," they say "O, Lamb of

God, I go." And the preacher, of course, is extending this invitation here, and "Yes, I see you there in the balcony," and "Won't you come," you know, but all of a sudden the preacher's changed too. "No, don't come up *here*," but some of them are confused and they start coming to the altar. "Don't! Get back. There's nothing up here!" "O, Lamb of God, I *go*." And as one we hear fifty thousand motors start, in the night at Yankee Stadium.

In a few hours the governor's phone begins to ring, and it is the warden at Riker's Island, and Clinton, and Attica, saying, "There's fifteen thousand people out here trying to get in."

And the governor says, "Well, what do they want?"

And he says, "They say they're looking for *God*, for *Jesus*."

[The governor responds,] "For God's sake, tell them to go to church. We don't have Jesus in there."

"Well, they say they went, and they didn't find Him. And that He told them that they could find him in the prisons, and in the nursing homes, and in the hospitals, and in the slums, and they say they want to see their Jesus."

That's what we can do. Nothing. But be what we are by our nature already reconciled to God, and all his creatures, and unable to endure the indignities and injustices that are heaped upon them.

My time is more than up.

Where do you do the ascription here? Where's the cross, Bill? Or is it all the cross? Wherever. Whatever.

In the name of the Father, and in the Son, and in the Holy Ghost. Amen.

B. To the Political Principalities and Powers

30

"White Liberals Are All Right in Their Place"*

CONTEXT: *In this essay, Campbell identifies with the so-called white liberals on "the race issue," but his form of political participation is chastised. In contrast to those who look to accumulate power in order to affect the right results, Campbell warns against such patronizing patriarchs (with an inflated opinion of their own importance). When it comes to politics Campbell asks white liberals to remain humble and vulnerable. Instead of jockeying for power and preening with self-importance, Campbell calls for a testing of all organizations and institutions. Endorse none, question all.*

The role of the white liberal in race relations today may be the distasteful one of standing aside. At least that is what he is being told. And no doubt for good reasons. He has never really been much of a factor in the first place.

The pattern we have seen develop in the civil rights struggle has been somewhat as follows: Negroes have grown tired of unfreedom. They have done something about it. In not one case has the leadership in the significant developments been furnished by whites. In Montgomery, Birmingham, Philadelphia, always it has been Negroes who have initiated the action. That, in the Christian understanding, is not as it should have been (bear ye another's burdens) but the way we might have known it *would* be (There is none good). Neither individual man nor society have been redeemed to the point where we are our brother's keeper or advocate very much of the time.

Yet all along there were those whites (referred to on these pages as "white liberals") who felt a deep urgency to join in from time to time. It

* Undated manuscript, Will Campbell Papers, University of Southern Mississippi. A version of this manuscript appeared in *Social Progress* (December 1963), 27–31.

should not be surprising that we are now being told by James Baldwin and others that we are simply in the way. I suspect that they are right where the Movement is concerned. Whether we like it or not, we are in the category of those against whom the revolt has been directed. True, some of us became traitors to whiteness because we knew we were on the wrong side of a moral question. But a defector is always suspect, even by those to whom he defects. Where the success of the revolution is concerned, that leaves us little alternative. If we are genuinely interested in its success we can only step aside with as much graciousness as we can find within us to display, permitting the revolutionary wagon to roll on to the station unencumbered by excess baggage. But that is if our primary commitment is to the Movement.

Before we move out of the picture, perhaps we would do well to see what we have been a part of and why, and then ask ourselves again if we are ready to leave, wanted or not. We have not really been involved in revolution but in "not quite revolution." It has been "not quite revolution" because if it had been true revolution it would all be over by now. For today Negro Americans have more than sufficient numbers, strength, courage, and world opinion on their side to stage a *genuine* revolution. True revolution is a political movement which seeks to overthrow a government. This is not what we have thus far experienced. Yet few question that it could have been accomplished and may yet be attempted. We have heard hints of it but only hints of bodies on runways, railroad tracks, and bus terminals to bring the flow of travel and commerce to a dead stop, jammed communication transmitters, demonstrations in legislative halls to halt deliberations of government; things calculated to pave the way for a new political order. The fact that it has not been done is not weakness among Negroes for their domestic strength, and certainly world support, is more than comparable to that which effected the American Revolution of 1775, the French Revolution of 1789, and provocation for it rivals that which brought on the Russian Revolution of 1917. But it has not happened. At least not yet. What has been happening has been *called* revolution, but it has not been. At least not yet. And I suspect the popularization of the label could be traced to white male (even liberal white) sources, perhaps as a technique by conservatives to divert attention from the true revolution, or by sentimental whites waiting to give the impression that the gains are of such significant proportion to merit the term.

If you ask why there has not been revolutions on the part of Negroes with all ingredients, potential, and provocation, why Roy Wilkins, Martin Luther King, and James Farmer have shown more restraint and demonstrated more patience than George Washington, the stormers of the Bastille, and Alexander Kerensky [of the Russian Revolution], I am not able to tell you. I can only guess that it is because they are basically reformers and not revolutionaries. Certainly they are patriotic Americans. But I am not particularly assured when I recall how many reformers within deteriorating political systems of the past have been displaced in the wake of true revolutionists with less patience and less confidence in the possibility of reform from within. But the true revolutionists are waiting in the wings, make no mistake about that, ready for their cue to enter the stage. The challenges to the reformers are daily mounting. One slight miscalculation in any major American city and the reformers will have to give way to the revolutionists. Their success has already been assured by white stupidity. All they lack is for a break of history to give them undisputed claim to leadership.

I, as a white liberal, feel comfortable—even pious—being a small part of the Movement for Reform because it asks so little and denies me nothing. (The truth is, it even affords me a means of livelihood.) But I refuse even to consider what my role, to say nothing of attitude, will be when the Movement for Reform is replaced by the restless giant of true revolution. For folks like me will be at most a pest to the revolutionists. Thomas Merton, in a recent letter to white liberals, said to, and of, my kind:

> When you come face to face with concrete reality, and take note of some unexpected and unlovely aspects of what you have hitherto considered only in the abstract, you yourself are going to be a very frightened mortal. You are going to see that there are more than ideas and ideals involved in this struggle. It is more than a matter of images and headlines. And you are going to realize that what has begun is not going to be stopped, but that it will lead on into a future for which the past, perhaps, offers little or no precedent. But since it is one of the characteristics of liberals that they prefer their future to the vaguely predictable (just as the conservative prefers only a future that reproduces the past in all its details), when you see that the future is entirely out of your hands and that you are totally unprepared for it, you are going to fall back on the past, and you are going to end up in the arms of the conservatives. Indeed,

you will be so much in their arms that you will be in their way, and
will not improve the shooting.

Those are hard sayings but difficult to argue with. Here then is the
dilemma for the white liberal. He has been a minor part of a Movement
for Reform. He has given no thought to involvement in true revolution.
Now he is being told—though significantly not by the King-Wilkins-
Farmers—that he is in the way. On the other hand, he is told that when
the real impact of revolution (when it comes) hits him he will flee to
the bosom of the conservatives. Only he is not to expect that he will be
received with the robe, the ring and the fatted calf. For he will be even
more in the way here. Better for him to have stayed on the farm for his
prospects for the future are not very bright.

But here is the key to the problem under discussion. It lies in his
prospects of finding a comfortable home in *any* camp. I assume that when
this journal talks of white liberals it really means white *Christian* liberals.
And this throws an entirely different light on the matter. For the *Christian*
liberal cannot consider whether or not he is wanted in the Movement,
effect, strategy, outcome, or any of the other things the Movement must
consider. As a *liberal*, one can expect that he will have some voice in the
settlement and that his future remains at least partially in his hands. As
a Christian, he had no such claim or expectation. What he must do, he
must do. Not for the success of the Movement for Reform. Not to head
off true revolution (self-preservation), but because, under God, he has
no choice. I have no doubt that Baldwin is correct. I have no doubt that
Merton is correct. But there are certain things the Christian liberal must
do because of his allegiance to the Sovereign God, and for no other reason. It's clear that he cannot stand aside, needed, wanted or not. He may
be irrelevant and a drag. At best he may be tolerated and patronized. If he
has been involved for the sake of the Movement, or because of some illusion about creating a kingdom, or for any reason other than obedience to
the Sovereign Lord, who has already created the kingdom and bids us (all
of us) enter it. Then Baldwin's and Merton's words are doubly right and
not only should he now step aside, he should never have been involved
in the first place. For such an involvement may have been nothing more
than another of his clear humanistic maneuvers to escape from faith and
responsibility before the living God. It is high time he abandoned his idol

for making civil rights the gospel. It is as much an idol as the one the segregationists have worshipped.

But if he has been involved as an act of faithfulness to God, to crash the idols of racism, to witness to the gospel truth of all man's common fallibility and humility before God who alone is sovereign, to invite men to enter the kingdom Jesus Christ established in which love, justice, and equality are an assumed fundamental, to challenge any false kingdom in which these fundamentals are denied even if it calls itself the church, then he will not, cannot leave the struggle at this juncture.

He cannot escape an involvement, wanted or not, because his mission is to hear and witness to the gospel. Whether he is welcome or wanted, in the way or not in the way, whether he perishes at the hands of the revolutionist or the conservative cannot be his concern. And whether his witness is made from a picket line, behind the bars of a jail (the jail of the racists or the jail of the revolutionist), from a pulpit, or wherever, it will all be an anthem of praise to God for life, to the Christian, is incarnational at its very center.

Why doesn't the white Christian liberal stay in his place? Because he has no place, no home except the comfort of having been a faithful servant and living in the grace of his Lord.

Why doesn't the white liberal stay in his place? Because he has no place. And no home. If he finds one, he's no longer a liberal because everyone has a "line," and violating questioning-lines is the work of the liberal.

The shame of the Christian liberal is the knowledge that he has been Christ's faithful servant.

31

"Up to Our Steeples in Politics"*

CONTEXT: *1968 proved a pivotal year in U.S. political history. The year began with the Vietcong's and Vietminh's Tet Offensive in Vietnam exposing the futility of U.S. military firepower and foreign policy. Weeks later, President Johnson announced he would not seek re-election. On April 4, Martin Luther King Jr. was assassinated in Memphis, Tennessee. Then in June, Bobby Kennedy was gunned down in Los Angeles just after claiming victory in the California Democratic primary. Later that summer, the Democratic National Convention found the streets of Chicago flowing with blood as protesters battled with police. With the presidential election scheduled for November, Americans longed for stability and certainty, many devout Christians expecting to find hope through the electoral system. Depending on one's political affiliation, either Richard Nixon, Hubert Humphrey, or George Wallace would fix what ailed the U.S.*

In this climate, Campbell and Holloway dedicated an issue of Katallagete *to assessing the faith many Christians place in the democratic process. Far from counseling the use of the system, they urged resistance. This editorial proved to be one of the more significant and controversial of the journal's history. So pointed was the essay, in fact, that* Christianity and Crisis *reprinted the piece in March 1969, inviting dialogue and debate. In 1970, Campbell and Holloway published much of the Fall 1968 issue in book form, adding a new introduction, which follows in the next chapter.*

Reactions to the thesis presented by Campbell and Holloway ranged from amused bewilderment to outrage against such political blasphemy. Either way, it is quintessentially iconoclastic.

* By Will D. Campbell and James Y. Holloway, from *Katallagete*, Fall 1968, 2–9. Reprinted with permission.

Our contributors in this issue have all talked of politics. They are a varied lot—black militant and white liberal, Klan spokesman and journalistic observer.

We believe each has spoken the truth: this nation and this people are in deep, perhaps irremediable trouble.

We of the Committee of Southern Churchmen wish to speak of politics also. But ours will be repeating, restating, rehashing, (but not revising) what we have been trying to say about our crises for three years. And that, stated simply, is that we believe the fundamental crises in our land arise from the obsession with politics, the faith that the political order (hereafter called Caesar) is the *only* source and authority to which we can and ought to repair for relief from what ails us as a community and as individuals. Because there is no real challenge to these obsessions, we believe that our crises will deepen, perhaps even beyond a point of no return, and that we shall become citizens of a technological police state because of the faith that a full use of political force and cunning is the only source we have to guarantee freedom and human dignity. Cases in point are the 70% plus of our good people who approve of the police work in Chicago last month—undoubtedly the same who were horrified at Sheriff Clark's work in Selma in 1965; and the effectiveness of "violence, crime in the streets, protestors and dissent" in the current election campaign. This suggests that while the technological barriers may not yet have been perfected, we may now be inside the compound and that our identification cards are already being notched and food allotments and medical services being prepared, and the tattoo needles being sterilized.

Look at us: politics prevails, and everyone believes that this is the only way it can be. Political troubles, political programs, political crises, political figures are all that count, and all that should count. "News" is what matters, directly related to football scores and the weather. Art, drama, novels, essays, poems, religion, dance, architecture, beads, pendants, psychedelia—to be real, every energy must somehow relate to politics. If not, it is irrelevant; not serious; obscurantist; old-fashioned; fundamentalist; sectarian; cloistered; a form of lunacy. Caesar is messiah: we are bones, sinew, and *politics*, period: and politics tells us what we shall do with our bones and our sinew. There is nothing wrong with us or our communities which political revolution, reordering, restructuring, reestablishing cannot overcome. How could we believe otherwise?

Perhaps what we are talking about is not new in the Western political tradition. Perhaps all this is simply a more extreme manifestation of what is characteristic of robust and healthy Western politics. We believe not. We are convinced of the basic accuracy of the social analyses of Jacques Ellul, the French Christian, who makes an overpowering case that because our new environment is now technique, not nature, the political implications are that technique and bureaucracy, not an exchange of ideas in political debates and elections, are the stuff of politics today. And this is unprecedented. As Ellul explains, "The decisions fundamentally affecting the future of a nation are in the domains of technology, fiscal technique or police methods. . . . fruits of the technician's labors." Politics in the traditional sense is an "illusion."

We have talked about these phenomena in this journal as political messianism, politics as Baal, technological concentration camps. Politics, a means to an end, have become *the* end. We have been gulled into believing that whatever ails us is tractable, and can be cured exclusively by political and social nostrums. God knows that there is much wrong with us politically, and the proper subject of political action is to adjust the external and relative arrangements, laws, institutions so that they function as instruments of social justice for all. But just here is the political tragedy, for what *is* wrong with us politically cannot be corrected so long as we insist by our political action that politics can correct *everything* that is wrong with us. To argue, as almost everyone does, that if politics cannot cure our every social ill, nothing can, is not to argue an alternative to what we are saying but to state the nature of our tragedy. We are convinced that just this is one very important reason why the very proper political (although constitutionally redundant) efforts in the so-called civil rights era failed to adjust political, social, and economic structures to meet the racial and social discrimination that had been welling up because of our racist tradition and advanced technological civilization. The ideology of the left and right, conservative and liberal, drew strength from the same myth: that the constraint of the police, law, federal marshals, national guards, bureaucracy (national, state, local), and the largesse of the federal budget was *all* that was necessary, indeed, all that could be done, to end what was a crisis that political adjustment could improve but not finally overcome. Racism is something which political adjustment could ease and ameliorate, but only if Caesar admitted his inherent limitation—not as an excuse for inaction, but as a reason for action. But pushed beyond its obvious point of effectiveness, politics in what Ellul calls the "techno-logical society" could only exacerbate, by unfulfilled promises, minority alienation and majority impatience and frustration, and in the end be used in a clearly totalitarian fashion by Caesar to impose its prejudice on the recalcitrants. Politics alone could not end the crisis and did not.

Examples? Specifics? What about those voices shrieking for mas-sive intervention by troops, marshals, and money and all the rest of the political power of Caesar, especially his federal apparatus, a scant four years ago to cure the *South's* racism—the same voices which now shriek for moderation and restraint in Caesar's use of his police power? Or, the pivots of 1954–1968: In 1954, the voices called for law and order, for obe-dience to the "law of the land, however distasteful"; in 1968, the voices say that to call for law and order is to call for racism.

Perhaps, as some believe, the civil rights activity of the 1960s was no more than an effort to balm the consciences of liberals who had no intention of altering their patronizing attitude toward black men when it would cost them a lot of money or jeopardize their (or their children's) status in the community or the establishment. But the real point is that the liberal conscience was susceptible of being soothed by laws and ex-ecutive orders because it has been cast in a tradition convinced that the beloved community could be overcome by political activity, guided by the enlightened opinion of a universally educated populace.

We are certain that so long as we persist in the belief that there are no limits to what politics can do for us because all that is critical about man is politics, it is inevitable that we shall try to tear each other asun-der, shear off into disillusioned and hateful factions, each with our own political nostrums which we shall brutally inflict upon those who do not share our nostrums because they have ones of their own. And all this in a political environment which Kierkegaard would call "sick unto death," because no one laughs at the regular and religious incantations about "in God we trust," and pious rhetoric about the greatest and most powerful nation in the history of the world being forged by free press, free speech, constitutional government, and the two-party system.

This is political messianism, Baalism. And, let us be specific: For three years this journal has tried to say to the Christian and to the church that an exclusive reliance on the political processes of the twentieth cen-tury exacerbates these very processes to the point that we drive ourselves into the technological concentration camp. "But they came to Baal-peor, and consecrated themselves to Baal and became detestable like the thing they loved" (Hosea 9:10). We have tried to say that this is not only a political calamity of an unparalleled order, but that it is blasphemous for Christians to exhaust their witness to the world in the processes Caesar determines for us. "The sure consequence," we said, "of relying exclusively on law and politics to resolve America's racism will be confirmation of that racism in and by our legal and political system."

The political activity of the ecumenical movement, social agencies, and seminaries of mainline (and most fundamentalist) Protestantism regardless of their theological orientation, have in large part, been expressions of just this Baalism. We have accepted with little or no objection the judgment about crises and the lists of priorities offered up by Caesar, the political order. Cold wars and wars of insurrection, racism, poverty, urban decay, etc., are the terminology of Caesar. But God's vicars in denominational social agencies, seminaries, pulpits, and religious journals have merely lined themselves and their constituency, money, and manpower behind Caesar's definition of the issues facing nation and people. All as if they, God's ambassadors, had nothing to say as God's ambassadors about man's nature and destiny, and how that might well assign a different set of priorities. All as if obedience to God demanded a realism that waited with shaking hands and bated breath for the latest white paper on the latest crisis from State, the latest views of the current justices of the Supreme Court, the latest study from Labor or Agriculture, the latest bulletin or in-depth report from the worldwide facilities of NBC News. All as if the inhabitants of the white ghettoes, north and south, rural and mountain and urban, were inhuman, without souls, subjects neither of God's grace and the church's compassion nor the liberal's largesse, as if they too were not those children of God impoverished and dehumanized by the affluence and the gimmickry of the liberal political-military economic establishment. All as if the real and only enemy of Christ were the jeering and spitting and sometimes murdering redneck and mountaineer transplanted to Dayton or Cleveland who give forth no newborn, bury no dead, have none of the hopes and dreads, joys and anguishes of the affluent, educated, and cultured product of the liberal system of politics, economies, and education. All as if there were no enemy in the wicked economic and social system lived from the down and looking up—from the paper mills and cotton mills and marginal filling stations and crossroads stores and sheriff's deputies and police patrolmen, unions and service clubs and political systems. All as if the Christian church were a folk church only in the South. All as if there were no enemy in the vapid and starved and century-old ineffective educational system of political and economic serfs. All as if Christ's vicars were under clear commandments to show only contempt and loathing, not compassion, for those whose economic and political and spiritual powerlessness in their own land made them immune and indifferent to the threats of the federal enemy and to the blandishments and intimidations and hatreds of liberal Christian activists.

God's prophets, not unlike Zedekiah the son of Chenaanah (1 Kings 22), are being cued and set in motion by Caesar, and away go their love gifts of money, personnel, new seminary curriculum, and what little moral suasion the social agency could muster in the track-rack at St. John's by the Gas Station and Boiling Springs Emmanuel Church at the Crossroads. Was it segregation in the schools? Or the freedom rides? Or the sit-ins? Or voter rights? Or peace in Vietnam (never Cuba or Latin America or the Middle East)? The witness of Christ's reconciliation was exhausted by supporting the (more or less) liberal forces of Caesar. The Good News became the legislative, court, and administrative victories of the liberal movements usually at the expense of those who could ill-afford another political or economic defeat. The Good News was McCarthy's victory in New Hampshire; or Senator Kennedy's decision "to enter," or President Johnson's decision to "stay out," or some hanky-panky with some draft cards or peace talks in Paris, etc., etc., etc.

We have learned . . . *nothing*. Four years ago we were told that a vote for Goldwater was a vote for some sort of manifestation of anti-Christ (the sort depended on where you lived). So Christians from bishops to the omnipresent concerned laymen spent themselves electing in the name of Christ crucified and resurrected. . . . Lyndon Baines Johnson, heir apparent to John Fitzgerald Kennedy.

The political consequences of the Death of God movement have always been its most significant and long-range manifestation. But the manifestation is completely misunderstood unless we realize that the theological expression of the Death of God simply ratifies what has been in fact the witness of the church of Jesus Christ in the United States for decades. We quote: "It is not an optimism of grace, but a worldly optimism. . . . it faces despair not with the conviction that out of it God can bring hope, but with the conviction that the human conditions that created it can be overcome, whether those conditions be poverty, discrimination, or mental illness."[1] This credo of the most publicized of the Death of God theologians in fact describes the totality of the recent witness of the body of Jesus Christ against man's murder—here and abroad of the one who was made his brother by the resurrection of the same Jesus Christ. Surely there is another way. That is, if God is not dead. Surely our calling as Christians is not summed up by a vapid, pathetic, and generally ineffective effort to inject morality and highmindness into political activity.

Our apostasy, therefore, is fundamentally the same one that St. Paul struck down in Antioch (cf. Galatians 1–2). It is our actions which stamp our doctrines as heretical. Thomas Merton wrote in an earlier issue of this journal: "To reconcile man with man and not with God is to reconcile no one at all." How, in the face of the last 2000 years or 200 years or two months or two weeks can we dispute the validity of that judgment? We are idolaters; we are Baal worshippers because we have rendered to Caesar the things that are God's and thereby have been unable to render to Caesar the things that are his. We have identified the witness to Christ's reconciliation with the effort of law and order (Caesar) alone to right human relations. For what other reason has ecumenical, mainline white Protestantism despised a witness to the impoverished white ghetto (despite black people's support of the effort) and become increasingly wary and disenchanted about maintaining (or beginning new) witnesses to impoverished black and Puerto Rican and Mexican-American ghettos? We have confessed with our deeds that God is dead: we have faced "despair not with the conviction that out of it God can bring hope, but with the conviction that the human conditions that created it can be overcome, whether those conditions be poverty, discrimination, or mental illness." And because we are in apostasy, we cannot as Christians render to Caesar the things that are Caesar's because we are sanctioning the efforts of Caesar to do the one thing that Caesar cannot do: be God and redeem man from sin and death.

That is why we do not believe that we are reactionary or fashionable when we observe in print that it bothers us to see preachers, nuns, priests, and other clergy up to their gills in politics and especially political conventions. Ours is simply a question derived from the fundamental ques-

---

1. William Hamilton, "The New Optimism: From Prufrock to Ringo," in Thomas J. J. Altizer and William Hamilton, *Radical Theology and the Death of God* (Indianapolis: Bobbs-Merrill, 1966), 169.

tion we are here raising: is obedience to Christ exhausted by immersing one's self in Caesar's definition of politics? Is witness to Christ's victory making all nations of men one blood best made by service to what Caesar judges as the urgent issues of our times? Might it not be that Caesar himself is confused, or is lying? There is evidence in the history of Western civilization to support both affirmations. Might it not be that, witting or unwitting, Caesar is diverting the Christian (and everyone else, for that matter) from an onslaught on the real centers of action by insisting that he, and he alone, define the critical issues of human life?

Before all this be read off as typical American fundamentalism, or modern Mennonitism or whatever, we hasten to explain that we, too, came through the liberal-to-neo-orthodox theological era, and we did it in what was then and is now considered to be the finest Ivy League tradition. That is not to boast (and maybe it is to apologize). It is to say that we have been exposed to and indoctrinated by the view that the principal Christian vocation in the twentieth century is to go where the action is, that is, into the muck and mire of politics, controversy, and "human existence wherever it is."

We were told that in order to be honest to our vocation, in order to be a Christian minister in the world-come-of-age, we had to become as knowledgeable in banking as John K. Galbraith and Merrill Lynch, etc., as wise in international affairs as George Kennan and Hans Morganthau, Dean Acheson and Rusk and John Foster Dulles, as expert in political science as David B. Truman and Robert E. Lane, in sociology as Talcott Parsons and Robert Merton, in psychology as Eric Erikson and Anna Freud. Unless, of course, we were to minister to the Town and Country Church, in which case we should know the 4-H Club pledge, the best of rural economics, and undertake agricultural and community surveys superior to the ones done by the county agent.

The evangelical notion "win them one by one" was the source of many funnies in the lecture halls, common rooms, and refectories. And we agreed, for we knew, from rides home after Sunday school with parents quarrelling about the grocery money, that culture would win them back faster than we as the Lord's spokesmen could win them or keep them. We missed the key, however: that what the evangelical notion was all about was what we were winning them *to*, and what culture was winning them *from*. A change of method or tactics in winning them may have been less important than a change in what winning them really meant. They told us about the cultural imperialism that was inextricably a part of the nineteenth century individualism of "winning them one by one," but this turned out to have been less real for us than the cultural imperialism of the gospel of "relevance and realism," winning the decision-makers, a culture, a political party, an entire industry, an art form.

Be that as it may. We came back South armed with Gunnar Myrdal and V. O. Key in one hand and Calhoun's *Lecture Notes* in the other; the Bible and Calvin's *Institutes* remained in the packing boxes until the awed laymen could get over to build the bookshelves in our "study." We were ready to go into the muck and the mire of politics and social controversy, to meet human existence wherever it was. We were set with many plans of how to do battle with the Devil, although nine-tenths of us were convinced that there wasn't such a thing, for what we remembered best about the New Testament was what demythologizing had disclosed about the social irrelevance of the three-storied worldview of biblical times.

Now, today, our questions have to do with the location of politics, or, at any rate, where we were supposed to go. As they say, where is the action? Where is the real politics, the muck and the mire, the site of human existence? Is it found where they told us to look for it—election politics (in one of the two or three or four parties)? In surveys to rival the county agent and the welfare workers? In Talcott Parsons? In supporting the forces of law and order because the Supreme Court initiated Christ's interest in man's inhumanity to man?

Fourteen years ago the Church American was enjoined by its leaders, experts, and theologians to support the forces of the "law of the land" because of what the Supreme Court had discovered about the inhumanity of segregation, in their wisdom changing their minds eighty years after they had last looked into the matter. Others warned that Christians had another authority for obedience to brotherhood that demanded precedence over any appeals for law and order. Nevertheless, as recent as three or four years ago many of our Christian leaders demanded the full weight of federal power to "end" racism, meaning the redneck racism of the Old Confederacy. Now we find that those who are almost hysterical about the Johnson-Nixon—Humphrey-Daley—Agnew-Reagan-Wallace-Muskie "law and order" nexus, and plea for restraint and de-escalation in Vietnam and for the moderation in the enforcement of law and order in the cities, were the same voices in 1954, '61, '63, '64, and '68 demanding that we preach support for the law of the land and pray that Congress and the president initiate new ones.

We do not have to say "we told you so," because there is the Democratic convention inside Fortress Chicago; there is the work of the Chicago Police Department, Hon. Richard J. Daley, mayor; there is the exploitation of fear in the appeal of all candidates for "law and order"; there are the ghettoes, north and south, urban and suburban and rural, black and white.

But we did what we were told to do when we returned [to the] South a decade or so ago. We tried the route of electioneering and party activism. We leaped into the movement for the election of "better" men (especially of our own omnipresent concerned Christian laymen) to the national, state, and local level. We attended the conventions of both parties in courthouses, in the prescriptions rooms of drugstores and in hotel suites. We registered and preached about Christian citizenship and responsibility and took carloads to the polls. (And some were beaten, unmercifully by other Christian citizens for their exercise of Christian citizenship.) But where has it taken us? Where has it taken us, and them? In part, it has taken us to the ethics professors who learned their lessons better than we did, who retain their objective impassion to be "relevant," and who tell us that our policy in Vietnam is more Christian than our policy in World War II because of our restraint: we are not this time demanding unconditional surrender. (Apparently, it is Christian realism to kill *some* babies and old people and young men, but it is not Christian realism to kill *all* babies and old people and young men.) It has brought us to the ethics professors, saying and writing wisely and seriously that, historically, the witness of America's statesmen (Rusk, McNamara, Ball, Kennen, Orville, Freeman) will prove more Christian than the witness of the Berrigans and [James] Groppi. It has brought us, on the same premises, to organizations of Christian concern coalescing around selective wars, selective conscientious objection, this-and-that about the draft as exercises in Christian realism. ("We disagree with the *tactics* of the Administration"; or, "American *interest* is not involved"; or, "We are not *pacifists*, God forbid! We supported the Kennedys in Cuba and Vietnam," etc.) It has brought the high-ranking religious officials to address national denominational gatherings on the efficiency and the weakness of our ICBM system. (From expertise in banking and psychology is such a short journey to expertise in military strategy.) It has brought most religious editors and seminary deans and associate deans worthy of their expense account to comment with the authority, seriousness, and unction of the modern Christian realist on every ripple and plop in the muck and mire of what Caesar says are domestic and international crises, to lecture expertly on economics and urban and suburban chaos, to muse about "the celebration of the arts and mass media," and to warn about the goings-on in communist China.

Were we poorly advised? Or did we misunderstand? To repeat: it seems to us that we were brought by all this to an acceptance of Caesar's judgment about what is good and bad; right and wrong; justice and injustice; critical and insignificant; law and chaos. This is the Baalism, the totalitarian quality of modern politics which we Christians have not only endured, but encouraged. It seems to us that, in permitting ourselves to be brought here, we have rejected the one vocation we Christians have in and to the world and have, and in the name of realism and relevance, accepted willy-nilly the world's inhumanity to man as normal, and the politics of Caesar as Lord and Savior. By doing so, we have denied our birthright as Christ's sons and brothers, bought at a price, whose only task as His sons and brothers is to witness to what the Risen Lord has already done for men: made each of us brother to the other so that there is no need to kill if the skin is different, the politics repugnant. So also are ours, but it no longer with us is a matter of life and death.

The theological doctors were right when they told us that the proper reading was "God so loved *the world*," not "God so loved *the church*." And we know they were right when they taught us that we ought to go into the world because that was what our Lord did. But what we are asking is whether or not there is any of *that* world in election politics, in political conventions, and in everything that necessarily precedes election politics and political conventions. We are not asking whether our Lord would have stayed out of political conventions and electioneering because of the deceit and compromise and chicanery that is properly a part of electoral politics: after all, he died for us who are filled with deceit and compromise and chicanery (cf. Romans 5:8). Moreover, an Ed King in 1964 as chairman of the Mississippi Freedom Democratic Party is one thing; clergy-delegates for Humphrey, McCarthy, Nixon, Rockefeller or Wallace is something else. Were there not the tens of thousands to accept gladly, greedily the posts held by the clergy-delegates who went to Chicago and Miami in 1968, just as there was the no-not-one who stood with Ed King in Mississippi (something quite different from standing with him in Atlantic City) in 1964?

We are asking whether the muck and mire we were told to immerse ourselves in can be found anywhere in electioneering and political conventions. We are asking whether, in the end, it is not ridiculous for Christians to exhaust their witness to Christ in pathetic efforts to inject morality and high-mindedness into politics by "being there" up to their steeple; we are asking whether political conventions and the whole affair that is today called the political process is nothing but a facade, an illusion, a diversion, a temptation to keep us away from where, in muck and mire, most of us human beings play out our lives. We are asking whether true human existence is to be found in electioneering, or is election politics today the place we spend our energies after the politicians and political experts have jammed scales over our eyes so that we cannot see what we ought to see, so we cannot attend what is happening in the streets, for example, on both ends of the billy clubs? In a word, we are convinced that in our day the world of politics is in large part the world of illusions. We are convinced that if we Christians persist in our frantic desire to be relevant to politics we shall end up by being court prophets and priests of Baal. We suspect that our main function today is a sanctification of political enterprises and adventures firmly contradicted by Christ and Scripture.

"Render unto Caesar the things that are Caesar's." What we must reject is the effort of the political order, of Caesar, to assert himself as the only authority on where the muck and mire of human existence is, to tell us that the only salvation for human existence is to be found in politics—as Caesar determines politics. And we must reject the church's leading us into this service of Baal. We must reject Caesar's illusion that politics is the messiah for the human condition, and the church's sanction of this illusion. We must reject Caesar's seduction that politics is the only reality, and that that reality can best be served by Christians participating up to their gills in politics, contributing ethics and high-mindedness to political decisions. We must reject the church's attempt to sanctify anything Caesar does by asking us to be priests of Baal so we can be prophets of Christ. Baalism is the confession that God is dead. And the Baalism of the contemporary church is why Christian opposition to the horrors of Vietnam and the violence of the forces of law and order in our streets and backroads is ineffective as well as ambiguous. "What is cheaply given can be cheaply had": who can take seriously church pronouncements on anything today? Some would say that we simply do not know what would happen in political affairs if the church did not try to bring morality to bear on the decision-making processes. We ask what, after all, did any clergy-delegate do or say at Miami or Chicago that was not done and said with more effectiveness, dignity and poise by the garden-variety delegate from Wisconsin, Nevada, Utah, or Kansas?

We must reject the church's—and Caesar's—insistence that only if Christians are concerned from moment to moment and crisis to crisis will their work in the muck and mire of human existence be relevant and a true witness to Christ's victories. Has not that demand of the church led us to Baal? What has Caesar to tell us about Christ's victory? We must reject the notion that the only word to the world the Christian has to offer is the cries in electioneering, petitions to the bureaucracy, and the participation up to the gills in political conventions. This merely sanctions all the ambiguities and idolatries of twentieth-century political messianism, and renders nothing but folly to Caesar. What kind of service is it to politics, to share the very illusions of messianism which have brought the world of the twentieth century from two global wars in an effort to restore peace, to the shadow of hydrogen apocalypse and world starvation to save us from communism and preserve freedom? How do we walk with our Lord into the world if we follow not Him but the very political messianism of Caesar which Christians, above all, are commanded to reject in obedience to the Lord, for the sake of Christ and the brothers?

The truth is, nothing happened in Chicago, Miami, or Montgomery. The truth is, nothing will happen November 5. So let the Christian act as if nothing happened, behave as if nothing happened. That would mean, at least, living the sign of Jonah and not the sign of the swastika or donkey or elephant or eagle or hammer and sickle or star on red background. That would mean that the Christian could render the only service he can make as a Christian to Caesar, to politics; the only vocation which would take him with no advice from Caesar into the muck and mire of human existence serviced by our Lord. When, after all, did Jesus "act as if something were happening" in the political order that required him to immerse Himself in it up to His gills? To live the sign of Jonah is to reject the temptation of Baal. To assert in the muck and mire by what we do and whom we visit that Christ arose is to render more service than a convocation's worth of clergy-delegates plunging heartily and with a briefcase full of analyses into political electioneering.

Anything specific in all this? We can weep not. And weep. Weep not for those who have "dropped out" of political participation convinced that it can only get more idolatrous than it is now, convinced that dropping out may be the only realistic way of moving back in. After all, to refuse to drop out, to stay in, is in effect to stay in under the domination of Nixon and Daley, Humphrey, Wallace and Agnew and all the rest. That is one of the chief reasons our political priests and experts regularly loose on us the cant that American democracy is identical with the two-party system. The Founding Fathers didn't think so. That is the real reason the American political system is paranoid today about both Wallace's candidacy and the youth who have decided to try to move politics into the street and away from the voting booths and law courts. It is not Wallace's racism that is offensive, nor the youth's radicalism. It is their refusal to play out their frustration and anger within the two-party consensus which has been for decades two-party in name only, not in reality or performance. Weep not for those who drop out.

But weep for those, especially the Christian those, who bit frantically and desperately, hook, line, sinker, and fishpole, the bait that the Christian—especially now as never before!!—must participate in the political processes to bring moral dimensions to the great issues, to the decision-makers. Weep for those. For the real decisions in Chicago and Miami, in Washington and Detroit, were taken in the streets, on both ends of the billy clubs, and in the offices of the city's bureaucrats and technicians, with the aid and support of the FBI, Secret Service, Pentagon, and concerns citizens. There was emotion and sentimentality, but there was no real politics in the shouting and singing led by Mayor Daley and Theodore Bikel of "God Bless America!" and "The Battle Hymn of the Republic," nor in the cheering and pseudo-TV-excitement about what happened or didn't happen on the Vietnam plank, or on the unit rule, or on speculations about a subordinate clause in the nominee's acceptance speech, or in the tears for a martyred leader. Weep for those who stayed in.

Anything specific? How about this? Some of our brothers are now pleading with Caesar to deny the clergy the temptation of privilege status regarding military conscription. We have a more simple, and we feel more relevant formula for those who would deny themselves, one that does not require the interest or even the approval of Caesar—at least not at the present time. Let all Christian ministers, priests, theologians, bureaucrats, and full-time Christian laymen deny themselves the temptation of Baalism, the temptation of political activism and participation. More specifically, let all ministers, priests, bureaucrats, theologians, and full-time Christian laymen renounce in a formal ceremony of the church *their "right" to vote.* Then we might learn something from them about living the sign of Jonah. God knows there would be no political loss, for what have we contributed to the ethical thrusts that was not more competently and elegantly contributed by the delegates from Wisconsin, Nevada, Utah, or Kansas?

What concerns us right now is that we Christians are rendering to Caesar the things that are God's. And that is the politics of Baal, not the sign of Jonah.

What concerns us right now is the Christian's complicity in setting the course irrevocably toward the technological police state, the Christian's effort to hand over the world. . . . *to politics.* And that is not the sign of Jonah but the politics of Baal.

32

Introduction to *Up to Our Steeples in Politics**

In one of his letters to the Christians in Corinth, St. Paul uses the imperative, *katallagete*: "In Christ's name, we implore you, be reconciled (*katallagete*) to God!" (2 Cor. 5:20). This word, directed to Christians and to
the Christian communities, is of interest to "the world" only if the world
finds it interesting, or if God should, in his own purposes, decide to interest the world in it. This book is primarily an effort to understand the
implications of Paul's imperative, *katallagete*, for Christians at the end of
the 20th century.

We agree with those who have reminded us in recent years that the
Christian faith is indicative (the fact that God reconciles the world in
Christ), not imperative (Go to church! Do not drink bourbon! Feed the
hungry! Search and destroy!). But we believe that St. Paul's imperative use
of "reconcile" calls attention to a special kind of behavior by the Christian
toward the world, behavior which "does" by being, "acts" by living—that
is, being and living as God made us in Christ.

This book is a series of statements about our understanding of why
St. Paul uses the imperative form of "to reconcile" and how that "why"
speaks clearly and unmistakably to what the world defines today as social
issues and political problems. It is, for that reason, a discussion of our
conviction that the Christian communities have failed in their calling,
their ministry, because (at their liberal best) they sought to do for the
world what God has already done for the world in Christ: the work of
reconciliation.

This book talks about our conviction that "already the axe is laid to
the root of the trees" (Lk. 3:9) because the church is trying to share shirts

* From Will D. Campbell and James Y. Holloway, introduction in *Up to Our Steeples
in Politics* (New York: Paulist, 1970), 1–6. Reprinted with permission.

and food with the poor and the hungry as imperative programs of social action, programs the church apparently believes are required by a law of God. We are trying to argue in these pages that St. Paul's imperative—Be reconciled to God!—means that God wants not doing, but being; not social action, but living; not welfare, but witness. Sharing? Yes! Not as a program, but as a parable, a thanksgiving, for what God has done for us in Christ!

In our day, we in the church have tried to do God's job, while at the same time rejecting the only job God puts before us. We have tried to reconcile people and groups of people by using every gimmick and technique that culture uses to sell its automobiles, deodorants, civil repression, and international warfare. We have tried surveys, group dynamics, T-groups, political activism, sociological and psychological processing, and all the well-known foolishness of church socials, retreats, picnics, bowling alleys, swimming pools, skating rinks, gymnasiums, counseling centers, marriage-and-the-family instruction, relevant ministries, and updated theological schools—all pleasant, on occasion even controversial, but having nothing, absolutely nothing, to do with the mission of Christians as ambassadors of, witnesses to, what God has done for all men in Christ.

But we in the church persist: we are still hopeful that through all those means we can build a kingdom in which all things will be set right between man and man (and occasionally between man and God), refusing to recognize that these means are an attempt to build a kingdom by our guidelines and blueprints, by our sociology and politics, not by what God's reconciliation has already done for the world in Christ. In this book we are trying to confess that the goals of the contemporary church—that is to say, the church of St. John's by the Gas Station, the Christian college, the denominational and interdenominational seminary—the goals of these Christian communities are blasphemous. The reconciliation the church is seeking to accomplish today by these subterfuges has already been wrought. The brotherhood—the "one blood" of Acts 17:26—that the church makes its goal today, is already a fact. And because this is so, that very fact judges our goals and our efforts to achieve brotherhood by social action as blasphemous, as trying to be God. Instead of witnessing to Christ, the social action of the church lends support to the totalitarianism of wars and political systems of the 20th century. By its social action, the church permits and encourages the state and culture to define all issues and rules and fields of battle. The church then tries to do what the state, without the church's support, had already decided to do: to "solve" all human problems by politics. And this is specifically the political messianism of contemporary totalitarianism and of Revelation 13. "Politics" by definition can only "adjust" and "rearrange." It cannot—as politics—"solve" anything. But the church's social action encourages the very movements in the contemporary political processes which are moving us straightaway into 20th-century totalitarianism.

The church has, in a word, tried to effect reconciliation where there already is reconciliation, while the only thing that God ever asked from the church was to live thanksgiving for others and so express thanksgiving for what he has done for us! Thus we talk in these pages about the Christian community in apostasy, for we believe that when the Christian community tries to do what God has already done, it is living a lie.

That is why we have failed as Christians. And failure to recognize the failure compounds our apostasy. St. Paul's imperative, "Be reconciled (*katallagete*) to God," inasmuch as we are reconciled to God, has no advice about what "to do." It has much to say about what "to be." We must be what we are—what we already are by God's doing, not ours. And what are we already? We are in Christ, reconciled to God and therefore to man. We believe that St. Paul's imperative leaves no room for what the church calls "social action." To engage in what the church calls "social action" is purely and simply to lie about reconciliation, to live as if it were obedience to law, to try to please God (and ourselves) by what we do by and for ourselves, and so reject the gift of what he did for us in Christ. Yet St. Paul's imperative—"Be reconciled to God"—is the only social action there is for the Christian: life as a thanksgiving to God. Such a life involves the giving of food to the hungry, drink to the thirsty, shelter to the homeless, and clothes to the naked—in other words, life as the Good News, life as thanksgiving for what God did for us. Not social action, for this rejects the gift of grace and contradicts the Good News by turning it into the Bad News of programs, strategies, imperatives, laws, and acts of obedience which, in trying to "please" God and ourselves with what we do for him, in fact recrucifies him.

In this book, we talk about racism, politics, war, poverty, education, and the coming of America's technological police state. But in no sense is this a handbook of social action or strategy suggestions for the Christian in politics. This is merely our effort to understand a fact—a fact, it must be emphasized, with which we had nothing to do. It is our discussion of the fact of God's reconciliation of all men as it bears on the racism, politics, war, poverty, education, and police states that characterize the 20th century.

But what about enmity, estrangement, alienation—realities which loom so large in the writings of St. Paul, despite his use of other (and probably more effective) words and descriptions? What of prejudice and the brokenness of the human family? How can we presume to say that man is already reconciled in Christ when all about us is the living hell of alienation, enmity and estrangement? We are not in these pages talking about being "reconciled" to racism's inhumanity, war's idolatry and death, education's totalitarianism or politics' messianism. We are saying that these blasphemies so characteristic of our age can be understood by the Christian and are judged by God only in the light of his reconciliation of all men in Christ. We are trying to talk in these pages about God's reconciliation of us, and not about our efforts to reconcile ourselves, efforts that have brought about the very enmities, estrangements and alienations that characterize the 20th century. We are talking about Thomas Merton's conviction that "to reconcile man with man and not with God is to reconcile no one at all."

We are reconciled to God, whether we know it or not, whether we want it or not. But this reconciliation is God's way of doing, not ours. It came to us as a gift, not as reward or law. As a gift, it is meant for us to accept. However, it can also—because it is a gift—be rejected, turned back, cursed, denied, and bring forth the fruits of enmities, estrangements and alienations and the blasphemies of social action. But because God did it, not man, because it is a gift and not a commandment, because it is life, not law, our blasphemies are not and cannot be the last word. The only Word is life, not death, resurrection, not annihilation. This is the fact. All the rest are the ideals of the social action which deny the Good News of what God did for us in Christ. And this means quite simply, in St. Paul's words, that "worldly standards"—beauty, sex, ugliness, money, race, poverty, complexion, politics, nationality, education, lack of education, shape, size, culture, culture-deprivation—these and any other such standards no longer hold power over the way we act toward God or toward others. We no longer need to behave as if "the world" or even we ourselves were making judgments on ourselves or on the world, or engage in the festivals which please the world or ourselves. Worldly standards no longer control the way we behave; they cannot alter this new and fundamental relationship which now exists between God and man, and between man and man, because of what God did by reconciling us to himself, beginning the "new creation" of men reconciled to each other in Christ. To proclaim—which is to say, to live—this news is the "service of reconciliation" of which St. Paul speaks, and this is the only thing God ever "asks." Not social action, not human engineering, not gimmicks or techniques that try to bring men together with other men—these deny that the news of Christ is good, since they affirm that he lived and died in vain and did not rise again for our salvation. God "asks" only that we live the whole of our lives so that it corresponds to, is a witness of, proclaims the truth about, what God has done for us all in Christ. Anything else for the Christian is to live a lie, because it lives as if the Event of Christ is of no account.

Do? Nothing! Be? What you are: a weak, helpless child whom God loves as Christ loves and has brought together (reconciled) in the Event, which is the imperative (*katallagete*) to live the truth of Christ—with no questions asked!—regardless of who we are and what we have done! That "service" is the imperative, *katallagete*, of the indicative, reconciliation.

That service is what these pages seek to discuss. Whether that notion is reactionary or radical, liberal or conservative, is of no concern to us. These terms are irrelevant to the biblical notions we are trying to uncover.

So whether or not you read further, whether you agree or disagree, we bid you, in God's name: *Katallagete!*

33

"On Mass Mobilizations"*

CONTEXT: *In this open letter, Will Campbell responds to the Southern Student Organizing Committee's statement on mass mobilization. Sometimes referred to as the "white SNCC," SSOC was eager to acquire political power so that they could utilize the mechanisms of government for good. Campbell, however, resisted their reasoning—questioning the wisdom of trying to alter the political system via the political system.*

Again, Campbell's diagnosis is that Christians have a misplaced faith in the political system, in what the government can and should do. Of all people, Christians should look neither to their own activism, nor the civil government to reconcile our social brokenness. Reconciliation is the work of the resistant church, not the nation-state.

Dear Folks,

I am responding to your statement—"On Mass Mobilizations"—before going to Washington. The reason is that I am not going to Washington. I did not go before. I did not go to Selma, Clarksdale, Memphis, Chicago, etc. Ten years ago I sat with a group of my fellow preachers from the North country who were planning strategy for a trip (mass trip) South. I insisted at the time that the vigil begin on the steps of the United Church Center in New York and on the steps of the federal courthouse there. Their response was that it was one thing to get local pastors to go to Albany, GA, to get put in jail, but they did not think most pastors could survive the local pressures of "praying on the steps of their own church houses." It was about at that point that I began being ruled out of "liberal" participation. My position then and my position now is that anything that does not

* Undated manuscript, James Holloway Papers, University of Mississippi.

exist locally, does not exist at all. I did not participate in the "Mississippi Freedom Summer" for the same reason. I did not see it as being serious. By that I mean that what's so hot about one summer except the weather. If they had been coming to locate in Mississippi, to have neighbors, friends, and kinfolks who would turn their backs on them when they raised hell and got thrown in jail would have been one thing. But to come on an excursion in which they would be lauded by their friends, neighbors, and kinfolks back home because some ignorant, mean ole redneck sheriff busted them on the head is quite another. I cannot be rejected by a stranger. I can only be rejected by those about whom I care. I cannot be hurt by someone I do not know. I can only be hurt by one I love.

Anyone who thought they would arouse the conscience of the nation by getting packed into a paddy wagon with a bloody head in Chicago was stupid. The nation (the state) HAS no conscience. There is nothing moral about the state—any state. By definition it can do anything it wishes to do. It exists for its own sake. The bloody heads and asses of all the Chicagoes, Washingtons, Selmas, etc., were nothing compared to the suffering of slaves and sharecroppers, the starving of Appalachia, the rejections presently suffered by the most tragic of all victims of the system—the poor misguided, exploited, lied to and about, Ku Klux Klansman because he is both victim and enemy. Or at least he is considered the enemy. I insist that he is not.

If the nation's conscience had not been aroused by the blood of centuries, it was not and will not be aroused by the blood of one evening or three days. It will cheer the blood, not repent over it. And it will do it WITH AN AROUSED CONSCIENCE, a conscience that tells them that the Stoic concept of an ordered rule is compatible with all that is holy, a conscience that tells them that a little band of dirty and bearded pot-puffing challengers is evil while a BIG band of dirty and bearded (ever spend three weeks at one time in a combat jungle?) partakers of stimulants far more potent than pot, but furnished as issue, not hustled, burning huts and villages, murdering women and babies and old men and young men, (not carrying picket signs) is good.

A nation has no conscience. How can it be aroused? A eunuch in bed with a doll is not disturbed.

But all of this we should have known. There is no point now in going into a rage because we did not succeed in arousing the conscience of the nation. The truth is, we did arouse the conscience, but it was an evil conscience. But to dwell on it now is like paying to sleep with a whore and then going into a violent rage when it is discovered there is no cherry. We should have known at the time. So what do we do? Precisely what you have suggested and if it is past the appropriate time—GO TO THE HILLS. But when you get there you will find no TV lights, no newspaper photographers, no one to tell your story, no fans to cheer you on. But you'll be where the action is. See you there. As for Washington? Well, maybe it's just that I don't like cowards.

Cordially with love,
Uncle Will

C. To the Academy

34

Excerpt from "Our Grade Is 'F'"*

CONTEXT: *In "Christ, the Hope of the World," John Howard Yoder wondered aloud how life in the academy might be different if disciples intentionally read their disciplines through the lens of the radical, scandalous Christ. Instead of Christians seeking to be good sycophants of the powerful and prestigious academic system—rewarded for their service with sabbaticals and tenure—what would happen if disciples privileged the sacrificial, nonviolent, reconciling Messiah? In the discipline of history, for example, Yoder imagined that such Christian historians would take narration "back from the grasp of the military historians and the chroniclers of battles and dynasties." No more celebrating the principalities and powers.*

In this excerpt from "Our Grade Is 'F'," Campbell carries this idea further. Christian colleges and universities are an embarrassing farce when they try to justify their expensive tuition by conveniently dropping in the name of Jesus here and there. Why are Christians in the academy so concerned to acquire the approval of that educational principality, anyway? A peculiarly Christian approach, *in other words, would not "graft Christ" onto a profession already defined by the maxims of the academic powers.*

Just as Campbell urged resistance toward institutionalized religion and power politics, so he counsels resistance to the academy.

The American colleges and universities (Christian and otherwise) have carefully guarded against any involvement in the racial crisis by worshipping at the shrine of academic excellence. The president of a great Southern university remarked to us a very few years ago—when it was decided, after all this time, to admit 5 or 6 *qualified black* students and

* From Will D. Campbell and James Y. Holloway, "Our Grade Is 'F,'" *Katallagete*, Fall 1969, 5–8. Reprinted with permission.

we had been summoned by someone other than the president to serve as "consultant" to the situation—"We do not contemplate any problem here because there won't be many to measure up to our high standards." He spoke the truth. So higher education washes its hands pure in the *Pilate* basin of academic excellence and sends the problem back to the racist, black and white. But it is doubtful that the shibboleth of academic standards is ultimately any more sacred to God than the hue and cry of racial intermarriage—the shibboleth of the Deep South racist—is sacred to God. Both, no doubt, contain an element of some sort of "truth": both are worshipping false gods.

The failure of education requires a closer look, in dimensions other than as well as the racial one. An important reason why the racial catastrophe is deep and probably irreversible is what America now means by and does with "education." Education's failure, and the perversion of education which came about in the process of failing in the racial crisis, is probably the most monumental calamity to befall an institution of American culture in the twentieth century. The refusal "to bus" to achieve some degree of balance leading toward an effective primary and secondary educational process, and the failure of higher education to seek out in order to serve the victims of this process, are simply the two most obvious manifestations of the same calamity.

We are concerned here, however, with the failure of education that falls as an especially acute judgment on the Christian in America. The New Testament proclaims the Good News that religion, that sickness which binds man to himself and to his idols and images, is conquered by the Resurrection. What concerns us is the fact that "education" has become a religion in the American democracy (and to the church) more sacred than American democracy (and Christ). The New Testament makes it clear that "education" is not "evangelism." What concerns us is the fact that the gamut of activities that goes by the name "education"—that activity which was to be the sure and certain guarantee that the American people would be come free and continue to live in freedom and democracy—education, along with and urgently supported by the political order, is preparing our minds and souls for the technological concentration camp.

We are concerned about more than a virtue become a vice, a thesis become an antithesis, a tragedy that is more than intellectual, because it involves the souls of the humanists and the birthright of Christians. We are convinced, for example, that the gut decisions that Christians will face in the next years and decades will not so much concern military service (it is more efficient to have a voluntary, professional army, anyway), but service to the idol of American "education." We believe that Christians will soon be forced to make decisions about whether to permit their children to attend institutions (kindergarten, upward, Christian and secular), spawned by educational systems and bureaucracies which are already hopelessly closed, totalitarian, beyond hope of internal or external renewal, and whose efforts bring forth a youth cynical at the manifest hypocrisy or brainwashed as to value and meaning in life. And Christians must make those decisions—like all decisions made as Christians—in the light of the fact that it is the Good News, and not "education", which liberates captives from the dungeons of idolatry.

Christians are more confused than anyone today about what "education" *is*. Or worse, perhaps most Christians are not even confused, but naively assume that they know what education *is*—and that, today is to be far, far worse off than to be confused. But the real charge that must be leveled against the Christian is that it was not us, but the plethora of revolts by blacks, youth, police, Indians, etc., etc., which challenged all our easy, liberal assumptions about what "education" *is*. Is education, for example, the objective transmission of information, data, facts, skills, about sundry subjects, liberating the recipient from ignorance about certain information, data, facts, skills—so that choices may be made on the basis of "reason" and that every choice made by those receiving this information, data, etc., is thereby "rational"? Perhaps so. But who decides what information, data, facts, skills, will be transmitted, and by whom, and why may we trust one person's objectivity and reject another's as subjective and emotional?

Or is education the appreciation of cultural, especially Western traditions, enabling one to better understand the world and the time in which we live? Perhaps so. But who decides how to present *what* about *which* tradition? About ours, to take an example close to hand: shall we agonize and assign term papers about the "meaning" of the Protestant Reformation, and the Age of Reason, and thus ignore the "meaning" of the introduction of the traffic in black lives from Africa to the "new" world by white Christian ladies and gentlemen? Shall we chart the battle for New Orleans and the Bloody Angle, and thus deny Christian genocide against the original inhabitants of what we now call North and Central and South America? Shall we memorize Talcott Parson's social theory of action, and overlook J. Edgar Hoover's? (If you substitute the right names in the proper places in the preceding sentences, you have the very sort of questions our political and social scientists are this very moment putting before our students as examples of today's "-isms", especially Marx's "isms.")

Some believe that education is the great equalizer in American democracy. Accessible to all regardless of race, creed, and color, it is the one sure vehicle which permits a son or daughter of a black mother and a white father to attend public schools anywhere without prejudice or impediment, secure admission into the crack universities or Christian liberal arts colleges, and become Abraham Lincoln, Richard Nixon, Betty Furniss, Jonas Salk, or Neil Armstrong. The fact is that tax-supported education (and *all* education, some Baptists and others to the contrary notwithstanding, *is* tax-supported) aids upper- and middle-income children far more than it supports these lower income folk. Indeed, these folk—because of who they are and what America has done to them and where they live—are the victims of the very educational system which their own tax dollars support in a higher proportion than do upper- and middle-income families. This fact we hereby commend for the earnest consideration of trustees in the small Christian college who are exercised about the separation of church and state, government support, etc., etc.—not that they accept government support but that they recognize an indebtedness to those who support *them*. And what about the black man's blackness, and the red man's redness, etc., etc., in education today? It is a "problem" which requires a "solution": those who are different because of skin color or "cultural deprivation" are made into "white"—in public institutions under the rubric of democracy, in Christian institutions under the rubric of brotherhood.

Some hold to a robust American pragmatism: we know what education is when we see what it does. On that score, also, we question an easy assurance. Education in the United States has studied war and the decision-making and political processes and power politics so thoroughly since the Second World War that a class of American mandarins has been created by our graduate schools. But this educational process (itself the object of critical professional inquiry only very recently, that is, after the barn has burned with the horses inside) has offered no alternative to the Cold War, to worldwide insurrections of race and poverty, to an understanding of the Middle Eastern crises that is surely wrenching Hitler's victims there into his own violent image, not without racial touches. As for Vietnam, it is the crown jewel of these scientists of human affairs (especially political affairs) who reject even the moral judgments of humanity as weal and subjective intrusions into the world of political realism.

Education today might well be judged by what it does. And what we see it doing is adjusting the student to the-system-which-is-everywhere—which is to say, dehumanizing the student rather than liberating him. Education, we think, should work toward an adjustment of the-system-which-is-everywhere to serve humanity. But because education today is an adjustment of the student to the system, the great people and the great literature and the great music and the great art since the Second World War have not been the work of those who are a part of the educational institutions in America. How could they be? And because this is so, our educational institutions are prisoners of the manifold fruits of a technology which the helpless and impoverished of the world and our land know only too well, from Hiroshima to Hanoi, from Canton in Mississippi to Ocean Hill-Brownsville in New York. And because this is so, education, whenever it might take place, must begin as a process of *dis*-adjustment to the-system-which-is-everywhere. And *that*, brothers and sisters, is about all we know about what education *is*, today.

Where are the Christian colleges in all of this? Where they have always been, led by Caesar and his educational institutions and bureaucracies. Except that, in most cases, we were early to segregate racially, in order to be relevant to our people; late to de-segregate because we had to preserve "unity"; and because of the strength of our conviction that our intentions are of the highest and purest, we are the last to understand that integration is, in fact, another way to control "them."

Whom does the Christian college serve? Whom do Caesar's colleges serve? Those same and precious few others. Certainly not the victims of Caesar's educational Gestapos (SAT, CEEB [College Entrance Examination Board]), for these are "high risk." And no one (Caesar's servants or Christ's) gives any thought to how high the risk *any* student runs by devoting four irretrievable years of his life to the sickness of present-day educational establishments. Certainly there is little enthusiasm in the Christian colleges today to resurrect those of whom Jonathan Kozol speaks in *Death at an Early Age*. For which among the present-day colleges has been more anxious about the dodges and deceits called "quality education" and "academic excellence" than the Christian liberal arts college? Which among them has been more anxious about accreditation than the Christian liberal arts college, even though it meant a service to Caesar and a denial of the service to Christ? Which among the educational institutions has competed more enthusiastically and energetically with Caesar for high-quality students (so as not "to scrape the bottom of the barrel"), and for basketball players, faculty, coaches, science centers, and athletic stadiums, than the Christian liberal arts college? Which among the colleges has ignored more effectively than the Christian liberal arts college the stranger lying bloody in the ditch (cf. Luke 10:29ff), the victim of the very educational system which now denies him?

Whom does the Christian liberal arts college serve when it echoes Caesar's concerns about "qualifications," academic standards, SAT and CEEB scores? In whose service is the Christian liberal arts college when it fails to strike head-on the very concept of "qualification," especially qualifications defined by the educational brigands who consigned the victim, bruised, naked, and half-dead, into the sewers of American society, dug in part by the educational brigands themselves? Whom does the Christian liberal arts college serve when it does not lead an onslaught against the totalitarianism of accrediting agencies? Where is the Christian liberal arts college which has compassion even on her own victims as well as Caesar's by pouring on oil (and, yes, wine) and paying the bill, not in reparations but as a neighbor (cf. Luke 10:29ff.)?

What we are asking is where in the Christian college is the white youngster we call "Kluxer" because he doesn't know which side of the plate the salad fork goes on and spends a lot of time talking about sex and automobiles? And where in the Christian college is the black whom we call "culturally deprived" and thus ineligible for admission to higher education because he has been deprived (or spared) our culture and belches or crepitates in public?

Our Christian colleges speak for mammon, not God. There is precious little evidence that they—which is to say, their trustees or administrators or faculties or alumni or students—will or desire the humility to do otherwise than be an agent of mammon. It may be argued against what we are saying that, well, at least the Christian liberal arts college is serving Christians—or at least the progeny of Christians in America. But when was the principal service to Christ ever the rendering of service to ourselves (cf. Luke 10:29ff.)? So in our Christian colleges we are in fact serving ourselves and not Christ, in the middle- and upper-income orientation of our curriculum and faculty and administration and trustees. Our distaste for the victims of our economics is never more evident than in our loud shouts about how many "Negros," or how many "high-risk" students we admit over the last year, over the state university, over the Ivy League colleges. If we were in the least bit serious about black and high-risk students, why would we have to say anything about *them*? Why not *be* like the man in Luke 10:29ff., *be* compassionate by binding up wounds and paying the bills and leaving, *incognito*?

Christian colleges, unlike the medieval universities we enjoy so much to deplore because of their authoritarianism, are contemptuous toward their environments—human and natural—which are exploited rather than served. Christian colleges have constructed buildings and obtained operational capital from a rape of the land and from the sweat and backs of Indians, blacks, rednecks, hillbillies, Kluxers, Chicanos, peckerwoods, etc., etc. The Christian colleges then use them as service or maintenance lackies, while their pathetic little culture-starved MAs and PhDs ridicule and scoff them and their music and their dress and their antics and drinking and fighting and sex life and prose and vocabulary and their support of George Wallace, and tell lies about them (and thereby about middle- and upper-income Americans and Christians) in their "required" courses.

Our Christian colleges serve themselves and not Christ when they explain in the most pained tones that they have only so "many" resources and that these must be allocated on the basis of priorities. And what and who are the priorities? Ourselves. Middle- and upper-income Christian Americans. And these are the priorities set by Caesar, not Christ. They are, the Christian colleges insist, committed to "quality education." And spelled out, this means that our Christian colleges will continue their commitment to the very same cycle of events which put and keeps the victims of the educational system, bloodied and bruised and half-dead, in the sewer of American society. And because he smells badly since he has been there so long, the Christian liberal arts college covers the victim not with oil and wine and compassion, but with surveys, institutional self-studies, statements of purpose, and massive foundation requests (that were rejected). An allocation of resources based on commitments to "quality education" is simply the educator's "white" lie that a commitment to the victims of the educational system in America is a compromise of "quality education." And this is quite simply the racism of white intransigence, which feeds on a conviction of superiority that crucified Christ and recrucifies Him anew.

Christ have mercy on us! What is the quality of "quality education" that rejects Christ's own dying for *all* men? Where is the quality in what our Christian colleges have taught about what Christian white people have done in wars and slavery to the people of color the world over, and what we have done in our own peculiar wars against each other? Where is the *excellence* that judges it "excellent" to allocate resources to support and preserve the very institution and ways of life that raped a people and a land and imported the children of God as draft animals, that digs new sewers in which to throw the new victims created by the new systems and methods and techniques of The American Way of Life?

Where is the service to Christ in that myriad of Christian liberal arts colleges whose only boast over the hated (because of the larger budget) state university is the lower student-teacher ratio (which never really works our to smaller classes in a meaningful way), easy access to the teachers, and the absence of student-faculty radicalism and hippie types? There is *no* service to Christ in all this, for the simple reason that there is no essential difference between what is happening on the campus of the Christian liberal arts college and the large state university. Recruit (and compete in recruiting) students, using the same formulas, for the same curriculum, taught by instructors indoctrinated by the same prejudices of the same professors in the same graduate and professional schools. Except that, instructors at the state universities were for the most part better all-round students, have stronger and more realistic and relevant views of today's society and (unbelievable as it might seem) are on the whole better classroom teachers. (What is the sense in bragging about smaller classes if the students are presided over by imperializing old maids, male or female?)

So there it is: Students sharing the same presuppositions because they must have them to finish high school and be "admitted" to college; faculty sharing the same ones because they have to get a "degree" and an "appointment" and tenure promotions and sabbaticals; administrators sharing them because they have to allocate resources according to the priorities set by society and by Caesar's universities, and by trustees drawn from the specialists in making and raising money in the American system. There it is: Christian college with state university, together and indistinguishable not under the Cross, but under the Great Yum-Yum Tree of Academic Excellence and Quality Education. No distinctions between "education" and "evangelism" wrought on the Cross. Rather, the "cross" in the "classroom" and not on *Golgatha*—evangelism in the service and at the beck and call of education-as-adjustment to the system-which-is-all-around-us.

But why should we emphasize failures only? Why not, for a change, speak of successes? Because . . . there are no successes. Because insofar as the Christian college is concerned, there will be no successes, absolutely not one, unless and until the nature and the depth of the failure is seen, and accepted. And this lies not in our hands, but God's. We are under His judgment.

It is clear that there will be no successes until the Christian college grasps the difference between teaching and evangelism as seen in the New Testament. Then it will cease evangelizing by education, by the cheap trick of trying to put "Christ in the classroom." Look for success, then, not in Christian colleges because they call themselves Christian. Look for success in a student here, a "call to discipleship" yonder, an insight there from a teacher which makes it impossible to "study" war or racism or the New Testament and come away the same person; impossible to study physics or chemistry and not dedicate one's career to opposing their enslavement to the horrors of twentieth-century technological inhumanity; impossible to study money and banking and come away lighthearted at what our economics have done to those who originally had property right to the land which supports us so richly, and to those whom we purchased as chattel and continue to treat as such. Look for success not where "Christ," but a Socratic Christian, is the classroom—that is, a teacher who will put *everything* under question, accepts *nothing* at face value, (especially himself and his discipline), not for the hell of it nor because he is possessed of a demon, but because the Cross and Resurrection put *everything* under question. Yesterday, today, forever. *Everything.*

Look for success in those places: for it is not under any circumstances essential that this kind of success occur only on the campus or in the classroom of the Christian liberal arts college. *That is the point.*

35

"What Do We Do about What Has Been Done"*

CONTEXT: *This presentation is another example of Campbell at his icono-clastic best. Speaking at Emory University's respected Candler School of Theology, he seems entirely unconcerned with formalities. Uninterested in the academy's approval, he does not seek it. (Remember that Campbell liter-ally pasted his handwritten ordination papers on top of his Yale Divinity diploma.) Instead, he uses the academy's pulpit to prophesy to the academy. His challenge of Candler's recent gift of $100 million dollars from Coca-Cola, for example, brings the scandalous message of Christianity to bear on a prestigious divinity school.*

Somehow "Dr. Campbell" just doesn't have a good ring to it. I'm Will Campbell, from Mt. Juliet, Tennessee, and it wasn't the Second World War. It was the Boxer Rebellion I was in, or the Spanish-American War—one of those.

They used to tell me shortly after that, when I was going to school under the GI Bill of Rights, from whichever war it was, that studying homiletics—do they still teach that?—that the first five minutes of any sermon or speech should be given over to sheer foolishness and non-sense, and I suppose this very gracious and lavish introduction has taken care of that. So I'll go on.

Let's see, this is the Methodist group, isn't it. I've got to come down to Atlanta next week, or the week after, sometime, to talk with the Presbyterians at your neighboring school, and I don't want to get the Calvinists mixed up with the Wesleyans. I always like to come to Georgia. How many of you know where Charles Wesley's first hymnbook was pub-

* Delivered at Emory University, January 22, 1986. Transcription by Richard C. Goode. Thanks to Mel Hawkins for providing a copy of the presentation.

lished? Just one? Savannah, I think. In fact, I'm sure. If none of you know, Charles Wesley's first hymnbook was published in Savannah, Georgia. That's a little Methodist trivia I thought I'd bring you today.

When Ms. Brown called me and told me what the theme of this gathering was—this was some time ago—she said, "Will you give me a title? We have to have a title for the flyer and the brochure and all that." I said, "Well, you know, the theme is good enough for me." She indicated that everybody would be talking about that, so we came upon this [title] together, "What Do We Do about What Has Been Done?" which seems to fit. No one has but one sermon, and I'm not sure that I've ever called my sermon that before, but it's as good a title for it as any.

By way of beginning to address this subject, I would like to read a few familiar words about what *has* been done. Has anything been done, really? We talk about what we do about what has been done, well what exactly has been done?

> By now it was about midday, and a darkness fell over the whole land, which lasted until three o'clock in the afternoon. The sun's light failed. TVA[1] just went out. And the curtain of the Temple was torn in two. Something happened in here. Then Jesus gave a loud cry and said, "Father into Thy hands I commit my spirit," and with those words he died.

Now one of those who came early to believe that story said, "From first to last, this has been the work of God."

He *has*. He has already reconciled us to himself through Christ, and he has enlisted us in this service of reconciliation. [This] always seemed a fair doctrine of the church, to me. What I mean is, God was in Christ reconciling the world to himself. No longer holding our misdeeds against us. None of them. No matter how atrocious. Good news.

Before this faith came, we were close prisoners in the custody of law—pending the revelation of faith. Thus the law was a kind of tutor—a kind of a college—in charge of us, until Christ should come when we should be justified through faith. And now that faith has come, the college's charge is at an end. Baptized into union with him, you have all put on Christ as a vestment—as a garment or robe. There is no such thing as Libyan or American. Black or white. Male or female. Now that, I take it, is what we have generally in mind when we talk about what has been done.

---

1. Tennessee Valley Authority, electricity supplier for the region.

It's a rather impressive bit—the way it came about, and what those earlier followers of the Way said that this meant. Now what can we *do* about this? What *should* we do about this? What *can* we do about it? Here we go again, Don Shriver. As the man said, "Nothing."

It took me a long time to figure out why a doctrine of unconditional grace won't peddle. You can't build a steeple on it. You can't build this on a doctrine of unconditional grace.

"Certainly, Will, there's something we've got to do for Mr. God, for doing this."

Well, *what*?

In every era, in every tradition, we have reverted to some kind of moralism. Sooner or later we get back to some kind of moralistic, legalistic code in response to what has been done.

Now when I was a little boy, growing up, as Clint told you, down in the alleged state of Mississippi, they used to tell us that the proper response to this—what it means to be "Christian"—is "don't smoke," and "don't drink liquor," and "don't mess around on Saturday night." Now even as a little shirttail boy in Amite County, Mississippi, when they talked about that being "good news," I got confused. Because I heard the high school boys talking down the hill, where the WPA had built this great big facility. I didn't see good news in that. It sounded like bad news. So I went off to college and universities, and Ivy League divinity schools to get educated and sophisticated. No, I didn't make it, but I tried. They tried. They told me that that is sheer nonsense. That God doesn't care about those little things. That what God cares about is the suffering of his people. I liked that. I had suspected it all along. That means, they said, don't discriminate across racial lines. Later, much later, perhaps—I hope not—but maybe too late, they added don't discriminate across sexual lines. Don't go to war. Don't segregate people. Don't pay your workers less than minimum wage—the minimum to be set by Mr. Caesar. And I bought into that, until it finally dawned on me that this is, after all, another moral code. Another set of legalisms. Even if I can do all those things, and upgrade them, I better not put it on the scorecard because when you get to thinking about that—if what God thinks about is the suffering of God's people—then last week I read in the newspaper that according to the learned doctors of the university, this [smoking] is going to kill more people than war. Cause more widows, widowers, and orphans, broken families, homes, and suffering, fill up more hospitals and cemeteries, than war—cigarette smoking.

So, if we take the logic that what God cares about is not little individual missteps, but what God cares about is the suffering of the people, then my primitive ancestors were more nearly right than the Ivy League. Because cigarette smoking, say nothing of drinking liquor, I don't know about messing around on Saturday night—well it killed some people. Leads to some people getting killed, I know that. But those things are going to lead to more of the suffering of God's people than the new, moral, legalistic code.

Now, what does that mean? Does it mean let's go back to the negative code? It doesn't mean that at all. It does mean, though, that *both* were wrong. That we both were betting on the wrong horse. Both were moralistic, legalistic. Well, what *can* we do in the face of what this God did in incarnation?

God *has* reconciled us, Paul said. It's over. It's done. How do we respond to that?

Well, we respond in a lot of ways. We respond in the sacraments. I'm high-church Baptist, by the way, so I can talk about the sacraments. Much as Methodists can. *United* Methodists, I'm sorry.

I am on record, and someone has reminded me of this story since I've been here this morning. I'm on record—written record—never to tell grandchild stories, but I lied and I'm going to tell [one]. Since I live under grace I can lie. I'm forgiven. I'm God's little liar. This [is] one grandchild story, and we don't have but one grandchild—a little boy. When he was about three, his mother wanted him baptized. Being a deep-water Baptist from Mississippi, and working on a book about the Anabaptists at the time—those people who got drowned in the Amstel River and tied on ladders and pushed on to brush heaps for *not* baptizing infants—I expressed some concern. She, knowing more about those matters than I, said "Well, anyone, even an unbaptized person since the Council of—I don't remember which council it was, some of you scholars know—don't even have to be baptized to baptize another person. So if you don't want to baptize your grandson . . ." "No, no," [I said.] "If he's going to be baptized then obviously I'm the appropriate one to do it."

My father was visiting us. I know I look too old to have a living father, but I do. He was six when I was born. We're all the same age, and grew up together. He was visiting us at the time. It was Christmas morning. And I said, "Daddy, what do you think about baptizing babies?" The way he handled it was to tell me this story, which I had heard before (but I'm not sure you have), but I was glad to hear it from him, about the Baptist preacher in Arkansas who was asked if he believed in infant baptism. He said, "Believe in it? Hell, I've actually seen it." Then he [Campbell's father] said, "Go ahead son. The little fellow may know more than you think."

The test in Baptist circles, to give you some instruction in Baptist doctrine here, is whether or not one has reached the age of accountability. So we baptized him, Christmas morning, at the breakfast table. When I had finished, he, still sopping the runny part of the egg with the last of his biscuit said, "Papa, what did you put on my head?" I said, "Water." He said, "Why?" His mother being sensitive and a good mother, didn't want her three-year-old traumatized by her Daddy's horse-and-buggy theology, kind of motioned me ["No,] let's don't get into that." But I tried to answer his question, and talked about sin, forgiveness, and reconciliation, and even guilt: "You know that lump you get in your throat when you're mean to your Mama? You don't have to have that. All our mischief is done away with because of what this means—putting water on your head."

He got to giggling while I was engaged in this little homily, which pleased his mother mightily. He didn't care about this one way or another. When I was finished, he jumped down and rushed off to his world of play, or reality, and then, though, turned and came back in the room and with a big belly laugh said, "Well, well, Papa, thank you then." My eighty-six-year-old Daddy looked across the table at me and winked. Two old deep-water Baptists knew that we need have no further qualms about his having reached the age of accountability. For what better response is there to a sacrament than a big belly laugh, and, "Well, thank you then"?

That is one response, but how do we say "thank you" like a little child? That was quite enough for me.

We say "thank you" in praise and song, in sacramental acts, and in worship, but I'm bothered by worship. I'm bothered by the luxury of worship, for what has evolved into worship in our culture is not affordable by the vast majority of human beings in the world.

I was at a retreat in another state, sponsored by another communion. I won't say which one. Some of you may be Episcopalians, for all I know, from Idaho. A part of this retreat was a long period of silence, from ten o'clock at night until twelve o'clock the next day. There was to be complete silence. I got along alright during the night. I don't talk a lot in my sleep anyway. But something started bothering me the next morning as we were making these little gestures to pass the grapefruit already sectioned out, and the English muffins, and the Canadian bacon, and a second cup of Columbian coffee, [all while] not speaking. After a bit, I said, "To hell with this nonsense!" [That] broke the silence, well, modestly. If I never believed in *glossolalia* before, I did then, because I found myself saying words which were really not my own, and I was not sure of the source of them. Yes, I broke the silence because more than fifty percent of our brothers and sisters around the world cannot afford to be silent. You can't be silent and push and scream and scrounge and shove for a half-cup of rice to feed your starving young ones. [Our neighbors cannot afford] the luxury of what we have come to call "praise" and "worship." There is something wrong in this kind of "Thank you then."

There is something wrong in a worship when the communion elements that go down our gullets have more calories in them than millions and millions of our brothers and sisters, young and old, more calories than they will have all day. What kind of "thank you then" is that?

When we proclaim our love for Jesus too much, and too often, in my judgment we're lying, and ought to quit it. We have it on good authority that even the taking of the sacraments, [according to] the Gospel of St. John, [we should] *stop this! Don't do it any more!* If you drink this blood and eat this flesh unworthily, you do so to your own damnation. You'd be better off to leave it off. Just quit it! When we proclaim our love for Jesus too much, religion has done got out of hand. When religion gets out of hand, it is a dangerous thing.

In my judgment, the problem with Christianity in our nation is not that enough people love Jesus. The problem is that *everyone* loves Jesus. The cross has been shined up, pretty. That [cross] is pretty, ain't it? What does it mean? Shined up? We've seen some cross shining going on this week, in this city. Now the Reagan Administration loves Martin Luther King Jr., sings "We shall overcome." *How dare you sir! Have you no shame? Have you no fear of God?* When 46 percent of black youth, who Martin King loved and died [for], can't find jobs, and 15 percent of all black adults—not counting those who have given up, quit looking for jobs and turned to the streets to survive like swine feeding on beech mash in the swamps—you dare stand on national TV and polish this cross? With Star Wars in your eyes, and "We shall overcome" and "We are not afraid" on your lips, somebody, sir, is lying. In the words of that great patriot, Governor Ross Barnett, who when he was turning James Meredith away from the University [of Mississippi] said, being a Southern gentleman, a person of some manners—as am I—I say so politely, "Somebody is lying."

What can we do to say "thank you" then? Are we back to nothing? Do nothing? Well, you don't have to do anything. I don't. I am your brother, no matter how many mistakes I make. No matter how many people I call liars. Even if I refer to God as "he," or "she," or "it," or whatever. There is something that has been done for me.

As long as we have dispensed with the scorecards, if you *want* to do something, by way of saying "thank you," I would make a few tentative and random suggestions. Nothing revolutionary. Nothing extraordinary. Nothing radical. We tend to mellow in our dotage. Just some little things, just little things. Not something that you put on your scorecard if you might want to do these things. Little things.

How many bishops are there in the United Methodist Church? I ran into a friend in the hall yesterday. I didn't realize it at the time, but when he was gone another friend said "He's now a bishop. Bless his heart. He's a nice fellow." We were talking and I asked him this question, "How many bishops are there?" He said forty-six, forty-eight, or something like that. I thought that there were more than that, but it doesn't matter. I had in mind suggesting that at the next General Conference. . . . Now I studied Methodist discipline once. If you want to know why I know all this about Methodist polity, I studied the Discipline. My rationale being that when I was in divinity school, up north they required that everyone take their own polity. Well, the person who taught Baptist polity was an absolute bore, and the person who taught then Methodist polity knew a lot of good stories, and was a very entertaining teacher, very popular. So, I told the dean that they didn't teach my polity there. "You don't teach Southern Baptist polity. This is American Baptist polity, and northern Baptist polity, and that's different. It's as different as Southern Baptist and Methodist," which was true. The dean didn't exactly look with great favor on that, but finally conceded the point. I was going to suggest that at the next General Conference that half—not quite half, being a chauvinist in my sin I am not willing to give women equal rights. [I was going to suggest that since] there are forty-six [bishops], twenty of these resign and elect twenty women bishops. That still gives us the edge. I believe we now have what, one or two?

Now I'm not going to suggest that. I thought about it, but that smacks of toadying—even of revolution. I've got a better idea. All of the bishops present don't resign. Hang in there. All current bishops remain, but let's have *three* bishops in each annual conference: one male, one female—all Americans and so presumably ethnically mixed—one male, one female, and then one scattered from the face of the globe. Parthians, and Meades, and Elamites, and dwellers of Mesopotamia, and in Judea and Cappadocia, and Pontus, and Asia, South Africa, and Vietnam, and Nicaragua, and Honduras, and the parts of Libya around Cyrene—a bishop from the Pentecost church. A little thing. You can do that. Don't tell me you can't. You've got to change the Discipline, right? No big deal. You do it all the time.

Nothing radical. Nothing revolutionary. But if you want to do something in response to what has been done, then open a part of the church houses around your cities, and towns, and villages so that the increasing number. . . . Did you read the paper this morning or last night? [Homelessness] up in some cities by 100 percent over a year ago. People who have no place to go, and who are turned loose—even the ones who have a place, who are brought in by the cities—at five o'clock in the morning are turned loose again on the streets. Just open one room [of the church house]. Let the word get around, "This door is open." Now they may pee on your carpet, understand that, and they may burn it down, but you can build it back.

Or, if you want to do something, just something that's possible, not any big thing. Any Christian institution that, let's say, comes into a lot of money—let's say $100 million. Just an arbitrary figure. I went to Wake Forest College, and let's just say that Wake Forest got $100 million from the Coca . . . um, the R. J. Reynolds Company. Now let's say that in the negotiation—now don't anybody tell me that this is not practical, because I want to be very, very practical this morning. Not revolutionary. Not outrageous. Not ridiculous. Just some little things that can be done. Now, in order to get that $100 million from R. J. Reynolds, somebody had to do some serious negotiating. What they used to call, "wheeling and dealing." Now these are good people that we're negotiating with, and we say, "Now you understand that we are from a tithing tradition, so [with] this money we are going to take 10 percent of this $100 million and get people off the streets. We are going to give people shelter and food, so that men, women, old, young, and now increasingly the little children, babies, don't freeze to death on the streets."

We're going to do that. Just some little thing. That we're going to use part of this, a tenth of this, to set the prisoners free. To restore sight to the blind. To bring good news to the poor. No big deal. We read that in the lectionary all the time.

Or, those of us who are preachers driving $16,000 cars, let's cut back to $11,000 cars. And if we wear $400 suits, let's cut back to $100 suits. Or rummage sales—they have some good stuff at rummage sales. [A] little thing to say "thank you."

Each congregation could, if it wanted to—don't have to, but if you want to do something—adopt one prisoner. Go once a week to the prison, and let him or her tell you their story, and you tell them your story. We've all got stories to share. I've long felt that if everyone locked up in prison had one person from the free world, and since I come from the Christian tradition I would hope that would be some Christian from the free world, to come once a week and visit with them and share the stories from free world to locked-up world, that this one act would lead to more prison reform than we're even ready to think about. Just a little thing.

Again, we read that [Luke 4 passage] all the time. Jesus said, "I have come to proclaim release to prisoners—to turn people loose." Now I know we exegete that and say, "Well, that means better libraries in the prison, or saltpeter in the food, or whatever to make their lives more bearable." I've always thought that as some kind of a conservative Christian, and not ready to concede all the biblical quarterbacking to the Falwellian syndrome. (Interesting to me how "Falwellian" rings so nearly like "Orwellian.") We read about Jesus saying, "I have come to proclaim release to captives." I think Jesus was at least as intelligent as the rest of us, and was capable of saying what he meant, when he quoted this passage from Isaiah. I think that is what he meant to say. That's a little thing we can do.

Or we could if we wanted to do something, pay commensurate taxes. What a *tremendous* tax break we get. We can say, "This is not right. We are going to set aside this tax, and we are going, in this nation, to set up a peace academy—as the government voted and then refused to finance—so that there will be some hope that we are not going to blow the whole creation of Almighty God to smithereens. Just a little thing.

Or we can take this commensurate tax and give the money to the poor of our enemies. Feed some people in Libya. They say they [the Libyans] are our enemies now. It varies from month to month. But the

Scripture that we read from is very clear on this issue of how we respond to our enemies—very clear on this.

Or any congregation that has a budget of say $100,000 or more could have a preacher-at-large. Find some young, middle-age, or old, man or woman, who is called of God, and say, "You are going to be our preacher out there in the world. We don't want you here. You can come if you want to, but we'd just assume you'd be doing something else. Now we're going to be busy up here at eleven o'clock on Sunday and some other times doing holy things. You are our preacher in the world. We're going to put in a pumpkin patch, or in a post office box, once a year a check for $12,000. You can do anything you want to do. We don't want any reports. We don't want you coming in here cluttering up quarterly conference—do you still have quarterly conference? But go out in the world, and take the message of reconciliation of what has been done, and by your life say, 'Well, thank you then.'"

There is one other option, of course, to what we can do about what has been done. It is not without precedent in our movement. We can walk away sorrowfully, for behold, behold, behold, we are very rich.

36

"The Computer Talks Back"*

CONTEXT: *After some introductory remarks and a story about his cherry walking cane, the transcription picks up with his parable about "The Chair of the Future" and the challenge of the gospel to the academy. Once he proceeds into heart of his presentation, Campbell's tone is considerably more serious and solemn than usual, but his redeeming iconoclasm is as poignant and objectionable as ever. Does the Christian liberal arts college have a distinct message and mission, or is it a weak imitation of all other institutions in the academy?*

This is the first time I've been on this campus. I commend the administration for never having invited me before, but I am happy that they have invited me this time. It occurred to me as I was walking around, a bit of a chill in the air, that I hope you that are students know—and I doubt if this is the case, but I hope you know—how very, very fortunate you are. I am not toadying at this point. I don't have to. I go to these big head factories, thirty, forty, fifty thousand students, being taught with tape recorders and electronic gadgets, who have not the slightest idea what their teachers' names are. Here you are in a situation where you are not being trained, like bird dogs, but you are being taught. You are getting an education. Now this will be painful to you as you go through life, because you will have a sensitivity that people who are trained [will not have]. There is a difference between being trained and being educated. You will have an understanding of what is going on in the world. I am glad that you are

* Delivered at Carson-Newman University, February 18, 1997. Transcription by Richard C. Goode. Thanks to Mel Hawkins for providing a copy of this presentation. This sermon is largely similar to Campbell's "The Computer Says 'Repent' (A Fable)," *Faith and Mission* 2 (Fall 1984) 77–81.

here, and again, I hope that you realize how very fortunate you are that you are here. I truly believe that the only place in America where real educating is going on is in your smaller liberal arts colleges, where people are still taught to think and make decisions on their own and are not robots, and who will in their dotage have no better sense than to crawl through airports on their belly. To not just defy or be a smart aleck, but as a demonstration that "I am a human being with a mind."

There was once an endowed professorship that was called the "Chair of the Future." The cue in establishing it had been taken from one of the world's foremost anthropologists who suggested that each great college should have something called "The Chair of the Future." She further suggested, in this case, that the chair should be automated. Equipment, she said, should consist of the most advanced computer technology. The professor's job would be simply to feed this machine, and reveal its fealty to the students, thereby, she insisted, enlightening them as to what the future holds for them and for the universe. The people of God, having already abdicated their other responsibilities for the welfare of society, will now be relieved even of apocalyptic interpretation. The church can give full-time [attention] to such matters as aerobic dance classes, weight-watchers clubs, marriage enrichment seminars, and other weighty matters of the gospel. Even prophecy will be handled by a machine.

It goes very well in the first semester. The academic fugitive from war games, faces his class of tomorrow's magnates with the result of months of data feeding in his hand. He has explained all along, still under the spell of out-dated classical learning, that the data used for each feeding is historical in nature. The final printout from the computer will reveal the future on the basis of past behavior.

Into the machine has gone the result of doctrines of manifest destiny, the roll call of the Iroquois and the Sioux, the Cherokee and the Navajo, the Crow and the Choctaw. In had gone the results of the ideas of racial supremacy and sexual supremacy. The roll of generations of slaves. The soldiers on both sides of a war that was to be a new birth of freedom. In had gone the casualties of great social movements dedicated to somehow alter the legacy of original sin. The patterns of greed, conformity, and blind obedience to witless authority, that would spell doom if left like genocide to follow their own grim logic. The rape of Mexico and the quelling of the Cuban Rebellion. Two global wars fought in part over who would gain control of the greater share of what they called "the Dark

Continent." Vietnam and the mining of Nicaraguan harbors. The slaughter in the Persian Gulf, fought against the weapons that we had furnished the enemy. In had gone the battered child, the father's murder spree, the execution of our mentally ill, and such contradictions as the condemnation of child abuse which would claim the lives of one hundred babies a year while accepting in cavalier fashion the termination of the lives of two million of the unborn each year. [In went] the mindless silence of those long beyond capacity for moral discrimination. [In as well went] the results of the great counter ideas: tolerance, helpfulness, neighborliness, the notion of life in community, and the greatest idea of all, that there be worship of no other gods than the one who said to Moses from a burning bush, "I Am Who I Am."

As the semester ends the ashen face of the professor turns with shaking hands and begins to speak. "Now young people, the computer says that in less than two years from the day of your commencement, the world will cease to exist. Anything except the most insignificant plant life will be gone."

A few ho-hums here and there. A few yawns and scattered snickers. They have heard all this before from left-wing peace marchers, and environmentalists who oppose an adequate national defense and champion spotted owls and forest trees, over lumber for building. But the professor is thorough in his explanation of any subject, so he continues. "Now you must understand, young people, this includes IBM, General Motors, General Electric, Boeing Aircraft, the ski slopes of Sugar Mountain, the golf courses of Pinehurst, Oak Ridge nuclear labs, the Atlanta Braves, and UT [University of Tennessee] football. You must understand further that these are not the words of some ecclesiastical hemophiliac, or soft-headed pacifist, this is the prediction of the highest technology ever known in human history." Snickers vanish and yawns give way to clinched-mouth consternation, as the now-concerned students envision their four years vanishing as a droll interlude in the flight into apocalyptic inevitability.

A young campus jock, who might also have been a Phi Alpha Epsilon, for all I know, had been dozing through it all surrounded by Dixie cups of tomato juice laced with Alka-Seltzer and other amenities necessary for an agonizing recovery from an extended weekend in the city. Hearing now for the first time that everything in the whole world, including the Atlanta Braves and UT football [would pass away], rose as one resolved to exert himself against the most robust odds. The equally stunned group, knowing of the inherent leadership capacity of this young jock, strong fellow that he is, appeared pleased with his assertive countenance. The big tough strode deliberately and resolutely and with an air of arrogance and took a stand beside the professor and his machine. "Alright professor, you just ask that blame thing, you ask that thing what we're supposed to do. We are a people of action and great accomplishment. We are people of world-feared power. Give us an ocean and we'll cross it, a mountain and we'll climb it, a war and we'll win it, problems and we'll solve them, but give us a clue, one little clue, as to what we should do." But the professor said that would take another semester.

So by executive order of the president and telephonic approval of the board the next semester begins. The Chair of the Future is the only course offered now. Math, Biology, Sociology, English, Bible, none of that. Just the professor with his Chair of the Future. The president, I am told, was put to work minding the auxiliary power station. The dean sandbagging the vault where grades and examination questions were kept. The more optimistic faculty relapsing occasionally into brief flirtations with self-study projects, curricular committees, and other things of previous high priority.

The appropriate data was fed into the machine. All the alleged advances and accomplishments of the new country called "America," were listed to lure the computer to a mood of leniency for us. The lone courage of Roger Williams standing against the religious intolerance of New England. The inspiration of those who at the foundation of this democracy stood for a principle of equal rights over and against the prerogatives of monarchs. The raw fortitude of Harriet Tubman and a thousand others who created the Underground Railroad to get slaves—owned like cattle—to freedom. The willing sacrifice of tens of thousands of tender and innocent American youth to stem the Nazi tide and keep alive the idea of freedom. The redeeming iconoclasm of our artists and their subjects from Hawthorne's Hester Prynne, to Twain's Tom Sawyer, to Ellison's Invisible Man, to Salinger's Holden Caulfield. The silent preservation of those in every generation who have chosen prison to blind obedience to the state and its authority. [Those] who have espoused the individualism of Thoreau, and rejected the simple dehumanizing submersion in the lonely crowd. Is there nothing in all this to save us?

The final day came and they were all there, the class having been long since been moved to the stadium. The lights of the machine whirled in rhythmic patterns, bells clamored and chimed like a covey of teletypes gone mad. The tape was finally deposited in the hands of the waiting professor. Students, teachers, trustees strained to hear the words of what they were to do to foil the predicted apocalyptic mischief. As if already he knew the answer, the professor turned casually to his hushed audience leaning forward to address the bevy of microphones before him directly. They were about to be told what to do to stop the end of the world.

"It says, 'Repent,'" the professor said. Having spoken, he dropped the tape upon the stage and took a seat among the baffled throng.

This time it was the senior valedictorian who spoke. Seeing that the big man on campus was "deep in the grape" and that a void of leadership was about to occur, she responded with the alacrity of a cobra, responding not to the professor but the machine itself. "Come on, iron brain. This is the twentieth century. We are an educated and sophisticated generation. Soon to be graduates of one of the nation's top academies, a place of much learning and high technology. We had to be first-rate intellects to get in this place, and we have to be first-rate intellects to stay. Tops. We are the best. We will leave here and administer the universe. And you tell us to 'repent,' simple brain? Repent, I ask you, of what?"

The computer with a voice of its own now, speaking with the tone and in the manner of a benign stand-up comic, yet as if programmed by some strange and unexpected epiphany, gave answer. "Perhaps," it said, "you can begin by repenting of *that*. Repent of your presumptuous much learning and sophistication. Repent of an educational system in America that too often has become a religion unto itself, as totalitarian as the other idols you have worshipped. Preparing minds and souls for technological concentration camps; camps judged not as slavery because they are of your own democratic construction. Ah, yes, you are the top. Consider then the bottom. Those whose sweat and blood, field, mine, and factory, have placed you in the ranks of privilege so that you might be here, but whose culture and plight are seen as trashy redneck or nigger still. Repent that the academy has not found ways to lose itself in the ghetto—black ghetto and white ghetto—with some delivering word beyond, 'Raise your ACT score and we'll let you in and teach you too.'"

Then as if partly programmed by the giant spirits of the classics department of bygone years, the computer begins an awkward paraphrase of Horace the poet. "O shame. O ignominy. O the academy with her upside down ways."

There is only the wisdom of silence now as the machine continues, "Even an iron brain knows that 'Repent' does not mean self-effacing breast-beating, but the turning right-side-up of that which is sunken. A change of direction, about face, and forward march. So let your tradition, you who turn soon to administer the academy and the universe, be to stand in the face of great resistance and opposition as teachers, and cry out, 'We are not here to train your warriors, like breaking wild horses. We are not here to fashion your young into robot facsimiles, rulers and technicians for commerce and industry; to produce corporate executives and upper echelon of the CIA, and robber barons of this present age. We are here to deliver young minds from the shackles of Caesar's slavery. We are here to release the captives. We are here to bring good news to the poor. Recovery of sight to the blind. In the name of Almighty God, we are here to set at liberty. Repent also of your own religiosity, of your righteousness in equating sixth-grade civics with the revolutionary gospel of Jesus Christ. For equating nationalism with the kingdom of God. Repent of your big spires and steeples casting their shadow on suffering and death, with [their] major commitment being to the growth, harmony, and prosperity of institutional structures. Repent of the electronic soul molesters, whose satellites fill the air with the gospel of 'Take up your cross and relax. Take up your cross in an edifice made of crystal. Take up your cross and get rich, praise the Lord, and send me the money.'"

The drunken big man on campus stumbles forward, devoid now of all arrogance, and stripped of all bravado, a picture of utter humility, kneeling humbly and reverently before the machine, he crosses himself and begins to sob. "Hey, Doc. Doc! Tell us something good."

The word comes back, "Unto us a child is born. Unto us a son is given."

The big man arises now, sober and serene, crosses himself again and races blithely through the crowd, laughing hysterically. Dancing, skipping sprightly as a gazelle, hugging freshmen, sophomores, professors, deans, men and women alike. Happy at the news.

The machine is alone now. It begins to groan and shake like the heavy spasm of death. Then, with a vibrating upheaval, making the sound of a gargantuan bull moose, the distant echo reverberating like the first rumblings of a volcanic eruption, it disintegrates into millions of almost invisible particles, spreading itself this way and that, like mercury poured on a slick marble surface. Suddenly the particles begin whirling round and round, like prairie grass caught in a summer whirlwind, rising slowly in a solemn ghostly ascension.

The woman with the Phi Beta key, the same one as before, moves forward again, watches this spectral preceptor disappearing behind the cloud, the cloud accepting and embracing it like a vacuum, and calls out with valedictory cynicism, "And what about the end of the world, thing?" From everywhere and nowhere, every direction and no direction, comes the mega phonic reply, "Unto us a child is born. And he shall reign forever and forever."

Scripture Index

Subject Index

Subject Index